This collection considers the relevance of the *Annales* "school" for archaeology. The *Annales* movement regarded orthodox history as too much concerned with events, too narrowly political, too narrative in form, and too isolated from neighboring disciplines. Annalistes attempted to construct a "total" history, dealing with a wide range of human activity, and combining divergent material, documentary, and theoretical approaches to the past. *Annales*-oriented research utilizes the techniques and tools of various ancillary fields, and integrates temporal, spatial, material, and behavioral analyses. Such an approach is obviously attractive to archaeologists, for even though they deal with material data rather than social facts, they are – just as much as historians – interested in understanding social, economic, and political factors such as power and dominance, conflict, exchange and other human activities.

Three introductory essays consider the relationship between *Annales* methodology and current archaeological theory. Case studies draw upon methodological variations of the multifaceted *Annales* approach. The volume concludes with two overviews, one historical and the other archaeological.

NEW DIRECTIONS IN ARCHAEOLOGY

ARCHAEOLOGY, *ANNALES*, AND ETHNOHISTORY

Archaeology, *Annales*, and ethnohistory

Edited by
A. BERNARD KNAPP
Macquarie University, Sydney

The right of the
University of Cambridge
to print and sell
all manner of books
was granted by
Henry VIII in 1534.
The University has printed
and published continuously
since 1584.

CAMBRIDGE UNIVERSITY PRESS
Cambridge
New York Port Chester
Melbourne Sydney

CAMBRIDGE UNIVERSITY PRESS
Cambridge, New York, Melbourne, Madrid, Cape Town, Singapore, São Paulo, Delhi

Cambridge University Press
The Edinburgh Building, Cambridge CB2 8RU, UK

Published in the United States of America by Cambridge University Press, New York

www.cambridge.org
Information on this title: www.cambridge.org/9780521102605

First published 1992
This digitally printed version 2009

A catalogue record for this publication is available from the British Library

Library of Congress Cataloguing in Publication data
Archaeology, *Annales*, and ethnohistory / edited by A. Bernard
Knapp.
p. cm.
Includes bibliographical references and indexes.
ISBN 0 521 41174 2
1. Archaeology and history. 2. History – Methodology.
3. Ethnohistory. 4. *Annales* school. I. Knapp, Arthur Bernard.
CC77.H5A69 1992
930.1 – dc20 91–10357 CIP

ISBN 978-0-521-41174-5 hardback
ISBN 978-0-521-10260-5 paperback

For Christina

Contents

PART III OVERVIEW AND PROSPECTS

Figures

Tables

Contributors

PROFESSOR RICHARD W. BULLIET
Department of History
Columbia University
New York

DR. PHILIP DUKE
Department of Anthropology
Fort Lewis College
Colorado

DR. ROLAND FLETCHER
Department of Anthropology
University of Sydney

DR. A. BERNARD KNAPP
School of History, Philosophy and Politics
Macquarie University
Sydney

DR. JOHN MORELAND
Department of Archaeology and Prehistory
University of Sheffield

DR. ANDREW SHERRATT
The Ashmolean Museum
Oxford

DR. MICHAEL E. SMITH
Department of Anthropology
State University of New York, Albany

Preface

Certain complex societies in the Old and New World alike generated numerous documentary records or prompted diverse ethnohistoric accounts. As a result, written evidence tends to dominate sociocultural interpretation, frequently at the expense of material evidence. In the study of past politico-economic or sociocultural processes, it is important to create a dialogue between material and written evidence, neither of which logically supersedes the other. In this regard, *Annales*-oriented research has been exemplary in its attempts to combine material, documentary, and theoretical approaches to the past into a single human science approach.

A series of seminars presented at the University of Sydney – Rhys Jones, Roland Fletcher, Bernard Knapp (Prehistory); I. Wallerstein (History and Economic History) – first suggested the possibility of producing a volume that would explore the concept of time in archaeology, and the *Annales* approach to the study of the past. Subsequently, at the First Joint Archaeological Congress (Baltimore, MD, January 1989), seven papers in this volume were presented in a symposium entitled 'Archaeology and *Annales*: Towards Resolution of the Archaeological–Documentary Dilemma.' Two papers presented in Baltimore (J. G. Lewthwaite, J. A. Greene) are not included in this volume; studies by P. Duke and A. Sherratt have been added, and R. Bulliet contributed the historical overview.

An *Annales* approach demands that equal consideration be given to continuity and change, whatever the medium that reveals them. It also forces the archaeologist, social scientist, or historian to realize (1) that certain variables must be weighed on different spatial or temporal scales, and (2) that such "objectivity" as is possible resides in the use of appropriate theory and method to elicit and elaborate on sociocultural or politico-economic issues. The goal is to generate an interdisciplinary, multivariate, human science that incorporates a broad spectrum of material, documentary, and behavioral variables.

Three introductory essays consider – from widely differing perspectives – the relationship between *Annales* methodology and current archaeological theory. Case studies draw upon methodological variations of the multifaceted *Annales* approach in order to examine the uncritical, often unquestioned comparison or contrast of archaeological and documentary evidence, and in order to bring together a range of data that bears upon issues of continuity and change in prehistoric, protohistoric, or historic-period society. Two overviews – one historical, the other archaeological – conclude the volume.

Individual acknowledgements and references are presented at the end of each chapter. In addition, I should like to thank Jessica Kuper, Editor for Anthropology and Archaeology at Cambridge University Press, for support and encouragement, but above all for insisting on firm editorial intervention in order to ensure a more integrated volume. The individual contributors I must also thank for enduring that repeated intervention, and for meeting a series of somewhat unrealistic deadlines. I am also grateful to Margaret Deith for her copy-editing and for the cordial correspondence that facilitated it. Finally, I wish to acknowledge the support of my wife, Christina Sumner (Powerhouse Museum, Sydney), who has sanctioned my pursuit of the past over three continents during the past decade: to the extent permissible in a multi-authored volume, I dedicate my contributions, at least, to her.

1 Archaeology and *Annales*: time, space, and change

A. BERNARD KNAPP

Introduction

> Microscopic problems of historical research can and should be made macrocosmic – capable of reflecting worlds larger than themselves. It is in this reflected flicker of truth, the revelations of the general in the particular, that the contribution of the historical method to social science will be found. (Postan 1939: 34)

> By and large, social scientists have not attempted to link the day to day events in the lives of individuals (ecological or synchronic processes) and the long term or large scale patterns of human societies (historical or diachronic processes). (Boyd and Richerson 1985: 290)

To inherit the past is also to transform it, or so a recent geocultural synthesis maintains (Lowenthal 1985: 412). As historians "auto-reflexively" narrate past processes or events by means of concepts and terms drawn from their own culture, so social anthropologists often treat the past as a "boundless canvas for contemporary embroidery" (Appadurai 1981: 201). Archaeology's most prominent historiographer regarded the past as something discovered chiefly through the filter of modern society's beliefs and attitudes (Daniel 1975).

Anyone involved in the study of the past realizes that is is difficult to relate our own ideas about the past to ideas actually held in the past (Hodder 1986: 2–6; Gallay 1986: 198–200; Trigger 1989: 351). Although archaeologists in general seek to study the past as an entity quite distinct from the present, many post-processualists, and particularly critical theorists (Leone 1981; Leone *et al.* 1987; Handsman and Leone 1989; Tilley 1989a; cf. Earle and Preucel 1987), maintain that the past

– created as the result of modern or recent-historical social transformations – cannot be viewed in isolation from contemporary human action or contemporary social concerns (Trigger 1981; 1989: 340–7; Wilk 1985; Gamble 1986: 239–40; Hodder 1986: 164–9; 1989; Shanks and Tilley 1987: 186–208; Lewthwaite 1988a: 87–90; Pinxten *et al.* 1988: 13; Gathercole 1989; Tilley 1989d). In the context of this volume, it must be observed that Marc Bloch – co-founder with Lucien Febvre of the *Annales* journal in 1929 – inaugurated the method of reading the past from the present, an "unorthodox" approach to time that resulted in new historical insight (Febvre, in Bloch 1966; Chirot 1984: 31).

The reconstruction of the past on various scales of time, i.e. through the evaluation of long-term processes or continuity, and shorter-term events or change, facilitates the investigation of "different world views, and the impact of space and time on human action" (Gamble, 1986: 238). Various aspects of time, space, and change attract the common attention of archaeologists, anthropologists, geographers, and historians. As David Clarke once observed, the metaphysical concepts of time and space form the boundaries of archaeological events, processes, and explanations (1973: 13).

Clarke, however, maintained that archaeological theory "either treats relationships of a purely archaeological kind, or processes with space and time scales for which there is no social terminology" (1973: 17), a viewpoint which Hodder believes has "in fact contributed to a continued blindness to the social construction of the archaeological past" (1987: 8). Clarke, however, was not insensitive to the role of material in the creation and maintenance of social relationships, nor was he as blind to social theory as he was dubious about its "primitive terms and correlated concepts" and how they could be related to the space, time, and sampling aspects of archaeological data (1973: 17). Furthermore, his insight into the (social) significance of documentary and ethnohistoric data for archaeological interpretation was unprecedented in the hypercritical, halcyon days of the New Archaeology, and stands yet as one stable mooring in the current quagmire of archaeological theory (Clarke 1973: 18):

> The new developments insist that the historical evidence be treated by the best methods of historical criticism and the archaeological evidence by the best archaeological treatment and not some selective conflation of both sets of evidence and their appropriate disciplines. The severe problems and tactical advantages which arise from integrating archaeological and historical evidence emerge as no more and no less than those arising between archaeological and physical, chemical, biological and geographical evidence. Indeed, work in text-aided contexts will increasingly provide vital experiments in which purely archaeological data may be controlled by documentary data, bearing in mind the inherent biases of both.

In a well-known passage, Clarke defined archaeology as "the discipline with the theory and practice for the recovery of unobservable hominid behaviour patterns from indirect traces in bad samples" (1973: 17). The fragmented, disproportionate, taphonomically transformed, and even non-representative material database of archaeology or parahistory has led, inevitably if not universally, to an analytical emphasis on deeper currents, on collective instead of individual behavior, and on socioeconomic or ideological trends instead of institutional decisions or political acts.

If long-term processes are regarded as inherent in the archaeological record of any place or time, short-term events might be regarded as more intrinsic to ethnohistoric or ancient documentary evidence. Yet the archaeological record bears witness to instants of change just as written materials reveal social patterns or politico-economic trends. Documentary evidence, wherever it exists, tends to dominate sociocultural and historical interpretation, whilst contemporaneous archaeological evidence is underemphasized. Although methodologically the information provided by archaeological and documentary or ethnohistoric records must be kept separate (Evans 1974: 17), in the study of the past it is necessary to develop a dialogue between the two.

> ... the historical document does not necessarily contain more truth than the artifacts recovered from the ground. Nor is the structure of phenomena as interpreted through history necessarily more valid than the structure observed and interpreted by the archaeologist. The historical and archaeological records are different analogs of human behavior, and they should not necessarily be expected to coincide. (Ferguson 1977: 7)

The use of general analogy provides an important means to relate ethnohistoric data to archaeological interpretation (Charlton 1981), and recent archaeological studies of ethnicity concur that the material and documentary records "measure similar behavioral trends ... with varying degrees of strength" (Pyszczyk 1989: 244; also Stevenson 1989: 271–4).

The dilemma that confronts human science in the evaluation and holistic interpretation of discrete types of evidence runs deeper than the rifts that divide traditional, processual, and post-processual archaeology, and that separate pre- or protohistoric archaeologists from historians. The roots of this 200-year-old debate lie in the division between humanistic, historiographic methodology, on the one hand, and social- (or natural-) science analytical procedure, on the other. Whereas brief consideration is given below to the dispute between history and the social sciences (see also Hodder 1986: 77–102; 1987: 1–3; Lewthwaite 1988b: 161–76; Knapp 1992), this volume aims to develop the potential for interdisciplinary co-operation, and to investigate how individual archaeological, social-science, or historical approaches to the study of the past might be recombined effectively in a non-positivist, human science approach.

Major theoretical differences have often separated historians or classical archaeologists from processual ("positivist") archaeologists who have steadfastly resisted any alignment with history (e.g. Binford 1962; 1968; Earle and Preucel 1987; cf. Renfrew 1980; Snodgrass 1988: 6–9; Trigger 1989: 356). The processualist approach emphasized model building, theory formulation and hypothesis testing, sought to establish general laws in human behavior (e.g. Watson *et al.* 1984; Watson 1986), and focused on systems theory and cultural process instead of culture history. Striking similarities nonetheless consistently outweigh trivial differences amongst the types of evidence that archaeologists, anthropologists, and historians employ, or within the range of absolute or relative chronological resolution at their disposal (Lewthwaite 1986: 61). Even the natural and social sciences increasingly re-examine historical aspects of their data in order to stimulate theoretical development (Boyd and Richerson 1985; Gould 1986; Grene 1988). Philosopher of science Stephen Toulmin anticipated this trend in the mid-70s (1977: 144–5):

> Nowadays, we seek to develop not so much timeless theories about the general nature of "social groups" and "social action" as historical insights into the character and experience of this or that human group or collectivity; to grasp not so much the general statics of cultural equilibrium as the dynamics of particular cultural changes; to achieve not so much the formal rigor of axiomatic systems as the practical testability and computability of programs and algorithms ... if the price of reestablishing this contact with actual experience includes breaking down the fences separating the established academic disciplines so that we can bring their varied techniques and theories to bear on some specific practical problems, so be it. These days, we are all prepared to be "interdisciplinary."

Archaeologists and anthropologists increasingly express the need for a more historically based, less theoretically abstract human science; historians increasingly acknowledge that anthropological enquiry has become critical for both narrative and quantitative history (Stone 1979: 13–14; Feeley-Harnik 1982; Hodder 1986: 153–5; 1987; McNeill 1986; Pinsky 1989; Trigger 1989: 336–40; Carrithers 1990: 189–91, and n. 4 with further references; Spencer 1990). The ahistorical, non-processual, derivative concept of culture esteemed by some social anthropologists has given way in many quarters to a realization that culture is rooted in social relations and plays an active role in shaping history (Sider 1986: 5–7). For Bourdieu, whose concept of *habitus* is increasingly utilized by post-processualists (Hodder 1986: 70–6; Tilley 1989b: 65–6; Moreland, this volume), history produces culture "in accordance with the schemes engendered by history" (1977: 78–84; Levi 1988: 607). Or, as Trigger recently put it (1989: 336): "Archaeology thus has an important role to play not only in unravelling the complex history of the past but also in providing a historical perspective for understanding the significance of ethnographic data."

Historical explanation involves both particular and global description, and description as such should not be opposed to explanation or theory (Finley 1977: 139–40; Hodder 1987: 2). Sahlins (1985) now argues that a false dichotomy has been created between structure and event, between myth and history, and that history is culturally ordered, just as cultural schemes are historically ordered. Because historical processes may constrain certain social factors, an understanding of historical meaning is necessary to put symbolism and ideology in context.

Annales-oriented research has always sought to produce human science by interweaving historical and social-science approaches to the past. Marc Bloch utilized the tools of history, sociology, economics, and anthropology forty years before the current cycle of human scientific practice became fashionable (Chirot 1984: 22). Both Durkheim and Bloch maintained that the individual could only be understood within the context of society, and that the structure of society manifested itself in concrete institutional and material remains (Iggers 1975: 49–50). With emphasis on the analysis of rudimentary material culture, on time, place, and social reality, and on the interdisciplinary study of their covariance, Annalistes share many of the aims and methods of contemporary archaeology. Archaeology, furthermore, provides an obvious link between social-science and humanistic approaches, particularly when the broader material and written record is applied to specific interpretive problems and issues.

Because the changing focus of archaeological emphasis triggers the search for new or different types of evidence, archaeological data will never be complete (Feeley-Harnik 1982; Yoffee 1982: 347). Furthermore, the stopping point in any archaeological explanation or historical reconstruction is never definitive, only incidental to the data selected for analysis. Both on the material plane of the prehistorian and in the documentary landscape of the historian, continuity and change are apparent in the spatio-temporal disposition of power strategies. To analyze such strategies, to study transformations in the material record, and to consider the association amongst society, economy, and ideology, it is necessary to theorize about patterns, processes, and breakpoints.

Amongst humanistic and social-science disciplines, archaeology alone is characterized by a nearly inexhaustible material record (including documentary evidence), an evolving – albeit imperfect – theoretical corpus, and the interdependence between the two. Archaeologists must enter into a dialogue between empirical findings and theoretical concepts (Wagstaff 1987: 34), a process that parallels the reciprocal movement from description to explanation, from the idiographic to the nomothetic, from structure to event, and from continuity to change. This dialogue has been expounded not only by sociologists (e.g., Weber 1956), anthropologists (e.g., White 1945: 245), and archaeologists (e.g., Hodder 1986: 11–17), but by all generations of Annalistes.

In what follows, I present first a broad overview of four generations of *Annales* scholarship in the context of the rift that developed in nineteenth-century scholarship between history and the social sciences (more substantive discussion of the philosophic underpinnings of *Annales* are presented by Lewthwaite 1986: 58–67; 1988b). Next I offer a general discussion of some common principles that link archaeology and *Annales*: temporal and spatial scales, chronology theory, continuity and change, a concern with human action. These principles are discussed in greater detail in the subsequent introductory essays by Smith and Fletcher, and are accommodated to various degrees in the volume's case studies (briefly summarized). The introduction ends with a statement that suggests why an *Annales* approach to the past may appeal to contemporary archaeologists, anthropologists, and ancient historians.

Origins: the *Annales* tradition

In 1929, the *Annales* approach to French history crystallized with the establishment of the journal *Annales d'Histoire Sociale et Economique* (since 1955, *Annales: Economies, Sociétés, Civilisations* [*Annales: ESC*]). Subsquent opinion on the methodology of *Annales*, an intellectual movement whose impact has been felt worldwide, ranges from decidedly enthusiastic to resolutely disparaging (e.g., Trevor-Roper 1973: 408; Kinser 1981a: 676). The pros and cons of this methodology and its ever-changing relationship with other historical or social-science methodologies have been discussed widely in several papers and monographs (e.g., Iggers 1975; Stoianovich 1976; Harsgor 1978; Braudel 1980; Wallerstein 1982; Clark 1985). Today *Annales* scholars draw inspiration and models as much from ecologists, psychologists, economists, art historians, and anthropologists as from other historians.

In his historical overview of the *Annales*, Stoianovich maintains that historical scholarship was born in classical Greece, nurtured in eighteenth- and nineteenth-century Germany (under Ranke's concept of history *wie es eigentlich war*), and matured in twentieth-century France within the *Annales* school (1976: 25–39; see also Harsgor 1978: 1–2). Wallerstein provides a useful counterpoint and discusses the origins, dispersal, and attempted reunification of history and the social sciences, as well as the *Annales* role in that process (1982). For Wallerstein, both history and the social sciences are nineteenth-century phenomena, born out of the French Revolution. The birth involved a process of separation between "universalizing" and "sectorializing" thought: knowledge begins with the particular and ends with the universal (or abstract). To the extent that all particulars were "equal," the universalist path ultimately formed the ideological basis of the more traditional, humanistic, Rankean historiography. The sectorializing mode of thought, devoted to the study of politico-economic and sociocultural phenomena, underpinned the five social-science "disciplines": anthropology, economics, geography, political science, sociology (Wallerstein 1982: 108–10).

Rankean history became an idiographic pursuit that

sought to reconstruct the past on the basis of individual state archives. The social sciences, meanwhile, became nomothetic in orientation, and sought general laws to explain universal phenomena. Both disciplines increasingly exhibited a narrow, "hyper-specialized," spatio-temporal focus of research: historians sought truth in the unchanging past, ethnographers in the unchanging present. Narrative history presented the past "as it really was"; ethnographers evaluated what made things happen in the "anthropological present." (It may be noted that as Victorian archaeologists extended the antiquity of humanity by outlining the stages of the Palaeolithic era, anthropologists were busy dismissing modern "primitives" as relicts of the Palaeolithic: Kuper 1988: 42–104; Bowler 1989; Trigger 1989: 94–109).

Toward the end of the nineteenth century, at least three major reactions had formed to challenge these well-established patterns of "universalizing–sectorializing" thought: *Staatswissenschaften*, Marxism, and *Annales* (Wallerstein 1982: 109–12). *Annales* was a relative latecomer, but its animosity towards the Rankean model then dominant in France – notably in the Sorbonne – was no less intense, if somewhat more eloquent and intellectual than that of the other emerging challenges (Bailyn 1977: 1033). The Annalistes emphasized holistic rather than "segmentalized" thought; economy and society rather than politics; long-term patterns rather than short-term events; global man rather than "fractional" man. They examined quantitative trends instead of chronological narrative, structural instead of political history. They rejected the uniqueness of history in favour of blending history with the social sciences (Wallerstein 1982: 110–11).

The principles of *Annales* methodology may be delineated through a glance at the work of its first three generations:

- 1st 1930–1950: Lucien Febvre (1878–1956) and Marc Bloch (1886–1944)
- 2nd 1950–1970: Fernand Braudel (1902–1985)
- 3rd 1970–1980: Pierre Chaunu, Georges Duby, François Furet, Jacques Le Goff, Emmanuel Le Roy Ladurie, Pierre Nora, and many others.

Through Febvre's teacher Gabriel Monod, both Bloch and Febvre traced their methodological lineage back to Jules Michelet (1798–1844). Amongst many aspects of Michelet's methodology, those most directly associated with the work of *Annales* historians are the "total" scope of history, the broad range of sources used in its reconstruction, and a concern with "ordinary people" and daily life (Burrows 1982: 78). Sociological input from F. Simiand represents another key influence in *Annales* methodology and mentality. His published attack (1903) on traditional historians at the Sorbonne renounced "surface history" and promulgated a new alliance of history with sociology, geography, anthropology, economics, and psychology, an alliance still intrinsic to the *Annales* (Forster 1978: 61–2; Simiand's essay was reprinted in *Annales ESC* 15 [1960] 83–119).

The final member of a triad who exerted notable impact on the *Annales* was Henri Berr, a philosopher of history who sought to recombine all aspects of historical study: political, social, economic; history of science, history of art; philosophy of history (Braudel 1973: 454–61). In 1900, Berr commenced publication of the *Revue de Synthèse Historique*, a journal that provoked traditionalists, and serves as a rallying point for those "active, lively, combative, conquering men" in the social sciences and history alike, a group similar to that which soon would rally round the *Annales* banner: Henry Hauser, François Simiand, Lucien Febvre, and later Marc Bloch (Braudel 1973: 459; further discussion in Lewthwaite 1986: 58–61;1988b: 161–76). *Annales*, in fact, coalesced and succeeded not least because of the philosopical support it enjoyed: *Annales* was a social product of its time (see also Sherratt, this volume).

Febvre and Bloch had a common vision of history, and subscribed to the Durkheimian principle that the individual must be studied within a social context. The practice of history, furthermore, entailed the study of material culture, social groups, economic trends, regional or local customs, even profound mental categories. Above all, in a context of interdisciplinary collaboration, history should strive for synthesis and comparison. Accordingly, the focus of *Annales* historical research shifted from the individual to the collective, from the political to the socioeconomic, from narrative description to analysis and interpretation, and from single-factor to multivariate explanation (Lucas 1985: 4). The first generation aspired to a synthesis of all the mental, physical, and material forces that shaped past human experience, and to a methodology that would relate all these forces within an interacting hierarchy.

As editors of the new *Annales* journal, and in their "passion for the past" (Braudel 1973: 467), Febvre and Bloch encouraged research based on a diverse range of written and material, socioeconomic, and mental data theretofore regarded as unsuitable for historical research. The methodological building blocks set up by the first generation of *Annales* were two:

(1) interdisciplinary research, particularly with geography and the social sciences;
(2) a "total" approach to historical reconstruction, through use of a broad and diverse database.

From the publication of *La Méditerranée et le monde méditerranéen* in 1949 (Braudel 1972) until he relinquished the editorship of *Annales* to its "young men" (Le Goff, Le Roy Ladurie, Ferro) in 1968, Fernand Braudel dominated *Annales* history and historiography, and the second generation of *Annales* may be attributed solely to him. Under Febvre's tutelage, Braudel heeded his mentors' call for social science input into history (Braudel 1973: 452–4). In France, socio-historical research converged on the study of people (*in sensu lato*), within the multidimensional context of time, space, and social reality. During Braudel's reign, the *Annales* eclectic approach to the past attained international recognition. Objects of historical study were defined and validated through the methodology of social science whilst the historical database diversified widely.

Braudel's major contribution to this dynamic attempt at human science, and a hallmark of *Annales* methodology, is the principle that macrophenomena are determinate and microphenomena indeterminate (Lucas 1985: 5). Historical events achieve significance only when evaluated in spatially extensive, diachronic contexts. In his own thesis (*The Mediterranean*), Braudel viewed the past from his now well-known tripartite perspective: long-term geographic or environmental structures (*la longue durée*), medium-term socioeconomic cycles (*conjoncture*), and short-term socio-political events (*l'histoire événementielle*). Although the weakest link in Braudel's trinitarian chain is the ecological determinism embedded in the concept of *la longue durée*, his intention was to balance the fleeting event and the persistent process in an unitary socio-historical account.

Within Braudel's schema, the multidimensionality of social time assumed a central place. In his structural history ("macrohistory"), physical or material factors that operate over long periods of time (*la longue durée*) act as constraints on human behavior. Macrohistory encapsulated centuries- or even millennia-long biological, environmental, and social interrelationships, what today might be termed human ecology (Chirot 1984: 32). Braudel's concept of structure is not some adjunct of a Lévi-Straussian scheme for ordering the world (*contra* Little and Shackel 1989: 496), nor is it concerned with the reciprocal interaction between spatial context and social organization; rather it assumes that there is a range of geophysical "structures" within whose confines human action takes place (Clark 1985: 183).

Braudel's conjunctural history ("mediohistory") occurs in five- or ten- to fifty-year spans, and is applicable to any form of human behavior that may be considered through its outline and its fluctuation around a norm (Kinser 1981b: 92–4). Braudel generalized the economic nature of a *conjoncture*, and reformulated it as a quantifiable sequence on either side of a normative activity; recurrent phenomena – prices, wages, accounts, demographic and technological change, and economic trends – form the object of study. The dynamic concept of the *conjoncture* made it possible to reconstruct historical life through measurable change in quantities of material. The inclusion and evaluation in historical analysis of a plethora of material and documentary data – even if initially ill-suited, inadequate, or poorly conceived – presaged the *Annales* foray into "serial history," and laid the foundations for a quantitative, quasi-statistical approach to historical data.

Braudel's *l'histoire événementielle* ("microhistory") represented little more than a concession to narrative political history. For Braudel, the short-term was ephemeral and events were infinite, mere "dust" in the diachronic sweep of historical pattern and process. This repudiation of the short term ultimately gave rise to serious contention within *Annales* historiography. Indeed human actions are not simply responses to deep structures, and here lies the crux of widespread dissatisfaction with this particular aspect of a Braudelian approach, both within and without the *Annales* camp (e.g., Adams 1984: 87–8). Events, viewed as historical realities lacking in pattern (Kinser 1981b: 94), ultimately proved to be basic to the *Annales* paradigm. Le Roy Ladurie (third generation) believed that events should be regarded as intersections that break patterns, and as such are critical to understanding and explaining change (1979: 111–16).

To the global historical approach and the interdisciplinary, social-science-based research that had been characteristic of the earliest *Annales*, Braudel added a trinitarian concept of time as a diachronic assemblage. In Braudel's "dialectic of time spans" (Clark 1985: 183), different spatial, politico-economic, or socio-ideological systems have characteristic rhythms, whilst time itself lacks any predetermined meaning. Since history, therefore, is a composite of different times moving at different speeds, historians must first define the object of their research, and subsequently determine the time span most relevant for data analysis (Furet 1984: 6–9; Lucas 1985: 6–7).

Braudel's methodology and writings inspired the epistemological views and research activities of the entire second generation of French historians. His intellectual overture to Lévi-Strauss (1980/1958) set the stage for several later issues of *Annales* devoted to structural anthropology, and so facilitated a dialogue with a discipline frequently hostile to history. By 1970, two decades of internal deliberation and external reaction led to the *émiettement* ("scattering") of *Annales*. This notion of fragmentation presumes a unity, but it would be misleading to think that an *Annales* "school" had amalgamated under Braudel. The "scattering" was in fact an opening of new avenues of research into traditional Annaliste concerns (Wallerstein 1982: 115).

The third generation of *Annales* carried out historical research global in scope and millennial in time, from prehistory (Bottero *et al.* 1973; Demoule 1982) to classical antiquity (Austin and Vidal-Naquet 1977; Vernant and Vidal-Naquet 1981), through the more customary realm of post-medieval to post-revolutionary France (e.g., Forster and Ranum 1977; Le Roy Ladurie 1979; 1981), to contemporary America, Israel, and Russia (Ferro 1980; Furet 1984: 153–206; Berelowitch *et al.* 1985). If the third generation was disinclined to tackle global history à la Braudel, their concern with social anthropology, demography, and the "unconscious world of *mentalité*" (Lucas 1985–8) – ideology, symbolism, cultural pattern – incorporated a vast new body of source material. The "scattering" usually associated with the third generation in some ways represents a return to concepts that inspired Febvre and Bloch: global history in the geographic sense was complemented by "total" history in the interdisciplinary sense (e.g., Le Goff and Nora 1985; Murra, Wachtel, and Revel 1986). Le Roy Ladurie observed that "history is the synthesis of *all human action aimed at the past*" (quoted in Harsgor 1978: 3, emphasis added).

Quantitative innovations, however, were perhaps most typical of third-generation research. Renewed emphasis on the systematic collection of data and an increased concern for statistical sophistication were the inevitable outcome of a preoccupation with measuring long-term cultural or historical patterns. Yet there is a certain paradox in that precise quantification requires that the time scale be more precise than the analysis, so that – in effect – the concept of structure in broader, non-specified time breaks down (Sturt Manning, personal communication). Quantification provided a means to distinguish amongst the trivial, the random, and the significant, whilst experimentation with systems analysis necessitated further quantification of similarities and differences within and between systems (Furet 1984: 40–53; Lucas 1985: 7).

Whereas the mania for statistics retains a prominent place in Annaliste research (Furet 1985; Bruguières 1985), the basis of a quantitative approach was and remains "serial" history (Chaunu 1985: 38–41). If serial history once denied punctuated change, more recently it has produced increasingly sophisticated analyses of discontinuity (Birnbaum 1978: 232). Yet even when data lend themselves to quantification, *Annales* historical research seeks chiefly to study the diachronic dimension of these phenomena, and to place material or documentary evidence into a temporal series of homogeneous and comparable units in order to measure fixed intervals of change and diversity (Furet 1984: 42). Indeed, the repetitive and comparative data of quantitative serial history replaced the elusive event: the breakdown of these data into different levels or subsystems ostensibly allowed the historian to use qualitative probabilistic analysis to consider the impact of internal relationships or external forces. But the contextual link between quantitative – often material – data and human action, and the theoretical link between data, human action, and interpretation, were yet to be established.

How closely is current, fourth-generation *Annales* methodology associated with that of previous generations, and what is the state of that methodology today? The most enduring characteristics of *Annales*-oriented research are three: (1) an emphasis on the multivariate nature of the historical discipline; (2) a commitment to an interdisciplinary relationship with the social sciences; and (3) an ongoing focus on the "sociale" (of the original journal-title), whose indetermination, as Febvre noted, helped to transform history into human science. Utilizing the techniques and tools of various ancillary fields, and integrating various levels of temporal, spatial, material, and behavioral analysis, *Annales* research still embraces a wide spectrum of socio-historical and cultural issues.

Braudel's trinitarian scheme not only instilled a temporal dimension into the study of human behavior, it also demonstrated that different time scales affect interpretations of environmental, politico-economic, or socio-ideological issues. Although subjects of narrower temporal and spatial scope have superseded those that emphasised *la longue durée* (Forster 1978: 64), the processes and events of the past are still seen as determined at least partly by unchanging physical forces (geology, climate), and partly by intangible but more volatile social forces (ideology, social formations) (Trevor-Roper 1973: 470). Such forces, or variables, may be viewed along a continuum from the biological/ecological through the socioeconomic to the political or individual. The temporal dimension has become subservient to the topic of research, whilst the nature of the question often determines the time scale for analysis.

If temporal concepts, therefore, still spark controversy amongst Annalistes, quantification – particularly when used to identify limiting and motivating forces – has had a more unifying effect. *Annales* quantification has been defined as a "halfway house" between cliometric and impressionistic history (Forster 1978: 69). For François Furet (1985: 13), however, the point of *Annales* quantitative history is

> to take the discipline of history in its widest possible sense, that is to say in its conceptual indetermination with all its multiplicity of levels of analysis, and from that point to devote oneself to the description of those levels and to the task of establishing simple statistical links between them, starting with hypotheses which, whether original or imported, are nothing more than the intuitions of the historian.

Although historical data cannot be reduced readily to mathematical formulation, at least they may be expressed in problem-oriented terms, and analyzed quantitatively with respect to regularities or differences, in order to consider basic elements in the process of change. Criticism directed toward an obsession with the quantitative (Lyon 1987: 206–7) at the expense of the qualitative has resulted in increased influence from social anthropology, cultural ecology, and demography (Forster 1978: 68; Lucas 1985: 9).

Braudel's call for a "new humanism" in history, and for the reaffirmation of social analysis within specific temporal dimensions (1957: 182), was echoed in the introduction of *Faire de l'histoire* (1974 publication of Le Goff and Nora 1985), when an appeal was made to history – in the face of "aggression" from the social sciences – to reassert itself (à la Bloch) as the "science of change, of transformation" (Lucas 1985: 9). Furet (1983: 409) also challenged the "scientistic illusion" and remarked that history's concern with human action was the

> best antidote against the misleading simplifications and illusory rigor inherent in the notion of a science of society. It is all the more effective an antidote for having dropped its traditional qualms about hypotheses and ideas, some of which it now borrows from the social sciences.

In Lawrence Stone's view, the number and diversity of historical variables have forced historians to adopt a "principle of indeterminacy" in which only middle-range generalizations can be made: "The macro-economic model is a pipe-dream, and 'scientific history' a myth" (1979: 13). In place of previous concerns with social groups or economic trends, the current, fourth generation of *Annales* emphasizes – often in a narrative mode of discourse – ideology and symbolism within the cultural context: *mentalité* (Duby 1985; Le Goff 1985).

The study of *mentalités* constitutes a direct link with Bloch and Febvre, albeit with divergent concerns: Bloch focused on mental phenomena closely linked to material and social life, whereas Febvre sought to explore the intellectual and psychological phenomena of a mental universe (Bruguières 1982: 433). The present emphasis on *mentalités* is regarded by Stone as "the end of the attempt to produce a coherent scientific explanation of change in the past" (1979: 19). Forster too argued over a decade ago that, along a spectrum from "scientific" to "humanistic" history, *Annales* scholars incline toward the latter, and practiced "qualitative empiricism" (1978: 74). Whereas certain ambiguities will always persist in the relationship between history and social science, it is useful to recall the words of Marc Bloch (cited in Bruguières 1982: 430): "Social realities are a whole. One could not begin to explain an institution if one did not link it to the great intellectual, emotional, mystical currents of the contemporaneous *mentalité* ... This [is an] interpretation of social facts *from the inside*."

In many respects, *Annales* history today remains faithful to its diverse ideological and interdisciplinary origins. In 1985, for the first time since its founding in 1948, the Sixth Section of *L'Ecole Pratique des Hautes Etudes* (since 1975 *L'Ecole des Hautes Etudes en Sciences Sociales*) has elected an anthropologist (M. Augi), not a historian, as its president. In France at least, *Annales* historians dominate the course and determine the trends of historical research, and the election of Augi perhaps signals as much the security and power of *Annales* history as a continuing commitment to interdisciplinary research. Furet nonetheless maintains that history must continue to diversify through an interdisciplinary methodology, and that it must remain "all-embracing" in order to comprehend the social phenomena with which it is most closely concerned (1983: 392).

If Braudel saw structuralism as a crisis for history in 1958, and Le Goff and Nora felt aggression from the social sciences in 1974, the current crisis stems from post-positivists, who maintain that history's newest challenge is no longer a self-critique, but rather a critique of the postulates of social science itself (Chartier 1988). It is argued that this crisis, which affects all human science, revolves around two themes: (1) the scale adopted for analysis, and (2) the cognitive implications of practicing and writing human science (*Les Annales* 1988: 291–3). These two themes are linked, it is argued, by the failure to acknowledge the relationship between the subjective human scientist and objective reality. If in previous generations nobody questioned the fundamental correspondence between historical or ethnographic sources (however falsified, perfunctory, or even lacking they may have been), on the one hand, and past reality, on the other, today's consciousness has undercut this implicit consensus, and forced human scientists to acknowledge that the sources themselves may have been constructed, in specific ways and towards specific ends (Chartier 1988: 45; Ginzburg 1990: 22).

However one regards the post-positivist critique, it must at least be acknowledged as an issue (or several issues – e.g., Tilley 1989a) that must be addressed. Chartier's (1988) account of philosophical introspection in history, its uncertainty about truth, reality, and practice, and its methodological limitations "dressed up as theoretical innovations ... , the same ultimate muddle" (Chapman 1989: 550), echo the refrains of critical theorists and post-processual archaeologists. To place archaeology in its dialectic context with *Annales*, and thus to examine the two-way relationship between social structure and human action (Hodder 1987: 7), it is necessary to look not only at the social generalizations of first- and second-generation Annalistes but also at the more integrative, behavioral efforts of the third and fourth generations (Bailey 1981: 106; Furet 1983; Hunt 1986; Lewthwaite 1988b).

Annales, archaeology, social theory and time

> The past is a foreign country; they do things differently there. (L. P. Hartley, *The Go-Between*)

Early *Annales* scholars pursued a "scientific history" and were confident that this would provide general laws to explain historical change (Stone 1979: 4–5). With their emphasis on *mentalités* and input from social anthropology, demography, and cultural ecology, the fourth generation has redirected research effort from matters global and systemic toward resolution of definable, more readily circumscribed problems (Lucas 1985: 8). The gap created by the collapse of Braudelian economic and demographic determinism, however, has yet to be filled by any ideological, ideational, or cultural model (Stone 1979: 13, 19).

Annales history, nonetheless, succeeded in substituting the study of anonymous people for that of great men, a model of continuity and discontinuity for a model based on change alone, and the analysis of rudimentary, material culture for the testimony of "great literature" (Furet 1984: 74). In Birnbaum's view (1978: 230), the tasks of "contemporary" *Annales* historical analysis are five:

(1) to establish distinctive temporal periods;
(2) to indicate major lines of development within each;
(3) to identify and measure regularities specific to each;
(4) to recognize innovation and the emergence of new structures within and between eras;
(5) to posit a range of elements that helps to isolate and explain continuity or change within and between periods.

Another recent focus of research published in *Annales: ESC* is the analysis of cultural systems, a shift in emphasis that poses for historians an array of questions already raised by archaeologists, anthropologists, sociologists, and philologists (Revel 1978: 17–18; Snodgrass 1982). Such a trend, however, is only the most recent *Annales* attempt to construct a positivist "total history," and to examine the "inner inter-connectedness" of culture and society (Birnbaum 1978: 232), pursuits already familiar to, if seldom undertaken by, most archaeologists.

One of the *Annales*' most significant achievements has been to force historical attention on social theory. Although Annalistes characteristically rejected any single theoretical principle, it was felt that major historical enquiries ought to contain a set of generalizations that would relate the model employed closely and clearly to an individual situation (Chirot 1984: 40). Concepts and theoretical formulations associated with *mentalité* postulate that human intentionality and *praxis* affect social change, a highly contentious issue in contemporary archaeological theory (Trigger 1989: 355). The *Annales* lack of a comprehensive theory of social change may be attributed to a skepticism over any approach whose propositions could not be verified empirically. Such skepticism, however, does not remove the need for theoretical formulations that treat social, behavioral, or politico-economic factors often disregarded by archaeologists and Annalistes alike: cognition, *praxis*, ideology, and power (Iggers 1975: 73; Stone 1979: 10).

Alain Schnapp (1981) has pointed out several areas of disciplinary overlap between archaeology and *Annales*:

(paleo-)ethnobotany, archaeometry, the concept of treating material/documentary patterns (e.g., seriation, "serial" history); he also emphasized that early Annalistes had somehow managed to overlook the major social and theoretical contributions of V. Gordon Childe (1981: 470–1). Whilst it is necessary to be aware of such links or omissions, the thrust of this overview is instead to highlight the major themes that permeate the outlook of the two disciplines.

With its emphasis on time, space and change, archaeology is structurally similar to history (Leone 1978: 30), particularly to *Annales* methodology in history. Furthermore, although archaeologists, like geographers, observe material data rather than social facts (Wagstaff 1987: 34), the two share a basic interest in modeling the spatial operation of power and dominance, conflict or co-operation, and other human action (Renfrew, 1983); in this light, Cherry suggests that archaeology, may be viewed as "political geography in the past tense" (1987: 146). Similarly, some *Annales* historians have sought to examine the ideological aspects of domination within sociocultural and institutional contexts (Le Goff 1971: 4–5).

Archaeology's unique frame of reference (as repeatedly noted) is the study of long-term diachronic change (e.g., Renfrew 1981: 264). Like the historian, the archaeologist can only interpret the past by looking through time-coloured lenses; different archaeological perceptions of time, however, diverge in the extreme (e.g., cf. Bailey 1983, with Shanks and Tilley 1987: 118–36). Nonetheless, within defined temporal boundaries, archaeology aims to interpret regularity or discontinuity in the spatial disposition of economic, social, and political relationships in human society, many of which are intended to overcome what Braudel called "distance, the first enemy" (1972: 355; Renfrew 1981: 267).

Most scholars who work today beneath the *Annales* banner find Braudel's structural–ecological determinism seriously flawed (Forster 1978: 64; Clark 1985: 189–96). Yet Braudel's hierarchical temporal rhythms – episodic, cyclical, structural – do not represent fundamentally different orders of reality (Binford 1981: 197), but rather inclusive aspects along a continuum. Such multiple, hierarchical time scales provide for archaeology an heuristic framework in which to conceptualize time and change in prehistoric or protohistoric society (Smith, Fletcher, this volume). The diachronic dimension of archaeological phenomena is central to their analysis: excavated data and documentary or ethnohistoric "facts" must be categorized abstractly, measured, compared, and – where possible – considered probabilistically.

With traditional archaeological and historical concepts of time, periodization attempts to define a sequence of events, represented as discontinuities but described in a narrative mode of continuity. In contrast, processual (and post-processual) archaeologists and serial historians attempt to discuss sequential "events" in a mode of discontinuity (Furet 1984: 48–52). Although Braudel always remained vague about the precise relationship between structure and event, and thus about discontinuity and change, his students and successors recognized that social structures could constrain human behavior, just as human behavior could have unintended consequences for social structure (similarly Giddens 1979). If human actions are regarded as points of articulation with social, politico-economic, or ideational structures, they may serve analytically as intersections that reveal configurational change in material and historical pattern. Events are not historical facts, but heuristic reconstructions, like structures and conjunctures, intended to provide insight into cultural pattern and process, and into human action.

Material culture forged the earliest and pre-eminent link between archaeology and the *Annales* tradition (Schnapp 1981: 469–70), and Leone recognized almost twenty years ago the significance and potential for archaeology of the material aspects of human behavior (1972: 18):

> At the moment, material culture as a category of phenomena is unaccounted for. It is scattered between interior decorators, advertising firms, and historians of technology. But when one considers how little we know about how material culture articulates with other cultural subsystems, one begins to see the potential. There exists a completely empty niche, and it is neither small nor irrelevant. Should archaeology become the science of material objects or technology, many of the aims, problems, methods, and data of the field would be completely transformed.

As the product of human behavior, material culture is not simply a passive reflection of past social systems, but rather an active entity in the creation and maintenance of social relationships (Hodder 1987:6–7). Although archaeology still lacks adequate theories on material culture (but see Moreland, this volume) and on the nature of the material component of human community life (Fletcher, this volume), the material "constructions" of cultural similarities and differences, of historical continuity and discontinuity, play a role in the dialectical relationship between structure and event (Hodder 1987: 8).

Table 1.1 *Concepts of time*

	Anthropological	
(Cultural relativists)		
	Cyclic	*Linear*
	Emic	**Emic/Etic**
Gurvitch	Multiplicity of "social times"	
Geertz	Stages within cycles (Balinese)	
Bloch	Ritual (ritualization of social relations) (Past time?)	Mundane
Leach	Repetitive/Reversible	Directional/Irreversible
Needham	Indo-Hellenic	Judaeo-Christian
Hall	Polychronic	Monochronic

		Historical (Annales)	
Braudel	**La longue durée** (Structural) Environmental	**Conjoncture** (Cyclical) Social	**Event** (Episodic) Individual
Le Roy Ladurie		*structure – event – structure* (material/documentary/material)	

		Archaeological	
	Prehistory (Lower–Upper Paleolithic)	**Protohistory** (Neolithic–Bronze Age)	**History/Historical archaeology**
	(Constraints)	(Patterns/Cycles)	(Sequences)
Bailey	Biological	Environmental	Social
Butzer	(Adaptive) Transformations	Modifications	Adjustments
Hodges	Environment	Groups/Groupings	Individuals
Adams	Stability/Maximization	Resilience/Survival	

		Process		**Representation**	
Bailey	(Simultaneity		Duration		Succession)
Butzer	Steady-state (Equilibrium)		Dynamic		Metastable
van der Leeuw		Simultaneous		Sequential	
Shanks and Tilley		Substantial		Abstract	
Gamble		Attritional		Accretional	

<----Repetitive--Sequential---->

	Time Scales	
Bailey	**Behavioral uniformitarianism**	**Time perspectivism**
	Hierarchical causation	Interactive causation
	Duration	Succession of events
	Repetitive/Steady-state	Directional/Sequential
	Continuity/Resilience	Change/Transformation

To examine interrelationships amongst material, sociocultural, politico-economic, or cognitive variables, archaeologists must explore the dynamic amongst scales of time, human action, and indicators of change. Yet as Gamble observes (1986: 230): "there have been few attempts, apart from stressing linear chronologies, to explore time concepts in the study of transformations. One difficulty is that whereas space can be measured, and behaviour inferred, comparable exercises with time produce ... no sensible patterns." And Frankel (1988: 47): "We do not have analogues, independent of archaeological ones, for considering the rate or scale of long-term changes in the more distant past, or for clearly isolating the factors which influence them." The theoretical importance of the past, and how to conceive of past time, continue to be particularly intractable issues, not only in archaeology (e.g., Bailey, 1981; 1983; "Time and Archaeology" issue of *Archaeological Review from Cambridge* 6.1 [1987]; Tilley 1989b: 38–9), anthropology (e.g., Bloch 1977; Appadurai 1981), and history (Rotenstreich 1987; Whitrow 1988), but also in the physical sciences (Hawking 1988), and even in more general media (Boslough 1990) or current "archaeological" novels (Ackroyd 1989).

Human behavior and human activity occur *in time*, even if all cultures do not explicitly recognize the modern, western notion of linear time as a distinct phenomenon. The manner of reckoning time may vary according to a society's economy, ideology, or sociopolitical makeup, but the existence of a social system necessitates not only some organization of time (measurement, scheduling, attitude), but also some awareness of temporal process. Although Malinowski argued that the past has no explanatory value and must be interpreted in terms of the present (Bloch 1977: 278; Appadurai 1981: 201), the anthropologist's "long conversation" with an informant began long before the latter was born; Bloch, therefore, argued reasonably that the past does have heuristic value (1977: 278–9).

As an aspect of human experience, two basic forms of time may be distinguished: the *cyclic* and the *linear* (Fraisse 1968:25) (Table 1.1). In linear ("sequential") time, events take place in a particular, directional order along a moving continuum; in cyclic ("durational") time, the span of events and of intervals between events is relative, and may be repetitive (Goody 1968: 30–1). Cultural relativists (e.g., Durkheim, Boaz, Evans-Pritchard) regarded concepts of time as fundamental cultural variables, social constructs closely bound to various types of social organization: such concepts of time may be classified as static or cyclic.

Bloch countered, however, that if every cultural group had a different concept of time, it would not only be difficult to carry on inter-group communication, it would also be nearly impossible to discuss time concepts in any meaningful, general manner (1977: 282–3). Following up Geertz's well-known study on the Balinese, who conceive of time as a conjunction of stages in different cycles (1973), Bloch maintained that there are only two possible notions of time, the mundane (linear), or everyday time, and the ritual (cyclic), where time is expressed in ritualized social terms within various individual cultures (1977: 283–90). Bloch cited several ethnographic cases to demonstrate that in certain (usually social/religious/state ritual) contexts, a different notion of time prevails from that of the everyday. Ritual time, therefore, is cyclic, often with a nuance of the past; Leach termed this notion of time repetitive or reversible. Everyday time, however, is linear and sequential; Leach termed this directional or irreversible time (1961). And whereas time might also be distinguished as emic and etic, the emic – in Bloch's terms – would include both ritual and mundane time. If time in society, therefore, tends to be (semi-)absolute, time for the individual tends to be relative.

Anthropological fascination with cyclic vs. linear time persists but the concerns reflect more contemporary issues, such as representation of the ethnographic "other" (Fabian 1983). If historical methodology accepts the fact that history is a construction made through time (Richardson 1990: 18), that is due at least in part to the *Annales* approach to the past, which challenged the reigning historical concept of linear time and reintegrated it with a more ethnological (cyclic), fragmented concept of space. Distinctions between cyclic (or past) time and linear (or current) time may be related directly to Braudel's hierarchical spatio-temporal rhythms (see Table 1.1), and to chronology theory in archaeology (Smith, this volume). Archaeologists tend to use time as a metaphor, but it is necessary to distinguish time – as a framework or context – from what happened in time. The scale of temporal measurement must not be confused with the relationships being measured (Clarke 1973: 13). As a conceptual term, time – like space – is relative to some observed system or phenomenon, not vice versa.

In a series of somewhat recondite essays (discussed to some extent by Smith, this volume), Bailey grappled with concepts of archaeological time (1981; 1983; 1987) and distinguished initially between two aspects of time:

(1) time as *process* (objective): the past explained in terms of the present;
(2) time as *representation* (subjective): the present explained in terms of the past, and the past in terms of large-scale, long-term, historical processes.

These are effectively methodological, not theoretical issues, and are therefore pursued no further in this context. Note, however, that Bailey discusses temporal horizons as fundamental, distinguishing characteristics of human behavior, and emphasizes that uniquely human attributes (language, conceptual thought, coordination of social activities in time and space) are closely associated with three fundamental features of time experience: succession, duration, simultaneity (Table 1.1).

Equally significant, Bailey associates time scales with causation through two concepts (1983: 182–4):

(1) *hierarchical* causation, which emphasizes differences between time scales: variables that operate over the long term act as constraints for those that operate over the short term;
(2) *interactive* causation, which emphasizes that closely interrelated processes operate over similar or intersecting time scales, regardless of the total time span involved.

The former closely approximates Braudel's hierarchical temporal rhythms; the latter is related to other analytical trends in *Annales* research, such as the *structure–event–structure* concept of Le Roy Ladurie (1979: 111–31). These concepts are discussed in more detail by Fletcher (this volume), who considers how significance may be attached to hierarchical levels of time.

Whereas cosmological, paleontological, and historical research often centers on a twofold division of time (closely corresponding to what is here termed linear and cyclic time), archaeological research into questions of prehistoric development or change has often been restricted to the directional aspect of time (Bailey 1981: 110), at least partially because archaeological data are inherently spatial in form (Bailey 1983: 171; Gamble 1986: 230–2). Although Bailey proposes to look beyond the one-dimensional, linear aspect of time, and furthermore maintains that a fuller understanding of the relation between time spans and human behavior will require archaeologists to break through the "flat, two-dimensional, single-scaled view of the past" (1987: 17), he observes continuity and change from a long-term perspective: major transformations take place alongside more resilient elements that persist beneath the flux of change as no more than contrasting notions in diachronic patterning (Bailey 1983: 185). The search for stable, long-term phenomena or constraints reflects Bailey's paleoeconomic approach and is not unlike Braudel's *la longue durée*, a sort of structurally determined continuum of associations between people and resources. Unlike Braudel's historical *longue durée*, however, an archaeological *longue durée* may last several millennia, and the former thus offers little insight for explaining long-term change.

Annalistes stress that the covariation of several kinds of production or other aspects of human action should be apparent in the data under consideration (Kinser 1981b: 96–7). In a similar manner, the diachronic dimension of archaeology facilitates analysis of transformations in material phenomena through time, in comparison, contrast, or association with typologically similar or stratigraphically linked material. Yet archaeology's diachronic perspective is often adopted only to provide a framework for the study of change, rather than to consider the possible effects of varying time scales on basic social, economic, and behavioral concepts (Bailey 1981: 102).

A crucial decision for the archaeologist, therefore, is to choose the appropriate time scale on which to weigh particular variables and, in the total time span of human behavior, to find suitable data and apt chronological resolution (Bailey 1987: 16–17). As with Braudel's hierarchical temporal rhythms, the point is not to abandon time but to spin it out and draw it in, to make it relevant to the problem at hand. The measurement of archaeological data occurring within relevant, agreed-on units of time, furthermore, may help to identify causative or relative variables.

In reconsidering the role of time scales as a key variable in explaining aspects of biological, ecological, or sociocultural process, one important tenet that underpins such arguments as Bailey's (and others, e.g., Hoffman 1972: 18) was first proposed by two geologists (Schumm and Lichty 1965: 110): "... as the dimensions of time and space change, cause–effect relationships may be obscured or even reversed, and the system itself may be described differently." For archaeologists, the corollary is that small-scale processes at work in everyday life – present or past – are not the only ones in operation; failure to take account of the long term can lead to misunderstanding of certain past "events." Large-scale processes, however, cannot be invoked to explain small-scale phenomena (Bailey 1987: 8; also Binford 1986: 473–4; McGlade 1987: 24; Frankel 1988). In fact, certain aspects of human behavior presumed to be universal are more likely culture-specific (Trigger 1989: 364).

Archaeology and time

If the *Annales* paradigm, like all others, fails to lead us directly through the maze of time, what may be said, in sum, about archaeology and time?

Unlike the more ahistorical, atemporal, and often non-spatial approaches of biology, ecology, or social anthropology, whence archaeologists derive many of their theories (Bailey 1983: 171–20), archaeology of necessity is concerned with diachronic issues of origin, growth, transformation, and collapse, and with the processes that frame these developments (Knapp 1990). Quantitative analysis of varying evolutionary tempos on different levels of social, ecological, or biological reality should help to break down the notion that sociocultural elements conform to some continuous, homogeneous, evolutionary pattern: instead it should encourage analysis within one or between two (or more) time scales, e.g., analysis of short, periodic, discontinuous variations within long-term trends. Quantitative trends identifiable in archaeological data analysis, moreover, may only be regarded as a background against which the relationship between structure and event is to be examined (Hodder 1987: 5).

A moment in time is bound up in the sweep of time: they are functions of one another (Leone 1978: 34–5). The concept of time, always difficult to grasp (Hawking 1987; Whitrow 1988: 170–6), varies on different levels of socio-spatial reality, and the impact of an "event" must be evaluated in terms of interrelated processes that operate over intersecting time scales. An archaeological "point-in-time," furthermore, may be a specific event or a millennium-long process taphonomically transformed into a two-centimeter stratigraphic sequence. Even if it is accepted that socioeconomic or ideological factors are relevant to the examination of short-term change, and biological or ecological factors important in the study of long-term developments (Bailey 1981: 112; 1987: 15–16; cf. Shanks and Tilley 1987: 121), archaeology's unique perspective should make it possible to consider the effect of various time scales on human behavioral trends, and to examine cause, association, and effect over relevant units of time. In turn, this should make it feasible to distinguish between proximate and ultimate causation, and so to formulate theory that not only takes account of individual action but also of emergent phenomena generated by the interaction of numerous individuals or events (Cowgill 1988).

Although archaeologists now have at hand a battery of high-tech means to measure absolute time, archaeology's essential dilemma persists: the dynamic, diachronic processes of the past exist only in a static, synchronic material state. Nonetheless, the previously predominant, unilinear "arrow of time" has been replaced by multilinear, evolutionary, spatio-temporal trajectories. Although the temporal and spatial constraints that channel and select human behavior cannot be ignored (Trigger 1989: 355), beyond absolute, linear time, there is no single aspect or quality of time that is universally valid, and any study of cultural dynamics must consider the social structuring of temporal existence (Pinxten *et al.* 1988: 18–20). As archaeologists probe further into the effects of selective pressure on long-term adaptive strategies in human evolution, and re-examine various aspects of social and behavioral transformation (agricultural, urban, politico-ideological, industrial), time – like space – must become "a focus for selection operated on by social and ecological systems" (Gamble 1986: 237–8).

Theoretical constructs and case studies

> The archaeological record we see today does not have any dynamic meaning, nor can we rigorously give it any simply by "explaining" it through recourse to untested ethnographic or historic analogies ... Ethnoarchaeological, or more importantly, historic studies, may well provide the means to begin to link dynamic cultural processes with the static record. I firmly believe that archaeologists will have to turn more and more to the historic record. What ethnoarchaeology has been in recent years to the study of hunter-gatherer groups, history will be, I predict, to research on complex societies. (Sabloff 1986: 116)

The case studies in this volume draw upon several methodological variations of an *Annales* approach to the past. Equal attention is given to continuity and change, and primary archaeological and ethnohistoric data sets – or the conjoint processes that may be identified in them – are analyzed independently before they are correlated. Composite models that result from comparison should not confuse these independent data sets (Smith 1987). Each case study marshals a wide range of relevant data in an attempt to understand processes of continuity or discontinuity in prehistoric, protohistoric, or historic-period society.

Most papers proceed in both *conceptual* and *methodological* dimensions: problems and data are analyzed implicitly within an *Annales* framework, without undue exhortation about the need to quantify, seriate, or *do* human science. The ethnohistoric component of each data set is delineated carefully, and close consideration is given to the potential of documentary and archaeological data for diachronic correlation.

Michael Smith's analytical overview takes a critical look, from the materialist stance of an Americanist, at the positivist New Archaeology prevalent in 1960s–1980s America. Smith discusses Braudel's hierarchical time scales in the context of the Binford–Schiffer debate ("Pompeii premise") and in relation to other theoretical and methodological trends in Americanist archaeology. Smith argues eloquently that archaeology, as an historical science, cannot take as its model the fundamentally synchronic time mode of ethnography, dominant in social anthropology and sociology. Rather archaeology requires a diachronic conceptual structure to treat its typically long time spans. Whereas Smith believes that the goal of archaeology is to document and explain sociocultural variability in the material record, his case study also attempts to integrate the native historical component, and thus elevates documents to a level of interpretive significance uncommon amongst Americanists.

Roland Fletcher discusses Braudel's hierarchical time scales in relation to contemporary archaeological (processual and post-processual) theory, assesses the suitability of a historically based science as a conceptual tool for dealing with the material components of human behavior, and reviews the role of social and biological evolutionary theory in explaining human behavior and in reconstructing (or deconstructing) the past. Some pitfalls of analogy, and problems with the (substantive) uniformitarian basis of explanation are outlined. Although Fletcher holds that an *Annales* approach is particularly significant for the primary role it assigns to the material component of human behavior, and for emphasizing that different sociocultural processes operate on different, hierarchical scales of time, he cautions that different scales of magnitude are only levels of enquiry, not an explanatory framework which integrates the material products of human action with other rates of cultural process on distinctive time scales. The implication is that archaeology still lacks an integrated theory to facilitate analysis of the material aspects of community life (as independent variables) on an appropriate, hierarchical time scale.

Most of the case studies disclose a penchant for the Braudelian concept of different temporal rhythms, and for its relevance and application to differing levels of material, sociocultural, and spatio-temporal reality (see also the overviews by Bulliet and Sherratt). And yet, as most papers also reveal, the Braudelian aspect is in many ways almost incidental to an *Annales* approach, and must not be regarded as fundamental, either to this volume, or to Annalisme in general. Since there is no straightforward application of *Annales* ideas to archaeology, nor any particular *Annales* theory that may best be exemplified archaeologically, the case studies are ordered from the material to the theoretical, from those that adhere closely to an *Annales*-type framework (Smith, Bulliet) to those that explore a more multifaceted approach (Knapp, Duke, Moreland).

In his application of Braudel's diachronic rhythms to the problem of correlating Postclassic central Mexico's archaeological and ethnohistoric records, Smith evaluates both empirical findings and theoretical constructs. If it is accepted that different environmental or social processes – and the nature of the associated variables – operate at different temporal levels, Braudel's multiple temporal rhythms can help the archaeologist to decide how much effort to invest in chronological refinement, given the nature of the phenomena under investigation. In applying these insights to his own case study, Smith considers how demographic, economic, and politico-military factors stand up to diachronic correlation between archaeological and ethnohistoric data. Smith argues that Braudel's conceptual framework influences not only how time and the past are perceived, but also how time is measured in order to document and explain the past.

Card-carrying Annaliste historian Richard Bulliet compiles a diverse array of ceramic and numismatic data from Nishapur, a site in northeastern Iran (excavated prior to World War II) to reconsider the process of urbanization in the context of the Middle East's Islamicization (AD 634–1000). In addition, he uses these data to examine a postulated relationship between ceramic style, on the one hand, and on the other socio-religious conflict and change prompted by the conversion process. Having argued in earlier publications for the existence within the new urban centers of an elite–populist division, rooted in the social consequences of conversion, Bulliet seeks to conceptualize ceramic style and distribution in terms of elitist and populist lifestyles. The recursive relationship between social construct and material or ethnohistoric data, central to an archaeological as well as an *Annales*-based approach to the past, is well exemplified and clearly argued in Bulliet's case study.

Knapp's case study adopts Le Roy Ladurie's *structure–event–structure* concept to re-examine independent documentary and material evidence related to the rise and collapse of social complexity in the southern Levant during the Middle and Late Bronze Ages (about 1800–1200 BC). The reciprocal relationship between structure and event, between material and ethnohistoric data and the recursive relationship of both to social change, are examined by focusing on two successive geopolitical structures – the locally dominated urban centers of the Middle Bronze and the imperially managed (Egyptian), quasi-independent city states of the Late Bronze – and on the matrix event that precipitated the transformation from one structure to another. A microscopic view of local production and change is combined with a macroscopic view of regional pattern and process in order to illustrate the dialectic of event and structure in historical analysis.

Philip Duke's study of North American, Northern Plains prehistory and ethnohistory draws upon *Annales* concepts of geohistorical structures and *mentalités* to assess, respectively, differing rates of cultural change in the material record, and the role of (prehistoric) processing and procurement activities, especially as reflected in gender relationships outlined in ethnohistoric documents. The difficulties of linking a Braudelian model to the resolutely prehistoric data are severe, and Duke's "events," for example, have varying time spans and may incorporate several stages. Duke nonetheless attempts to interweave the long- and the short-term, and argues that certain structures, as identified in economic activities, were transformed through a recursive relationship with human action, made manifest in specific events: the introduction of the bow and arrow; the adoption of ceramics; the arrival of Europeans. Duke conjoins a post-processual approach with Annaliste conceptions of duration and change in order to break down barriers between the prehistoric and ethnohistoric past, and to consider structural continuities between material-culture patterning and human behavior.

John Moreland's study of *incastellamento* – the process of settlement-pattern shift from dispersed village to hilltop site during the early Middle Ages in central Italy – reflects the influence of *Annales* historians Jacques Le Goff and Georges Duby, who accentuate the social construction of reality and the dialectic between social structure and individual human agent. Such emphasis on the behavior of the individual actor in the work of third- and fourth-generation Annalistes stands in stark contrast not only to Braudel's geohistorical structuralism, but also to the "scientific rationalism" of a positivist approach. In analyzing changes in habitat, and the correlative, intensified use of documents, Moreland discusses the recursive relationship amongst social structure, human action, and the material products of human action. People, maintains Moreland, are not bound by structures, but live within them and are active in changing them. Material data, including documentary evidence, are likewise active in maintaining or transforming social relationships, a concept that makes it possible to consider archaeological and ethnohistoric witnesses to the past within the same interpretive framework. The rich material culture of the hilltop sites of early medieval Italy, and the extensive documentation used to facilitate administration and information processing therein, strongly suggest that they were focal points for social control over local populations. At the same time, *incastellamento* served to establish social bonds that superseded elementary structures of kinship. In such a way peasant producers became a potent force in establishing and legitimizing power relations amongst competing elites; the hilltop settlements themselves were physical manifestations of these power relations.

Annales: retrospect and prospect

In 1949, Lucien Febvre, disgruntled with the miasma that history had become, argued that the word had lost meaning (1973: 43 n. 9 [1949]):

> But what word would we use to replace [history] to contain at one and the same time the ideas of man, change and duration? "Archaeology" has already been used up, and leads us back to that quite inept definition of history, "science of the past"; it does not contain any suggestion of humanity or of duration. Anthropochronology, ethnochronology – philistine inventions which would need explaining before anybody would understand them.

More recently, Foucault observed that although archaeology once emulated history and attained meaning only in the recreation of historical discourse through description and interpretation, the tables had turned, and *Annales* history aspired to the condition of archaeology by transforming documents into monuments (Foucault 1972: 6). The document and narrative discourse have become but two elements amongst many which provide a means to define sociocultural and historical entities, totalities, series, and relations (Foucault 1972: 7; Stone 1979). Stone, bone, ceramic, or metal "monuments" represent traces of past human actions; they should be studied as material refractions of rules, beliefs, and past social practices – outside the limits of homogeneous time (Tilley 1989c: 312) – that delimit the parameters and govern the practice of archaeological research (Handsman 1982: 63–4).

To conclude this overview and set the stage for what follows, I add a final observation, pessimistic as well as optimistic and thus in the enduring spirit of *Annales* scholarship. Fletcher and Moreland (this volume) question not only the general appeal but the specific value of *Annales* methodology in assessing archaeological and ethnohistoric material. Similarly, amongst the many reviews of Braudel's *The Mediterranean* (1972), at least one sought to understand the wide-ranging appeal that extended even to readers with no specific interest in the subject matter: "it is the very anti-definitiveness of the master-text that outlines its authority" (Kellner 1979: 217).

Perhaps, then, the appeal of an *Annales* approach lies in its fundamental ambivalence, and in its capacity to adapt and grow with the demands of an always-shifting method and theory, and an ever-changing database (as in archaeology), or with the social and moral dictates of society, which often propel revisionist trends in both history and the social sciences.

My own feelings find appropriate expression in the words of the Belgian medievalist Henri Pirenne, written almost eighty years ago. Pirenne's impact on Marc Bloch and the *Annales* was substantial (Lyon 1987), and his observations perhaps prompted Bloch's much later statement that history is the science of change (Pirenne 1912: 57–8; Lyon 1987: 206 n. 30):

> All those engaged in searching for the truth understand that the glimpses they have of it are neces-

sarily fleeting. They glow for an instant and then make way for new and always more dazzling brightness. Quite different from that of the artist, the work of the scholar is inevitably provisional. He knows this and rejoices in it because the rapid obsoleteness of his books is the very proof of the progress of his field of knowledge.

Acknowledgments

I should like to thank Sturt Manning (Jesus College, Cambridge) and James G. Lewthwaite (Department of Archaeology, University of Sheffield) for reading and commenting on an earlier draft of this paper. I am grateful to Alain Schnapp (CNRS, Paris) for providing relevant offprints. Suggestions from the Editorial Board of the New Directions series led to reorganization of this chapter.

References

Ackroyd, P. 1989 *First Light*. London: H. Hamilton Ltd.

Adams, R. McC. 1984 Mesopotamian social evolution: old outlooks, new goals, in T. K. Earle, ed., *On the Evolution of Complex Societies: Essays in Honor of Harry Hoijer 1982*, pp. 79–129. Other Realities 6. Malibu: Undena.

Les *Annales* 1988 Histoire et sciences sociales: un tournant critique? *Annales: ESC* 43: 291–3.

Appadurai, A. 1981 The past as a scarce resource. *Man* 16: 201–19.

Austin, M. M. and P. Vidal-Naquet 1977 *Economic and Social History of Ancient Greece*. London: Batsford.

Bailey, G. N. 1981 Concepts, time scales and explanations in economic prehistory, in A. Sheridan and G. Bailey, eds., *Economic Archaeology*, pp. 97–117. British Archaeological Reports, International Series 96. Oxford: BAR.

1983 Concepts of time in Quaternary prehistory. *Annual Review of Anthropology* 12: 165–92.

1987 Breaking the time barrier. *Archaeological Review from Cambridge* 6: 5–20.

Bailyn, B. 1977 Review of T. Stoianovich, *French Historical method: The* Annales *Paradigm* (Ithaca, NY: 1976), in *Journal of Economic History* 37: 1028–34.

Berelowitch, W., J. Sapir, L. Haimson, R. Robin and M. Ferro 1985 Histoire de l'URSS. *Annales: ESC* 40: 717–899.

Binford, L. R. 1962 Archaeology as anthropology. *American Antiquity* 28: 217–25.

1968 Archaeological perspectives, in S. R. Binford and L. R. Binford, eds., *New Perspectives in Archaeology*, pp. 5–32. Chicago: Aldine.

1981 Behavioral archaeology and the "Pompeii premise." *Journal of Anthropological Research* 37: 195–208.

1986 In pursuit of the future, in D. J. Meltzer, D. D. Fowler, and J. A. Sabloff, eds. *American Archaeology Past and Future*, pp. 459–79. Washington, DC: Smithsonian Institute.

Birnbaum, N. 1978 The *Annales* School and social theory. *Review* 1: 225–35.

Bloch, Marc 1966 *French Rural History: An Essay on its Basic Characteristics*. Berkeley: University of California Press.

Bloch, Maurice 1977 The past and the present in the present. *Man* 12: 278–92.

Boslough, J. 1990 The enigma of time. *National Geographic* 177 (3): 109–32.

Bottero, J., O. Buschenschutz, S. Cleuziou, P.-M. Duval, A. Laming-Emperaire, A. Schnapp and A. Wasowicz 1973 Préhistoire, archéologie, sociétés. *Annales: ESC* 28: 52–76.

Bourdieu, P. 1977 *Outline of a Theory of Practice*. Cambridge Studies in Social Anthropology. Cambridge: Cambridge University Press.

Bowler, P. J. 1989 *The Invention of Progress: The Victorians and the Past*. Oxford: Blackwell.

Boyd, R. and P. J. Richerson 1985 *Culture and the Evolutionary Process*. Chicago: University of Chicago Press.

Braudel, F. 1957 Lucien Febvre et l'histoire. *Annales: ESC* 12: 177–82.

1972 *The Mediterranean and the Mediterranean World in the Age of Philip II* (volume 1). New York: Harper and Row.

1973 Personal testimony. *Journal of Modern History* 44: 448–67.

1980 History and the social sciences: the *longue durée*, in *On History*, pp. 25–54. Chicago: University of Chicago Press.

Bruguières, A. 1982 The fate of the history of *mentalités* in the *Annales*. *Comparative Studies in Society and History* 24: 424–37.

1985 Demography, in J. Le Goff and P. Nora, eds., *Constructing the Past: Essays in Historical Methodology*, pp. 123–50. Cambridge: Cambridge University Press.

Burrows, T. 1982 Their patron saint and eponymous hero – Jules Michelet and the *Annales* School. *Clio* 12: 67–81.

Butzer, K. 1982 *Archaeology as Human Ecology*, Cambridge: Cambridge University Press.

Carrithers, M. 1990 Why humans have cultures. *Man* 25: 189–206.

Chapman, M. 1989 Review of R. Chartier, *Cultural History: Between Practices and Representations*, in *Man* 24: 550–51.

Charlton, T. H. 1981 Archaeology, ethnohistory, and ethnology: interpretive interfaces. *Advances in Archaeological Method and Theory* 4: 129–75.

Chartier, R. (trans. L. G. Cochrane) 1988 *Cultural History: Between Practices and Representations*. Oxford: Polity Press.

Chaunu, P. 1985 Economic history: past achievements and future prospects, in J. Le Goff and P. Nora, eds., *Constructing the Past: Essays in Historical Methodology*, pp. 28–46. Cambridge: Cambridge University Press.

Cherry J. F. 1987 Power in space: archaeological and geographical studies of the state, in J. M. Wagstaff, ed., *Landscape and Culture: Geographical and Archaeological Perspectives*, pp. 146–72. London: Blackwell.

Chirot, D. 1984 The social and historical landscape of Marc Bloch, in T. Skocpol, ed., *Vision and Method in Historical Sociology*, pp. 22–46. Cambridge: Cambridge University Press.

Clark, S. 1985 The *Annales* historians, in Q. Skinner, ed., *The Return of Grand Theory in the Social Sciences*, pp. 177–98. Cambridge: Cambridge University Press.

Clarke, D. L. 1973 Archaeology: the loss of innocence. *Antiquity* 47/185: 6–18.

Cowgill, G. L. 1988 Onward and upward with collapse, in N. Yoffee and G. Cowgill, eds., *The Collapse of Ancient States and Civilizations*, pp. 244–76. Tucson: University of Arizona Press.

Daniel, G. 1975 *The Idea of Prehistory*. Harmondsworth: Penguin.

Demoule, J.-P, 1982 La préhistoire et ses mythes. *Annales: ESC* 37: 741–59.

Duby, G. 1985 Ideologies in social history, in J. Le Goff and P. Nora, eds., *Constructing the Past: Essays in Historical Methodology*, pp. 151–65. Cambridge: Cambridge University Press.

Earle, T. K., and R. Preucel 1987 Processual archaeology and the radical critique. *Current Anthropology* 28: 501–38.

Evans, J. D. 1974 The archaeological evidence and its interpretation: some suggested approaches to the problems of the Aegean Bronze Age, in R. A. Crossland and A. Birchall, eds., *Bronze Age Migrations in the Aegean: Archaeological and Linguistic Problems in Greek Prehistory*, pp. 17–26. Park Ridge, NJ: Noyes Press.

Fabian, J. 1983 *Time and the Other: How Anthropology Makes its Objects*. New York: Columbia University Press.

Febvre, L. 1949 Vers un autre histoire. *Revue de métaphysique et de morale* 58: 225–47.

(ed. P. Burke) 1973 *A New Kind of History: From the Writings of Febvre*. London: Routledge and Kegan Paul.

Feeley-Harnik, G. 1982 Is Historical Anthropology possible?, in G. M. Tucker and D. A. Knight, eds., *Humanizing America's Iconic Book*, pp. 95–126. Chico, CA: Scholar Press.

Ferguson, L. 1977 Historical archaeology and the importance of material things, in L. Ferguson, ed., *Historical Archaeology and the Importance of Material Things*, pp. 5–8. Society for Historical Archaeology, Special Publication 2.

Ferro, M. 1980 *October 1917: A Social History of the Russian Revolution*. London: Routledge and Kegan Paul.

Finley, M. I. 1977 "Progress" in historiography. *Daedalus* 106(3): 125–42.

Forster, R. 1978 The achievements of the *Annales* school. *Journal of Economic History* 38: 58–75.

Forster, R. and O. Ranum (eds.), 1977 *Rural Society in France: Selections from the* Annales. Baltimore: Johns Hopkins University Press.

Foucault, M. 1972 *The Archaeology of Knowledge*. London: Tavistock.

Fraisse, P. 1968 Time: psychological aspects, in D. Sill, ed., *International Encyclopaedia of the Social Sciences*, volume 16, pp. 25–30. London: Collier-Macmillan and Free Press.

Frankel, D. 1988 Characterising change in prehistoric sequences: a view from Australia. *Archaeology in Oceania* 23: 41–8.

Furet, F. 1983 Beyond the *Annales*. *Journal of Modern History* 55: 389–410.

1984 *In the Workshop of History*. Chicago: University of Chicago Press.

1985 Quantitative methods in history, in J. Le Goff and P. Nora, eds., *Constructing the Past: Essays in Historical Methodology*, pp. 12–27. Cambridge: Cambridge University Press.

Gallay, A. 1986 *L'Archéologie demain*. Paris: Belford.

Gamble, C. 1986 Archaeology, geography and time. *Progress in Human Geography* 11: 227–46.

Gathercole, P. 1989 Childe's early Marxism, in V. Pinsky and A. Wylie, eds., *Critical Traditions in Contemporary Archaeology*, pp. 80–7. Cambridge: Cambridge University Press.

Geertz, C. 1973 Person, time and conduct in Bali, in *The Interpretation of Culture*. New York: Basic Books.

Giddens, A. 1979 *Central Problems in Social Theory*. London: Macmillan.

Ginzburg, C. 1990 *Les 'Annales': renouveler la reflexion methodologique*. *Le Monde*, vendredi le 19 janvier: 22.

Goody, J. 1968 Time: social organisation, in D. Sills, ed., *The International Encyclopaedia of the Social Sciences*, vol. 16. pp. 30–42. London: Collier-Macmillan and Free Press.

Gould, S. J. 1986 Evolution and the triumph of homology, or why History matters. *American Scientist* 74: 60–9.

Grene, M. 1988. Hierarchies in biology. *American Scientist* 75: 504–10.

Gurvitch, G. 1964 *The Spectrum of Social Time*. Dordrecht: Reidel.

Hall E. T. 1966 *The Hidden Dimension*. London: Bodley Head.

Handsman, R. G. 1982 Machines and gardens: structures in and symbols of America's past, in E. Tooker, ed., *Ethnography by Archaeologists*, pp. 63–78. Washington, DC: American Ethnological Association.

Handsman, R. G. and M. P. Leone 1989 Living history and critical archaeology in the recognition of the past, in V. Pinsky and A. Wylie, eds., *Critical Traditions in Contemporary Archaeology*, pp. 117–35. Cambridge: Cambridge University Press.

Harsgor, M. 1978 Total history: the *Annales* School. *Journal of Contemporary History* 13: 11–13.

Hartley, L. P. 1953 *The Go-Between*. London: Hamilton.

Hawking, S. 1987 The direction of time. *New Scientist* 1568: 46–9.

1988 *A Brief History of Time*. London: Bantam.

Hodder, I. A. 1986 *Reading the Past: Current Approaches to Interpretation in Archaeology*. Cambridge: Cambridge University Press.

1987 The contribution of the long term, in I. A. Hodder, ed., *Archaeology as Long Term History*, pp. 1–8. Cambridge: Cambridge University Press.

1989 This is not an article about material culture as text. *Journal of Anthropological Archaeology* 8: 250–69.

Hoffman, M. A. 1972 Process and tradition in Cypriot culture history: time theory in anthropology. *Anthropological Quarterly* 45: 15–34.

Hunt, L. 1986 French history in the last twenty years: the rise and fall of the *Annales* paradigm. *Journal of Contemporary History* 21: 209–24.

Iggers, G. G. 1975 The *Annales* traditon – French historians in search of a science of history, in G. G. Iggers, ed., *New Directions in European Historiography*, pp. 43–79. Middletown, CT: Wesleyan University Press.

Kellner, H. 1979 Disorderly conduct: Braudel's Mediterranean satire. *History and Theory* 18: 197–222.

Kinser, S. 1981a Capitalism enshrined: Braudel's tryptich of modern economic history. *Journal of Modern History* 53: 673–82.

1981b Annaliste paradigm? the geohistorical structuralism of Fernand Braudel. *American Historical Review* 86: 63–105.

Knapp, A. B. 1990 Paradise gained and paradise lost: intensification, specialization, complexity and collapse. *Asian Perspectives* 28: 179–214.

1992 *Society and Polity at Bronze Age Pella: An* Annales *Perspective*. Sheffield: Sheffield Academic Press.

Kuper, A. 1988 *The Invention of Primitive Society: Transformations of an Illusion*. London: Routledge.

Le Goff, J. 1971 Is politics still the backbone of history? *Daedalus* 100: 1–19.

1985 *Mentalités*: a history of ambiguities, in J. Le Goff and P. Nora eds., *Constructing the Past: Essays in Historical Methodology*, pp. 166–80. Cambridge: Cambridge University Press.

Le Goff, J. and P. Nora (eds.) 1985 *Constructing the Past: Essays in Historical Methodology*. Cambridge: Cambridge University Press.

Le Roy Ladurie, E. 1979 *The Territory of the Historian*. Chicago: University of Chicago Press.

1981 *The Mind and Method of the Historian*. Brighton: Harvester Press.

Leach, E. 1961 Two essays concerning the symbolic representation of time. *Rethinking Anthropology*. London School of Economics, Monographs in Social Anthropology 22. London: Athlone Press.

Leone, M. 1972 Issues in anthropological archaeology, in M. Leone, ed., *Contemporary Archaeology: A Guide to Theory and Contributions*, pp. 14–27. Carbondate, IL: Southern Illinois University Press.

1978 Time in American archaeology, in C. Redman *et al.*, eds., *Social Archaeology*, pp. 25–36. New York: Academic Press.

1981 Archaeology's relationship to the present and the past, in R. A. Gould and M. B. Schiffer eds., *Modern Material Culture: The Archaeology of Us*, pp. 5–14. New York: Academic Press.

Leone, M. P., P. B. Potter, Jr., and P. A. Shackel 1987

Towards a critical archaeology. *Current Anthropology* 28: 283–302.

Levi, J. M. 1988 Myth and history reconsidered: archaeological implications of Tzotzil-Maya mythology. *American Antiquity* 53: 605–19.

Lewthwaite, J. G. 1986 Archaeologists in academe: an institutional confinement?, in J. L. Bintliff and C. F. Gaffney, eds., *Archaeology at the Interface*, pp. 52–87. British Archaeological Reports, International Series 300. Oxford: BAR.

1988a Living in interesting times: archaeology as society's mirror, in J. Bintliff, ed., *Extracting Meaning from the Past*, pp. 86–98. Oxford: Oxbow Books.

1988b Trial by *durée*: a review of historical–geographical concepts relevant to the archaeology of settlement on Corsica and Sardinia, in J. L. Bintliff, D. Davidson, and E. Grant, eds., *Conceptual Issues in Environmental Archaeology*, pp. 161–86. Edinburgh: Edinburgh University Press.

Little, B. J. and P. A. Shackel 1989 Scales of historical anthropology: an archaeology of colonial Anglo-America. *Antiquity* 63: 495–509.

Lowenthal, D. 1985 *The Past is a Foreign Country*. Cambridge: Cambridge University Press.

Lucas, C. 1985 Introduction, in J. Le Goff and J. Nora, eds., *Constructing the Past: Essays in Historical Methodology*, pp. 1–11. Cambridge: Cambridge University Press.

Lyon, B. 1987 Marc Bloch: historian. *French Historical Studies* 15: 195–207.

McGlade, J. 1987 Chronos and the oracle: some thoughts on time, timescales and simulation. *Archaeological Review from Cambridge* 6: 21–31.

McNeill, W. H. 1986 Mythistory, or truth, myth, history, and historians. *American Historical Review* 91: 1–10.

Murra, J., N. Wachtel and J. Revel 1986 *Anthropological History of Andean Politics*. Cambridge: Cambridge University Press.

Pinsky, V. 1989 Commentary: a critical role for the history of archaeology, in V. Pinsky and A. Wylie, eds., *Critical Traditions in Contemporary Archaeology*, pp. 88–91. Cambridge: Cambridge University Press.

Pinsky, V. and A. Wylie (eds.) 1989 *Critical Traditions in Contemporary Archaeology*. Cambridge: Cambridge University Press.

Pinxten, R., E. Soberon, D. Berboven, and K. Snoeck 1988 Cultural Dynamics: a vision and a perspective. *Cultural Dynamics* 1: 1–28.

Pirenne, H. 1912 *Manifestation en l'honneur de M. le Professeur Henri Pirenne*. Mons, Belgium.

Postan, M. M. 1939 *The Historical Method in Social Science: An Inaugural Lecture*. Cambridge: Cambridge University Press.

Pyszczyk, H. W. 1989 Consumption and ethnicity: an example from the fur trade in western Canada. *Journal of Anthropological Archaeology* 8: 213–49.

Renfrew, A. C. 1980 The Great Tradition versus the Great Divide: archaeology as anthropology. *American Journal of Archaeology* 84: 287–98.

1981 Space, time and man. *Transactions, Institute of British Geographers* n.s.6: 257–78.

1983 Geography, archaeology and environment: 1, Archaeology. *Geographical Journal* 149: 316–23.

Revel, J. 1978 The *Annales*: continuities and discontinuities. *Review* 1: 9–18.

Richardson, M. 1990 Enough Said: reflections on Orientalism. *Anthropology Today* 6(4): 16–19.

Rotenstreich, N. 1987 *Time and Meaning in History*. Boston Studies in Philosophy of Science. Dordrecht: Reidel.

Sabloff, J. 1986 Interaction among Classic Maya polities: a preliminary examination, in C. Renfrew and J. F. Cherry, eds., *Peer Polity Interaction and Socio-Political Change*, pp. 109–16. Cambridge: Cambridge University Press.

Sahlins, M. 1985 *Islands of History*. Chicago: University of Chicago Press.

Schnapp, A. 1981 Les *Annales* et l'archéologie: une rencontre difficile. *Mélanges de l'Ecole Française de Rome, Antiquité* 93: 469–78.

Schumm, S. A. and R. W. Lichty 1965 Time, space and causality in geomorphology. *American Journal of Science* 263: 110–19.

Shanks, M. and C. Tilley 1987 *Social Theory and Archaeology*. Cambridge: Polity Press.

1989 Archaeology into the 1990s. *Norwegian Archaeological Review* 22: 1–54.

Sider, G. M. 1986 *Culture and Class in Anthropology and History: A Newfoundland Illustration*. Cambridge Studies in Social Anthropology 60. Cambridge: Cambridge University Press.

Smith, M. E. 1987 The expansion of the Aztec empire: a case study in the correlation of diachronic archaeological and ethnohistorical data. *American Antiquity* 52: 37–54.

Snodgrass, A. 1982 La prospection archéologique en Grèce et dans le monde méditerranéen. *Annales: ESC* 37: 800–12.

1988 *An Archaeology of Greece: The Present State and Future Scope of a Discipline*. Sather Classical Lectures 53. Berkeley: University of California Press.

Spencer, C. S. 1990 On the tempo and mode of state formation: neoevolutionism reconsidered. *Journal of Anthropological Archaeology* 9: 1–30.

Stevenson, M. G. 1989 Sourdoughs and cheechakos: the formation of identity-signaling social groups. *Journal of Anthropological Archaeology* 8: 270–312.

Stoianovich, T. 1976 *French Historical Method: The* Annales *Paradigm*. Ithaca, NY: Cornell University Press.

Stone, L. 1979 The revival of narrative: reflections on a New Old History. *Past and Present* 85: 3–24.

Tilley, C. (ed.) 1989a *Reading Material Culture: Structuralism, Hermeneutics, and Poststructuralism*. Oxford: Blackwell.

1989b Claude Lévi-Strauss. Structuralism and beyond, in C. Tilley, ed., *Reading Material Culture: Structuralism, Hermeneutics, and Poststructuralism*, pp. 3–81. Oxford: Blackwell.

1989c Michel Foucault: towards an archaeology of archaeology, in C. Tilley, ed., *Reading Material Culture: Structuralism, Hermeneutics, and Poststructuralism*, pp. 281–347. Oxford: Blackwell.

1989d Archaeology as socio-political action in the present, in V. Pinsky and A. Wylie, eds., *Critical Traditions in Contemporary Archaeology*, pp. 104–16. Cambridge: Cambridge University Press.

Toulmin, S. 1977 From form to function: philosophy and history of science in the 1950s and now. *Daedalus* 106(3): 143–62.

Trevor-Roper, H. R. 1973 Fernand Braudel, the *Annales*, and the Mediterranean. *Journal of Modern History* 44: 468–79.

Trigger, B. 1981 Anglo-American archaeology. *World Archaeology* 13: 138–55.

1989 *A History of Archaeological Thought*. Cambridge: Cambridge University Press.

Van der Leeuw, S. E. 1982 How objective can we become? Some reflections on the nature of the relationship between the archaeologist, his data, and his interpretations, in C. Renfrew, M. J. Rowlands, and B. A. Seagreves, eds., *Theory and Explanation in Archaeology*, pp. 431–57. New York: Academic Press.

Vernant, J.-P. and P. Vidal-Naquet 1981 *Tragedy and Myth in Ancient Greece*. Brighton: Harvester Press.

Wagstaff, M. 1987 The new archaeology and geography, in M. Wagstaff, ed., *Landscape and Culture: Geographical and Archaeological Perspectives*, pp. 26–36. Oxford: Blackwell.

Wallerstein, I. 1982 Fernand Braudel: historien, l'homme de la conjoncture. *Radical History Review* 26: 104–19.

Watson, P. J. 1986 Archaeological interpretation, 1985, in D. J. Meltzer, D. D. Fowler, and J. A. Sabloff, eds., *American Archaeology Past and Future*, pp. 439–57. Washington, DC: Smithsonian Institution.

Watson, P. J., S. A. LeBlanc, and C. Redman 1984 *Archaeological Explanation: The Scientific Method in Archaeology*. New York: Columbia University Press.

Weber, M. 1956 *The Sociology of Religion* (translated by E. Fishchoff). Boston: Beacon Press.

White, L. A. 1945 History, evolutionism and functionalism: three types of interpretation of culture. *Southwestern Journal of Anthropology* 1: 235–47.

Whitrow, G. J. 1988 *Time in History. The Evolution of our General Awareness of Time and Temporal Perspective*. Oxford: Oxford University Press.

Wilk, R. A. 1985 The ancient Maya and the political present. *Journal of Anthropological Research* 41: 307–26.

Wright, H. T. 1986 The evolution of civilizations, in D. J. Meltzer, D. D. Fowler, and J. A. Sabloff, eds., *American Archaeology Past and Future*, pp. 323–65.

Yoffee, N. 1982 Social history and historical method in the late Old Babylonian period. *Journal of American Oriental Society* 102: 347–53.

PART I
THEORETICAL CONSTRUCTS

2 Braudel's temporal rhythms and chronology theory in archaeology

MICHAEL E. SMITH

This chapter relates Fernand Braudel's model of hierarchical temporal rhythms to current theoretical work on time and chronology in archaeology. The debate between Lewis Binford and Michael Schiffer over the existence of a "Pompeii premise" in Americanist archaeology serves as a point of departure, and it is shown that Binford's distinction between "ethnographic time" and "archaeological time" is encompassed by Braudel's model. The varying temporal rhythms associated with diverse socioeconomic processes are relevant to the methods of chronology-building, periodization, and cultural reconstruction. It is argued that these associations need to be considered not only at the level of interpretation, but also at the levels of research design and data recovery. Chronology-building is an integral part of the research process, and Braudel's formulation contributes to an understanding of the dialectical relationship between changing research questions and chronological refinement.

Introduction

Archaeology as a historical science

Since the early days of the "New Archaeology," one of the primary goals of archaeology has been the explanation of past culture change. The long time span represented in the archaeological record is seen as one of the most important resources for archaeology, and the analysis of processes of change is often viewed as archaeology's major contribution to knowledge (e.g., Plog 1973). Because of long-standing disciplinary and intellectual ties between American archaeology and anthropology (see Willey and Sabloff 1980), Lewis Binford and the other new archaeologists took sociocultural anthropology as the model for their vision of archaeology's future. Archaeology was to be part of anthropology ("Archaeology as anthropology" – Binford 1962), specifically the part concerned with change ("Diachronic anthropology" – Plog 1973).

Unfortunately, sociocultural anthropology with its ethnographic foundation operates in a fundamentally synchronic mode, and ethnography simply cannot provide observations or models of change (or stability) over the long time spans typically dealt with in archaeology. As a "historical" discipline concerned with temporal processes, archaeology requires a conceptual structure quite different in orientation from that of non-historical disciplines like sociocultural anthropology or the other social sciences. In a theoretical treatment of this problem, Dunnell identifies two "underlying views of the nature of reality: space-like and time-like frames" (1982: 8). His argument that archaeology requires a time-like view (rather than the space-like view of the social sciences) in order to document adequately and explain the archaeological record is paralleled by Ernst Mayr's (1982: 32–67) discussion of the distinctiveness of evolutionary biology in relation to the physical sciences. As a historical field of study concerned with evolutionary change over time, biology has its own methods, theories, and epistemology that make it a very different kind of science from physics or chemistry, two fields that are often viewed as models for scientific procedure (see also Gould 1986).

These concerns are not limited to archaeology or biology, as Toulmin and Goodfield (1965) point out in their treatment of the development of the various historical sciences.[1] These sciences, including physical cosmology, geology, evolutionary biology, and human history (both documentary history and archaeology) all confront a fundamental methodological obstacle – the past cannot be observed directly. Historical disciplines must therefore devise indirect means to investigate the past. While the particular indirect methods are necessarily distinctive for each discipline, this common problem has produced some basic methodological parallels among historical disciplines (see Gould 1986). Toulmin and Goodfield make this point as follows:

> Throughout the centuries of intellectual endeavor, the growth of men's historical consciousness across subjects ranging from physical cosmology at one extreme to theology and social history at the other, took closely parallel forms ... where disciplines with quite different subject-matters have faced common forms of problem (e.g. the problem of establishing a well-founded temporal sequence of past epochs), they have – it seems – resorted again and again to similar strategies. To this extent, we conclude, physical cosmologists today may have more to learn than they yet recognize from the theoretical quandaries facing their predecessors in geology, and even in political theory. (Toulmin and Goodfield 1965: 15)

Similarly, archaeologists may have more to learn that we yet realize from the methods and theories of the other historical disciplines.

Some Americanist archaeologists recognize this, and have turned to aspects of evolutionary biology for models of sociocultural change based upon natural selection (e.g. Dunnell 1980; Rindos 1984; Leonard and Jones 1987). For the study of complex societies, however, models from the discipline of history may be more appropriate. While Americanists have often borrowed data from history (particularly ethnohistory), most have ignored the methods, models, and theories worked out by historians. This is a consequence of a dichotomy proclaimed by the New Archaeologists between history, viewed as particularizing and thus bad, and science, portrayed as generalizing and thus good (e.g. Binford 1964; 1972; Watson, LeBlanc, and Redman 1971: 165–70). This is a false dichotomy, however, and it reveals a profound misunderstanding of the nature of both history and science (see Walker 1972 for an early critique of Binford in this regard). Scientific history, referring to a concern with comparison, generalization, and rigorous explanation, has a long pedigree that includes such scholars as Marx, Weber, Bloch, Braudel, and Wallerstein. Science, on the other hand, is not a unitary pursuit concerned only with generalization; the investigation of particular unique events is a crucial component in all of the historical sciences (Toulmin and Goodfield 1965; Mayr 1982: 71–6; Gould 1987).

The relevance of history to archaeology is nothing new to archaeologists in Britain and Europe, where the two pursuits have long-standing disciplinary ties (Lewthwaite 1986). However, this relationship needs to be stressed in Americanist archaeology, which has yet to sort fully the wheat from the chaff of the New Archaeology (Trigger 1984; Kohl 1984; Dunnell 1986; Schiffer 1988). This paper explores the archaeological relevance of a particular historical construct – Fernand Braudel's notion of hierarchical temporal rhythms. This model ties in closely with current theoretical and methodological work on time and chronology in Americanist archaeology. Braudel's model not only helps place that work in a wider context, but it also contributes to the clarification of archaeological goals and explanations. In a separate paper in this volume (Smith), Braudel's insights are applied to the archaeological and ethnohistoric records of socioeconomic change in Postclassic central Mexico. In addition to showing the relevance of hierarchical temporal rhythms to archaeology, the case study also demonstrates their value in the correlation of parallel historical and archaeological data on long-term change.

Rhythms of temporal change in history and archaeology

One of Fernand Braudel's most important contributions to the study of history is his notion that different historical processes operate at different temporal rhythms or levels (Braudel 1972; 1980; see also Lewthwaite 1987; Knapp 1992; this volume). Briefly, Braudel discusses four hierarchical levels of temporal change. *Events* concern the individual actions that Braudel (1972: 21) calls "traditional history": kings, battles, treaties, and the like. The *conjuncture* (from the French *conjoncture*, not from the English sense of the term) is Braudel's term for two intermediate levels of historical duration; Braudel calls the study of conjunctures "social history, the history of groups and groupings" (1972: 20). Braudel divided conjunctures into two kinds: *intermediate-term conjunctures*, which include wage and price cycles, rates of industrialization, and wars; and *long-term conjunctures*, which refer to secular changes like "long-term demographic movements, the changing dimensions of states and empires (the geographical conjuncture as it might be called), the presence or absence of social mobility in a given society, [and] the intensity of industrial growth" (1972: 899).

The *longue durée* represents Braudel's most significant innovation in temporal categorization. This level describes "man in his relationship to the environment, a history in which all change is slow, a history of constant repetition, ever-recurring cycles" (1972: 20). In Braudel's two major historical analyses (*The Mediterranean* and *Civilization and Capitalism*), the *longue durée* forms an almost unchanging, centuries-long background that furnishes constraints and opportunities for the dynamic operation of change at the levels of conjuncture and event. It is an arena dominated by "structures," which for Braudel are "defined then first of all by duration and second by their effects on human action" (Santamaria and Bailey 1984: 79; see also Stoianovich 1976 on Braudel's notion of structure).

From an archaeological perspective, Braudel's conception of the *longue durée* as a structural rather than a dynamic factor presents problems, since archaeologists deal with many examples of changes on time scales equivalent to and often much longer than the *longue durée*. Archaeology needs a construct that can treat 200–400 year intervals in a dynamic, not static, framework, and it needs additional temporal constructs of even longer duration. Such issues are dealt with by Karl Butzer (1982), who applies concepts from ecology and systems theory to the evidence for cultural change in the archaeological record. Butzer defines three "dynamic modes of adaptive systems," two of which correspond to Braudel's temporal rhythms. (1) *Adaptive adjustments* are short-term readjustments within a dominant adaptive strategy which resolve social and economic crises. As examples, Butzer lists "geophysical disasters, epidemics, famines, destructive wars, and dynastic changes" (1982: 290); this level corresponds to both Braudel's events and the shorter type of conjuncture. (2) *Adaptive modifications* involve "substantial revision of adaptive strategies within the context of a viable and persistent adaptive system" (Butzer 1982: 290), and include cases of agricultural intensification, demographic expansion, and cycles of growth, florescence, and decline of civilizations. These changes correspond to both Braudel's longer conjuncture and the *longue durée*. (3) *Adaptive transformations* involve the development of radically different adaptive modes, including late Pleistocene cultural diversification, agricultural origins, the formation of states, and the industrial revolution; this level of change is not treated in Braudel's scheme.

Butzer's scheme extends and improves Braudel's conception of temporal rhythms in two ways. First, it supplies an additional longer perspective (the adaptive transformation) required in many archaeological studies. Second, Butzer's dynamic ecosystem perspective corrects Braudel's static view of the environment by stressing both environmental change (Butzer 1982: 24) and the dynamic nature of the relationship of human populations with their environment (1982: 279–320).

Braudel's association of each temporal level with a suite of relevant sociocultural processes and constraints (personal and political processes at the level of the event; social and economic processes at the level of the conjuncture; environmental constraints at the level of the *longue durée*) represents an empirical finding that arose out of his research for *The Mediterranean* and finds support in *Civilization and Capitalism*. Comparative work in archaeology, history, and the social sciences suggests that these associations are valid (case studies, this volume), and thus Hexter's (1973: 533) assertion that they are "arbitrary" is incorrect.

Bailey's work (1981; 1983; 1987) on "time perspectivism" in archaeology reaches similar conclusions independently, although he frames the issue in different terms. Bailey utilizes the concept of hierarchical causation, "in which causes at one [temporal] scale are treated as logically independent of causes at other scales" (1983: 182). Thus Bailey focuses on the nature of the variables that influence human behavior and adaptation at different time scales while Braudel focuses on the nature of the social processes that operate at different temporal rhythms. The basic principle of recognizing a diversity of hierarchical temporal rhythms is the same, however, and the work of Braudel, Butzer, and Bailey has important implications for the archaeological study of change.[2] This approach parallels recent theoretical work on biological evolution (Gingerich 1983) and changes in ecosystems (O' Neill *et al.* 1983), where hierarchical concepts of time and change (referred to as temporal scaling) are becoming important.

Braudel and chronology theory

Binford, Schiffer, and the "Pompeii premise" in Americanist archaeology

Braudel's work on temporal rhythms can contribute to conceptual advances in an area that might be called archaeological chronology theory. The debate between Lewis R. Binford and Michael B. Schiffer over the existence of a "Pompeii premise" in Americanist archaeology illustrates some of the issues involved. Robert Ascher (1961: 324) first used the phrase "Pompeii premise" to refer to the "erroneous notion, often implicit in archaeological literature ... [that archaeologists recover] ... the remains of a once living community, stopped as it were, at a point in time." Binford (1981) reviews Ascher's remarks and places them in the context of his own views of the archaeological record as a static contemporary phenomenon that was formed by dynamic processes operating over a long period of time in the past. According to Binford, the archaeological record relates to a different order of time from that of a living, functioning community. An ethnographer observing contemporary events and episodes operates in "quick time," while the archaeologist recovers artifacts and patterns produced over long intervals of time representing a "different order of reality" (1981: 197). I will refer to these two levels of time as ethnographic time and archaeological time.

From this perspective, Binford (1981) criticizes Schiffer (1976a) for advocating the application of transformations that would allow archaeologists to reconstruct Pompeii-like "fossilized" assemblages reflecting events on the level of ethnographic time. Binford (1981: 199, 201) quotes a passage in which Schiffer (1976a: 12–13) supposedly reveals that, in his archaeological research, he "wants to find Pompeii" (Binford 1981: 201). In Binford's opinion, Schiffer is wasting time by trying to reconstruct phenomena pertaining to ethnographic time. Rather than viewing the archaeological record as a distorted picture of past behavioral systems, archaeologists should treat it in its own right and confine themselves to the scale of archaeological time. Schiffer (1985) responded by noting that there are a number of different types of archaeological deposits, each created through the operation of distinct formation processes, and that Pompeii-like assemblages represent only one of many kinds of archaeological situation. Binford's critique focuses on Schiffer's discussion of house-floor assemblages, so Schiffer concentrates on this kind of deposit in his reply:

> the real Pompeii premise is that the archaeologist can treat house-floor assemblages at any site *as if* they were Pompeii-like systemic inventories ... by ignoring, overlooking, or downplaying the operation and effects of formation processes, especially cultural formation processes, investigators *tacitly assume*, in the employment of certain analytical strategies, that their assemblages have a Pompeii-like character. (Schiffer 1985: 18, 20; emphases in original)

This statement is backed up by detailed reanalyses of the work of Hill (1970) and others on house-floor assemblages in the American southwest (Schiffer 1985; 1987: 323–38). On this basis, Schiffer argues that it is Binford (e.g. 1964: 425) and his early students like Hill and Longacre who adhered to a Pompeii premise. Schiffer (1985: 18) points out (quite correctly) that Binford (1981) distorts his views, and reminds Binford that much of Schiffer's analysis in *Behavioral Archaeology* (1976a) is based upon secondary refuse whose accumulation is measured over the rhythms of archaeological time, not ethnographic time.

The chronological issues concerning the "Pompeii premise" may be discussed in two dimensions, the conceptual and the methodological. The conceptual dimension deals with the ways we interpret and assign significance to the different levels of time, and the methodological dimension concerns the possibility of measuring different time scales and temporal rhythms with archaeological data. These are discussed in turn by focusing first on Binford's notions of ethnographic and archaeological time, and then on the questions of periodization and chronological refinement.

Binford's distinction between ethnographic and archaeological time

In a 1986 article, Binford discussed his views on the different levels of time referred to here as ethnographic and archaeological:

> The archaeological record presents us with information vastly different from that which was available to the participants within past systems ... The archaeological record also demonstrates temporal durations or a tempo of chronological change that is very different from that perceived by persons who participated in it. The rates of change for most archaeologically known eras are much slower than the rates of generational replacement for participants in those systems. This fact must be appreciated in two ways. First, the beliefs and perceptions of the past participants could not have been germane to a reality of which they could not have been aware, the macrotemporal scale of systems change and the factors that were conditioning it. Second, the observations by ethnographers and historical figures, while perhaps documenting something of the internal dynamics of cultural systems, cannot be expected to be necessarily germane to an understanding of a much slower and larger-scale process of change and modification. Thus the reality with which we deal is one that living, breathing persons have in fact never directly experienced. (Binford 1986: 473–4)

These two levels of time clearly parallel Braudel's distinction between the event and the *longue durée*, but there is a significant difference between the two formulations: for Binford, the distinction is fundamental, a qualitative difference between two "order[s] of reality" (1981: 197), while for Braudel, the distinction between levels is more quantitative in nature. Braudel's alternative temporal rhythms represent convenient sections along a continuum rather than distinct, fundamentally different phenomena. Binford is quite right in stating that the *longue durée* of much of the archaeological record represents a reality "that living, breathing persons have in fact never directly experienced" (Binford 1986: 474); indeed, Braudel makes the same point, referring to the *longue durée* as "unconscious history" (1980: 39). However, rather than insisting on the existence of two fundamentally different levels of time (ethnographic and archaeological), it is more useful for archaeologists to take advantage of the insights of Braudel's formulation of the issue and thereby recognize the existence of multiple temporal scales. The problem then becomes methodological. No archaeologist would deny the relevance of the *longue durée* and our ability to monitor stability and change at this level. But is it possible to study the faster rhythms of the conjuncture or the event with archaeological data?

Periodization and chronological refinement

Because of the methodological and conceptual impossibility of dealing with instantaneous occurrences, any consideration of temporal change must begin with periodization, the division of the time continuum into analytical units. There are special conditions in which an archaeological "period" may be very limited in time (e.g., knapping a block of flint), but the discussion here is not concerned directly with such temporal divisions. Periods are synchronic constructs in that events and conditions occurring within a given period are treated as analytically contemporaneous (see Michels 1973: 11). From the Neolithic stage onward, the most common kind of archaeological period is the ceramic phase, and archaeological studies of change usually consist of comparisons of variables and conditions across such units. Some archaeologists have voiced dissatisfaction with this procedure, which appears to impose a step-wise model of change upon the archaeological record. Plog (1973; 1974), for example, argues that change should be viewed as continuous rather than step-like, and that change can and should be monitored in the trajectories of individual variables without the necessity of synchronic reconstruction of conditions for each period (see also Dunnell 1982; Blake 1985).

The continuous-versus-steps issue is a question of scale and methods. In order to make comparisons between different points in time, periodization is required, because it is methodologically not possible to study "continuous change." The methods do not exist that can isolate and analyze instantaneous occurrences, and even if this were possible, which of the nearly infinite instances would we choose to analyze? The real issue is then the degree of refinement of the chronology employed; this issue is discussed below. Plog's second point is also problematic, as Schiffer pointed out in a review of Plog (1974):

> his claim that [the archaeological] record can be read without making synchronic statements (reconstructing past lifeways) seems curiously

> inconsistent. He suggests that to obtain the temporal trace of any past variable it is sufficient to construct quantitative indices from artifactual and other data, applicable to several points or periods in time. This approach would seem to depend on synchronic statements, and of course these are what Plog actually presents. (Schiffer 1976b: 183–4)

The necessity of using synchronic data and analyses to make diachronic statements does not commit the archaeologist to making complete reconstructions of life in two or more periods before studying change in selected variables, nor does it require viewing chronological differences as epistemologically equivalent to synchronic spatial differences, as Dunnell (1982: 13, 19) suggests. Mayr (1982) and Gould (1986) discuss the situation in biology, where knowledge of the diachronic processes of past evolution is based upon analyses of synchronic patterns in the present (Gould's [1987] discussion of the development of uniformitarian thought in geology is also relevant here).

In the study of change, we are thus required to construct periods or phases and then make comparisons among them. The issue of continuous change is a red herring, and the crucial question is how finely can we measure past time, or how refined can we make our chronologies? Chronology-building and refinement are costly and time-consuming activities, so the issue must be dealt with in two parts: (1) what degree of refinement is *possible* for a given archaeological situation? and (2) what degree of refinement is *needed* to address specific research objectives?

The major factors that determine the levels of chronological refinement possible in various archaeological situations are the following: the age of the contexts under study, the kind of cultural adaptation, the capabilities of chronometric dating techniques, the specific archaeological deposits encountered and analyzed, the archaeological recovery techniques employed, and the level of effort and funding invested. (1) The *age of the contexts* under study is a major determinant of the possible level of refinement, with more recent archaeological contexts susceptible to greater chronological control than more ancient contexts. This is due to a number of factors, including the time ranges of available chronometric techniques, progressive changes in the kinds of cultural adaptations present in many areas, and increasing population sizes and densities in most parts of the world. (2) The *kind of cultural adaptation* influences chronological refinement in several dimensions. Because of the nature and quantity of archaeological remains produced, chronological refinement can generally proceed further for sedentary societies than for mobile societies, in complex societies relative to simple societies, and in societies with large dense populations compared to small dispersed groups. (3) The *capabilities of chronometric dating techniques* (e.g. Michels 1973) clearly influences chronological refinement, and the increasing sensitivity of most techniques (e.g., Hester 1987) will help to refine sequences in many parts of the world.

(4) The nature of the *specific archaeological deposits* encountered and analyzed exert a degree of control over chronological refinement. For example, architectural contexts often permit finer temporal control than non-architectural contexts, and structures which exhibit a high degree of modification and rebuilding can produce relatively fine chronological control (e.g. Blake 1985). In addition, burials and caches can provide abundant time-sensitive artifacts, and secondary refuse is more appropriate than primary refuse[3] for chronological seriation, and thus permits finer control. (5) Finally, *archaeological recovery techniques* strongly influence the possibilities of chronological refinement. It is almost always possible to obtain finer sequences with excavated deposits than with surface material, and such excavation questions as natural versus metric levels, the size of grid squares, and the use of screening play important roles in determining the degree of refinement possible.

Chronological refinement and archaeological goals

Some of the constraints listed above are beyond the archaeologist's control and others are largely determined by the nature of his or her research goals. However, some of these factors are the direct result of fieldwork decisions, and to the latter must be added a final constraint – (6) *the level of effort put into chronology in both fieldwork and analysis*. Most existing archaeological sequences are capable of refinement if only the necessary time, resources, and funds are invested. However, chronological work is an expensive endeavor in both time and funds. How does the archaeologist decide what level of investment is appropriate? Should chronology comprise a large or a small portion of one's research activities? Braudel's work on temporal rhythms can help resolve this issue.

Because different sociocultural processes operate at different time scales (Braudel), or because different variables become significant at different times scales (Bailey), the level of chronological refinement required in archaeology depends heavily upon the kinds of sociocultural variables and processes under investigation.

Studies of large-scale demographic patterns or subsistence strategies can be carried out successfully with phases of several centuries' length, while analyses of the changing social or economic conditions of states or empires require finer phases, on the order of a century or less. Archaeological work on such questions as warfare, domestic cycles, or price movements, processes operating at the scale of the shorter conjuncture, requires even shorter periods, on the order of decades.

Chronology-building and chronological refinement should proceed in a dialectical fashion with other research activities. It is generally acknowledged that some form of chronology is needed as a first step in the archaeological investigation of a new area (e.g. Thomas 1979: 137–40). Once a basic spatial and temporal framework has been erected, archaeological research typically turns to other issues. As new research goals and issues arise out of the results of fieldwork, analysis, interpretation, or theory-building, finer chronologies may or may not be needed. As suggested above, Braudel's work can help the archaeologist decide how much effort to put into chronological refinement given the nature of the phenomena under investigation. If the existing sequence is not adequate, it can be amended, extended, or even replaced by a more sensitive periodization. For this reason, archaeological chronologies should not be viewed as final and unchanging, but rather as working constructs whose modification or abandonment will probably be needed periodically (see Hole *et al.* 1969: 5; Smith 1987).

Unfortunately, this attitude is often not carried into practice, and archaeological research in many areas continues to try to fit new problems into the inappropriate framework of old chronologies. There is a sentiment among many archaeologists that chronology-building is a necessary evil that must be gotten out of the way before we can address interesting questions (note the title of Redman *et al.* 1978, *Social Archaeology: Beyond Subsistence and Dating*). Some explicit attention to Braudel and the work of Butzer, Bailey, and others would help ameliorate this situation.

Temporal rhythms and cultural reconstruction

Braudel and cultural reconstruction

Beyond the relevance of Braudel's model for chronology-building and diachronic analysis in archaeology, the notion of varying temporal rhythms also comes into play in the area of synchronic analysis or cultural reconstruction. When an archaeologist constructs a model of a past society or culture during a specific phase or period, what levels of temporal processes are represented in the archaeological remains? Ethnographic analogues are often used to interpret archaeological remains, but do the ethnographic and archaeological records pertain to compatible levels of time? This is the issue that prompted Binford's critique of Schiffer and his subsequent remarks on ethnographic versus archaeological time (see above). While Schiffer shows that in some cases it is indeed possible to monitor short intervals of time (Schiffer 1985; 1987), Binford is correct that in most archaeological situations, the "quick time" of ethnography is compressed so that the deposits recovered by archaeologists – including those working with the material remnants of complex societies – pertain to blocks of time beyond the life span of past individual actors.

Many of the social groups analyzed by ethnographers, such as families or households, extended kin groups, work parties, neighborhoods, associations, and the like, are relatively short-lived phenomena and thus the archaeological record for such groups often consists of the compressed remains of several or many successive examples at a single location. As Binford (1982) stresses, the archaeological record reveals more about the *places* where past activities were repeatedly carried out than about the individual episodes and activities themselves. In other words, the nature of the deposits we excavate may limit our temporal resolution to the level of the *longue durée* or the longer conjuncture, whereas the ethnographic analogues frequently called on to interpret the archaeological record pertain to groups and processes that exist on the level of the event. This disjunction between ethnography and archaeology, discussed above in reference to Binford's work, can make ethnographically derived interpretations of the archaeological record problematic. The example of "household archaeology" illustrates this point.

"Household archaeology" and time: some problems

The household as a social group is defined by ethnographers in a variety of ways, in some cases emphasizing kinship and in other cases residence, while more recently functional attributes have come to the fore in household studies (see Yanagisako 1979; Netting, Wilk, and Arnould 1984). An anthropological focus on households has a number of advantages in the study of agrarian societies, for households are usually the primary units of production, consumption, and reproduction. The increasing attention being paid to households by anthropologists parallels recent trends in social history and the social sciences, and the cross-cultural and cross-temporal study of households, domestic groups, and families is now an important social science subfield in its own right.

Archaeologists, particularly those working in Mesoamerica, were quick to jump on the household bandwagon, citing the same justifications for household study as are found in the literature of anthropology and other disciplines. In addition to the social-theoretical and comparative benefits of the household focus, there are two strong attractions of the household as a unit of analysis in archaeology. First, the study of households helps tip the balance of archaeological research away from temples, tombs, and palaces and toward the bulk of the population in ancient societies. Second and perhaps most attractive to archaeologists is the simple fact that houses are relatively prominent in the archaeological record, and this is a methodologically convenient scale of analysis (see Wilk and Rathje 1982; Rathje 1983; and Wilk and Ashmore 1988 for programmatic statements and case studies of household archaeology).

In their rush to study ancient households, archaeologists have ignored the issue of the temporal scales discussed in this article. The warnings of Dunnell (1982) and Binford (1981; 1986) on the compatibility of archaeological and ethnographic data are not acknowledged in this work. How do archaeologists isolate the remains of a single household in the past? This only happens in those cases where we have a catastrophic abandonment event (e.g., Pompeii), or in rare situations when new houses are built and occupied for only one generation before being abandoned (e.g., Snow 1989). In most agrarian societies, however, houses are used for more than one generation and the refuse deposits associated with a house contain the compressed remains of several successive households that occupied the structure. If archaeologists cannot identify and study individual households, then where does this leave "household archaeology"?

A brief example from my own research illustrates the problem that time creates for studies of ancient households. In 1986 the Postclassic Morelos Archaeological Project excavated 44 Late Postclassic houses at the sites of Capilco and Cuexcomate in Morelos, Mexico (see Smith *et al.* 1989). House remains consist of stone foundation walls and floors, and fragments of adobe (mud brick) were recovered adjacent to the walls. Relative and chronometric dating work indicates that over half of the houses were occupied for a century or less, with the remainder occupied for about two centuries. This accords with ethnoarchaeological observations of nearby modern adobe houses with stone foundations that often have a use-life of a century or more. While the excavated houses have relatively dense middens in association, artifacts in those deposits cannot be assigned to temporal units finer than ceramic phases of about a century. Thus it is impossible to isolate the remains of single "households" from these sites, although it is likely on comparative grounds that households did indeed inhabit the houses. This situation of long-lasting houses and temporal phases of 100 years or more is not unusual in the archaeology of agrarian states. If we cannot identify or isolate a single "household" in these domestic remains, then what kind of social category is relevant to their interpretation?

An acknowledgement of the temporal problems involved in cultural reconstruction leads to a different approach to the social analysis of archaeological remains. Rather than simply borrowing analytical units from ethnography, as in the case of household archaeology, archaeologists should construct their own interpretive units to assign sociocultural meaning to the archaeological record. For the social interpretation of permanent housing in agrarian societies, I suggest the concept of "household series" as a replacement for "household" (see Smith 1989). The household series may be defined as the sequence of households that successively inhabit a given structure or house over a span of more than one generation. This analytical unit follows Binford's (1982) call for a place-orientation in archaeological systematics and has the advantage of being a unit that is relevant and detectable in many archaeological situations.

On the other hand, the household series has the disadvantage of being a construct whose social significance is virtually unknown. The social correlates of archaeological categories need to be established with comparative evidence, yet the ethnographic record tells us little or nothing about the nature of successive households at a single house-site over several generations, much less on the material expressions of such a phenomenon. Studies of the family developmental cycle (Goody 1958) are relevant but insufficient for dealing with changes over more than two generations. Can we make the assumption that the socioeconomic situation and activities of the successive inhabitants of a given house-site over several generations were relatively consistent through time? If the fortunes and conditions of household series fluctuate greatly from one generation to the next, then there may be a significant amount of synchronic socioeconomic variability that is masked by the compressed nature of most archaeological deposits. There is a clear need for comparative data on such phenomena so that sociocultural analogues for archaeological remains will pertain to appropriate levels of time. Key social issues that need to be investigated involving the household series include the inheritance and sale of houses and property, changes in residence, and generational continuity in wealth, occupation, and other conditions. Archaeologists need first to assemble comparative ethnographic and historical data on these phenomena and consider the causal forces influencing intra- and inter-cultural variation, and then to develop appropriate models or correlates of their material expressions.

In the process of building models and analogies appropriate to the archaeological study of residences, archaeologists can turn to the historical record. Unfortunately, Braudel has little to say about households and their changes through time. This area is part of "material civilization," which is treated as a structural element in volume 1 of Braudel's *Civilization and Capitalism* (1981). The burgeoning field of "family history" has produced voluminous data on changing patterns of household demography and organization (e.g., Goody, Thirsk, and Thompson 1978; Netting, Wilk, and Arnould 1984), but the unit of analysis and comparison is the single household or the community, not the individual building.

A few French family historians have begun to explore relevant issues like the relationship of peasant households to individual house-sites, and the socioeconomic conditions of "lines" of peasant families, over several generations (e.g., Lamaison 1979; Segalen 1986). This is clearly an area that archaeologists need to pay attention to. Sabloff has recently suggested that "what ethnoarchaeology has been in recent years to the study of hunter-gatherer groups, history will be, I predict, to research on complex societies" (Sabloff 1986: 116). Sabloff's primary reason for making this statement is the lack of modern enthographic analogues to the preindustrial state-level societies of the past. Beyond this factor, archaeologists also need history to provide comparative information on social units and social processes over longer time spans. This kind of information is required not only for studies of change, but for synchronic reconstructions as well. While Braudel's work makes few specific contributions to changing conditions on the household or family level, his temporal frameworks can be extended to this level, as is shown by recent *Annales* work (e.g., Lamaison 1979).

In sum, one of the major determinants of the level of comparability between the ethnographic/historical record and the archaeological record is the scale of time represented in the two sources of data (Binford 1981; 1982). Before archaeologists can make effective use of ethnographic and historical analogues in the interpretation of synchronic phenomena, they need to consider the issue of varying temporal rhythms. As in the case of diachronic analysis and chronology-building, Fernand Braudel's work is of clear relevance to the common archaeological procedure of cultural reconstruction.

Conclusion

The various socioeconomic processes that characterized past societies operated at different temporal scales, and Braudel's work demonstrates that archaeologists need to take this issue into account in their models. The significance of varying temporal scales is implicated not only at the level of interpretation and explanation, however, but also at the level of research design and methodology. The design and planning of archaeological research must include careful consideration of chronological issues in both the theoretical (temporal rhythms) and practical (archaeological sequences and chronological refinement) dimensions. Braudel's work ties in closely with current thinking by Bailey, Butzer, Binford, Dunnell, Schiffer, and others concerned with the theoretical and methodological bases of modern archaeology. A recognition of this linkage may help lay to rest the unproductive anti-historical orientation of the new archaeology while yielding a new appreciation of archaeology as a fundamentally historical science.

Notes

1 This paper takes the position that archaeology is and should be a scientific discipline concerned with the documentation and explanation of sociocultural variability as expressed in the archaeological record (*contra* Shanks and Tilley 1987). Most Americanist archaeologists would probably concur, and a materialist orientation is dominant in New World archaeology (e.g., Thomas 1979; Butzer 1982; Kohl 1984; Binford 1986).

2 The notions of time and chronology found in the work of Braudel, Butzer, and Bailey are based upon a materialist epistemology that incorporates a scientific approach to the study of the past. Shanks and Tilley (1987: 120–6) present an alternative "post-processual," anti-objectivist critique of Bailey's time perspectivism. While their remarks may have some relevance in the ethnographic study of perceptions of social time, their denial of the dimensionality of time and the possibility of an objective knowledge of the past is counterproductive for archaeology. Rudwick's (1985: 451–5) discussion of cartography as a metaphor for scientific enquiry, discussed by Lewthwaite (1986: 57), is useful in showing the necessary contributions of both "discovery" and "construction" in the historical sciences. While Shanks and Tilley are correct in observing that many new archaeologists may have tipped the balance too heavily toward objective science ("discovery") in archaeological interpretation, these authors'

rejection of objectivity in archaeology is a clear case of throwing out the baby with the bathwater.

3 Secondary refuse is the most appropriate kind of deposit to use for quantitative seriation techniques because of the variety and abundance of artifacts and the general lack of functional specificity of such refuse deposits (Smith 1983: 205–6). Seriation can often produce a very fine-grained ordering of deposits, but these refined sequences are usually collapsed into coarser phases for analysis just as adjacent stratigraphic levels are often lumped into phases. There are three reasons for this lumping, which reverses the normal direction of chronological refinement: comparability, sample size, and precision. Archaeologists need to make comparisons among deposits, and coarser phases are easier to use than the finer sequence of individual deposits (see Drennan 1976: 54). Also, individual deposits often have too few artifacts for confident quantification, and lumping chronologically adjacent deposits into phases enlarges the size of the artifact sample. Finally, a seriation curve may be accurate, though at a coarser scale than the sequence of individual deposits; lumping deposits into phases cancels out the potential lack of chronological precision in the exact order of deposits (see Smith 1983: 244).

Acknowledgements

I would like to thank Bernard Knapp for the opportunity and encouragement to write this paper, for stimulating correspondence on some of these issues, and for helpful comments on earlier drafts of the paper. Roland Fletcher also provided useful comments on an earlier draft. Geoff Bailey and James Lewthwaite kindly sent me reprints of articles relevant to the themes discussed here. I have had fruitful discussions on archaeological time and related issues with Michael Blake, Robert Dunnell, Cynthia Heath-Smith, Kenneth Hirth, Donald Lathrap, Scott O'Mack, and Dean Snow. My thinking on households and temporal rhythms was stimulated by a graduate student at the University of Washington who asked the right question at the wrong time. Finally, I would like to acknowledge Donald W. Lathrap's positive influence on my thinking about the role of chronology in archaeology.

References

Ascher, R. 1961 Analogy in archaeological interpretation. *Southwest Journal of Anthropology* 17: 317–25.

Bailey, G. N. 1981 Concepts, time-scales and explanations in economic prehistory, in A. Sheridan and G. Bailey, eds., *Economic Archaeology: Towards an Integration of Ecological and Social Approaches*. pp. 97–117. British Archaeological Reports, International Series 96. Oxford: BAR.

1983 Concepts of time in Quaternary prehistory. *Annual Review of Anthropology* 12: 165–92.

1987 Breaking the time barrier. *Archaeological Review from Cambridge* 6: 5–20.

Binford, L. R. 1962 Archaeology as anthropology. *American Antiquity* 28: 217–25.

1964 A consideration of archaeological research design. *American Antiquity* 29: 425–41.

1972 The "Binford" pipe stem formula: a return from the grave. *Conference on Historic Site Archaeology Papers* 6: 117–26.

1981 Behavioral archaeology and the "Pompeii premise." *Journal of Anthropological Research* 37: 195–208.

1982 The archaeology of place. *Journal of Anthropological Archaeology* 1: 5–31.

1986 In pursuit of the future, in D. J. Meltzer, D. D. Folwer, and J. A. Sabloff, eds., *American Archaeology Past and Future*, pp. 459–79. Washington, DC: Smithsonian Institution.

Blake, M. 1985 Canajaste: an evolving Postclassic Maya site. Ph.D. dissertation, Department of Anthropology, University of Michigan.

Braudel, F. 1972 *The Mediterranean and the Mediterranean World in the Age of Philip II* (translated by Sian Reynolds). 2 vols. New York: Harper and Row.

1980 *On History* (translated by Sarah Matthews). Chicago: University of Chicago Press.

1981 *The Structures of Everyday Life: The Limits of the Possible* (= *Civilization and Capitalism 15th–18th Century*, volume 1) (translated by M. Kochan and S. Reynolds). New York: Harper and Row.

Butzer, K. W. 1982 *Archaeology as Human Ecology: Method and Theory for a Contextual Approach*. New York: Cambridge University Press.

Drennan, R. D. 1976 *Fábrica San José and Middle Formative Society in the Valley of Oaxaca*. University of Michigan, Museum of Anthropology, Memoirs 8. Ann Arbor.

Dunnell, R. C. 1980 Evolutionary theory and archaeology. *Advances in Archaeological Method and Theory* 3: 35–99.

1982 Science, social science, and common sense: the agonizing dilemma of modern archaeology. *Journal of Anthropological Research* 38: 1–25.

1986 Five decades of American archaeology, in D. J. Meltzer, D. D. Fowler, and J. A. Sabloff, eds., *American Archaeology Past and Future*, pp. 23–49. Washington DC: Smithsonian Institution.

Gingerich, P. D. 1983 Rates of evolution: effects of time and temporal scaling. *Science* 222: 159–61.

Goody, J. (ed.) 1958 *The Developmental Cycle in Domestic Groups.* New York: Cambridge University Press.

Goody, J., J. Thirsk, and E. P. Thompson (eds.) 1978 *Family and Inheritance: Rural Society in Western Europe, 1200–1800.* New York: Cambridge University Press.

Gould, S. J. 1986 Evolution and the triumph of homology, or why history matters. *American Scientist* 74: 60–9.

1987 *Time's Arrow, Time's Cycle: Myth and Metaphor in the Discovery of Geological Time.* Cambridge, MA: Harvard University Press.

Hester, J. J. 1987 The significance of accelerator dating in archaeological method and theory. *Journal of Field Archaeology* 14: 445–51.

Hexter, T. 1973 Fernand Braudel and the monde Braudellian. *Journal of Modern History* 44: 480–539.

Hill, J. N. 1970 *Broken K Pueblo: Prehistoric Social Organization in the American Southwest.* University of Arizona, Anthropological Papers 18.

Hole, F., K. V. Flannery, and J. A. Neely 1969 *Prehistory and Human Ecology of the Deh Luhran Plain: An Early Village Sequence from Khuzistan, Iran.* University of Michigan, Museum of Anthropology, Memoirs 1.

Knapp, A. B. 1992 *Society and Polity at Bronze Age Pella: An* Annales *Perspective.* Sheffield: Sheffield Academic Press.

Kohl, P. L. 1984 Force, history, and the evolutionist paradigm, in Matthew Spriggs, ed., *Marxist Perspectives in Archaeology,* pp. 127–34. New York: Cambridge University Press.

Lamaison, P. 1979 Les stratégies matrimoniales dans un système complexe de parenté: Riennes en Gévaudan (1650–1830). *Annales: Economies, Sociétés, Civilisations* 34: 721–43.

Leonard, R. D. and G. T. Jones 1987 Elements of an inclusive evolutionary model for archaeology. *Journal of Anthropological Archaeology* 6: 199–219.

Lewthwaite, J. G. 1986 Archaeologists in academe: an institutional confinement?, in J. L. Bintliff and C. F. Gaffney, eds., *Archaeology at the Interface,* pp. 52–87. British Archaeological Reports, International Series 300. Oxford: BAR.

1987 The Braudelian beaker: a Chalcolithic conjoncture in western Mediterranean prehistory, in W. H. Waldren and R. C. Kennard, eds., *Bell Beakers of the Western Mediterranean: Definition, Interpretation, Theory, and New Site Data,* pp. 31–60. British Archaeological Reports, International Series 331. Oxford: BAR.

Mayr, E. 1982 *The Growth of Biological Thought: Diversity, Evolution, and Inheritance.* Cambridge, MA: Harvard University Press.

Michels, J. W. 1973 *Dating Methods in Archaeology.* New York: Academic Press.

Netting, R. McC., R. R. Wilk, and P. J. Arnould (eds.) 1984 *Households: Comparative and Historical Studies of the Domestic Group.* Berkeley: University of California Press.

O'Neill, R. V., D. L. DeAngelo, J. B. Waide, and T. F. H. Allen 1986 *A Hierarchical Concept of Ecosystems.* Princeton: Princeton University Press.

Plog, F. T. 1973 Diachronic anthropology, in C. L. Redman, ed., *Research and Theory in Current Archaeology,* pp. 181–98. New York: Wiley.

1974 *The Study of Prehistoric Change.* New York: Academic Press.

Rathje, W. L. 1983 To the salt of the earth: some comments on household archaeology among the Maya, in E. Z. Vogt and R. M. Leventhal, eds., *Prehistoric Settlement Patterns: Essays in Honor of Gordon R. Willey,* pp. 23–34. Albuquerque: University of New Mexico Press.

Redman, C. L., M. J. Berman, E. V. Curtin, W. T. Langhorne, Jr., N. M. Versaggi, and J. C. Wanser (eds.) 1978 *Social Archaeology: Beyond Subsistence and Dating.* New York: Academic Press.

Rindos, D. 1984 *The Origins of Agriculture: An Evolutionary Perspective.* New York: Academic Press.

Rudwick, M. J. S. 1985 *The Great Devonian Controversy.* Chicago: University of Chicago Press.

Sabloff, J. A. 1986 Interaction among Classic Maya polities: a preliminary examination, in C. Renfrew and J. F. Cherry, eds., *Peer Polity Interaction and Socio-Political Change,* pp. 109–16. New York: Cambridge University Press.

Santamaria, U. and A. M. Bailey 1984 A note on Braudel's structure as duration. *History and Theory* 23: 78–83.

Schiffer, M. B. 1976a *Behavioral Archaeology.* New York: Academic Press.

1976b Review of *The Study of Prehistoric Change* by F. T. Plog. *American Anthropologist* 78: 182–4.

1985 Is there a "Pompeii premise" in archaeology? *Journal of Anthropological Archaeology* 41: 18–41.

1987 *Formation Processes of the Archaeological Record.* Albuquerque: University of New Mexico Press.

1988 The structure of archaeological theory. *American Antiquity* 53: 461–85.

Segalen, M. 1986 *Historical Anthropology of the Family* (translated by J. C. Whitehouse and Sarah Matthews). New York: Cambridge University Press.

Shanks, M. and C. Tilley 1987 *Social Theory and Archaeology*. Albuquerque: University of New Mexico Press.

Smith, M. E. 1983 Postclassic culture change in western Morelos, Mexico: the development and correlation of archaeological and ethnohistorical chronologies. Ph.D. dissertation, Department of Anthropology, University of Illinois.

1987 The expansion of the Aztec empire: a case study in the correlation of diachronic archaeological and ethnohistorical data. *American Antiquity* 52: 37–54.

1989 The spatial organization of settlement at late postclassic sites in Morelos, Mexico, in S. MacEachern, D. J. W. Archer, and R. D. Garvin, eds., *Households and Communities: Proceedings of the 21st Annual ChacMool Conference*, pp. 450–9. Calgary: The Archaeological Association of the University of Calgary.

Smith, M. E., P. Aguirre, C. Heath-Smith, K. Hirst, S. O'Mack, and T. J. Price 1989 Architectural patterns at three Aztec-period sites in Morelos, Mexico. *Journal of Field Archaeology* 16: 185–203.

Snow, D. R. 1989 The evolution of Mohawk households, A.D. 1400–1800, in S. MacEachern, D. J. W. Archer, and R. D. Garvin, eds., *Households and Communities: Proceedings of the 21st Annual ChacMool Conference*, pp. 293–300. Calgary: The Archaeological Association of the University of Calgary.

Stoianovich, T. 1976 *French Historical Method: The* Annales *Paradigm*. Ithaca, NY: Cornell University Press.

Thomas, D. H. 1979 *Archaeology*. New York: Holt, Rinehart, and Winston.

Toulmin, S. and J. Goodfield 1965 *The Discovery of Time*. Chicago: University of Chicago Press.

Tourtellot, G. 1983 An assessment of Classic Maya household composition, in E. Z. Vogt and R. M. Leventhal, eds., *Prehistoric Settlement Patterns: Essays in Honor of Gordon R. Willey*, pp. 35–54. Albuquerque: University of New Mexico Press.

Trigger, B. 1984 Archaeology at the crossroads: what's new? *Annual Review of Anthropology* 13: 275–300.

Walker, I. C. 1972 Binford, science, and history: the probabilistic variability of explicated epistemology and nomothetic paradigms in historical archaeology. *Conference on Historic Site Archaeology Papers* 7 (3): 159–201.

Watson, P. J., S. A. LeBlanc and C. L. Redman 1971 *Explanation in Archaeology: An Explicitly Scientific Approach*. New York: Columbia University Press.

Wilk, R. R. and W. Ashmore (eds.) 1988 *Household and Community in the Mesoamerican Past*. Albuquerque: University of New Mexico Press.

Wilk, R. R. and W. L. Rathje (eds.) 1982 Archaeology of the household: building a prehistory of domestic life. *American Behavioral Scientist* 25 (6).

Willey, G. R. and J. A. Sabloff 1980 *A History of American Archaeology*, 2nd edition. San Francisco: W. H. Freeman.

Yanagisako, S. 1979 Family and household: the analysis of domestic groups. *Annual Review of Anthropology* 8: 161–206.

3 Time perspectivism, *Annales*, and the potential of archaeology

ROLAND FLETCHER

This paper discusses the need for a hierarchical arrangement of explanations used by archaeologists to deal with processes that occur over different scales of space and time. The aim is to define what type of hierarchy is needed. In a hierarchical structure of theories, large-scale processes cannot be reduced to small-scale ones and small-scale ones are not determined by large-scale ones. By contrast, a reductionist view holds that the nature of the smallest component sufficiently explains the largest system or is essential for a basic understanding of it. Hierarchical explanations are usual in the biological sciences, the earth sciences and the hard sciences, contrary to much misapprehension about them by humanistic disciplines. The trend is toward these integrative explanatory structures.

A version of hierarchical explanation introduced to history by the *Annales* school (Braudel in particular) suggests that it is not incompatible with studies of human beings. Biologists such as S. J. Gould have no difficulty in arguing that history – in the sense of successions of unique events – matters in a study of the vast patterns and processes of biological evolution, and is consistent with "science." It follows that a history/science dichotomy in archaeology or any study of human beings is founded on suspect premises about the significance of uniqueness and determinism. Since biological, geographical, and historical theories are regularly used in archaeology, tacit hierarchical arrangements of theory are accepted but without a rigorously defined hierarchy of explanation.

This study stresses that the hierarchies proposed in *Annales* history are defective and will undermine the prospect of developing an effective integration, because they are insufficiently coherent to carry the burden put upon them. The weakness is even more severe in archaeology. The crucial hiatus in the hierarchies of explanation so far proposed is the lack of a coherently defined level of process for the operational effects of the material component of human behavior on the functioning of human communities.

Introduction

> Theory generally should not be an attempt to say how the world is, rather, it is an attempt to construct the logical relations that arise from various assumptions about the world. (Lewontin 1980: 65)

Archaeology is the only form of academic enquiry that looks at the nature of human behavior over very long spans of time. The discipline is also concerned with data from periods of time within the domains of documentary history and has even gained a role in the study of contemporary society (Gould and Schiffer 1981). In consequence archaeologists have to deal with a vast range of time perspectives – millions of years for ancestral hominids, thousands of years in the Upper Paleolithic, hundreds of years or decades in the Bronze Age and the Classical world, and decades or years in the modern world of the eighteenth century AD. Now included are contemporary hunter-gatherers (Whitelaw 1983), garbage in twentieth-century Tucson (Rathje 1979), and disposal of the dead in Cambridge (Pearson 1982). None of these differing contexts, nor their appropriate time scales, are preferable to the others; each is valuable for asking questions about differing issues of cultural behavior. Either there is no cogent association between them or, as seems more likely, they may be viewed as interrelated parts of a general enquiry into the relationship between human beings, things, and time.

There are three main ways of logically relating these different perspectives: reductionism/determinism, explanatory compression, or hierarchies of explanation. Reductionism specifies that some fundamental minute phenomenon determines the nature of all the more complex, large-scale entities and processes derived from it. The deterministic corollary is that the large scale defines what happens at the small scale. In a compressive theoretical viewpoint some level of order, such as political functioning, is given an elemental significance to which other phenomena and processes are subsidiary (Shanks and Tilley 1987a: 71–5). The third option, which differs markedly from the restricted orientation of the others, is to acknowledge a hierarchy of processes operating at differing scales and rates over different magnitudes of time. This viewpoint requires a theoretical construct which will tie the various explanatory levels together and facilitate the explanation of why the particular differing rates of process occur.

Though an integrated hierarchy of explanations may be feasible and necessary in archaeology and history, it is not as yet rigorously articulated because of theoretical inconsistencies in both disciplines. This factor poses a significant problem. The lack of integration in a discipline which considers a wide range of time scales is liable to cause the fragmentation of its analytical goals. No logical constraint exists to prevent competition between proponents of different, particular scales of enquiry. At the most extreme, even the evidence for differing scales of process may be rejected. Particular explanatory scales are liable to be reduced to minor aspects of some larger process or, conversely, a more detailed perspective, on a smaller time scale, may be elevated to an unwarranted level of significance. Disciplines in this condition are likely to display obvious characteristics of theoretical divergence, with trends toward very large and very small perspectives; disputes between theoretical positions actually concerned with different magnitudes of process; and a strong trend toward methodology. The latter trend seeks to improve the nature of the data (as if it possesses defects that are the source of the interpretative dilemma), rather than reassess whether the questions being asked are appropriate.

Archaeology currently displays these characteristics and some of its practitioners are seeking to resolve the problems by using various time-scaled forms of enquiry (Fletcher 1981a; Bailey 1983; Jones 1986; Hodder 1987). Since a hierarchical explanatory structure has already been developed by the *Annales* "school" of history, it should provide a useful guide and caution to archaeology. The essential point to be gained from *Annales* is that a hierarchical scaling of enquiry provides useful insights and can be applied appropriately to the study of human behavior. But we should not assume, therefore, that a generalized version of the Annaliste approach will necessarily suffice for a rigorous, integrated approach to time scaling, since this is not now defined as an aim of *Annales* scholarship. To produce an integrated hierarchy requires more than just a cogent recognition of differing time scales of analysis.

The *Annales* experience is valuable because we can use

it as a basis for assessing the qualities and defects of hierarchical analysis. The logical problems and consequences of the resultant diversity in *Annales* have been noted by several commentators (Kinser 1981; Furet 1983; Clark 1985; Lucas 1985). Archaeologists thus have the advantage of being able to see the problems because of Annaliste efforts in establishing the hierarchical approach and in assessing its weaknesses. In addition, more experience of the logic which can be used to manage hierarchical scale explanations has been gained since the 1960s (Koestler and Smythies 1969). Hierarchies of explanation have become familiar and prevalent topics of discussion in the natural sciences and substantial analysis of their characteristics has occurred since the 1970s (Eldredge and Salthe 1984; Grene 1987). Because it has to address a wide range of time scales and in addition must connect with the hierarchical scaling of biological evolutionary theory in the study of early hominid behavior, archaeology will eventually need to devise a hierarchical approach capable of integrating historical, behavioral, and biological perspectives. To tie together such a vast explanatory hierarchy, archaeology will eventually need a rigorous, non-deterministic, uniformitarian framework as well as explanations of the particular rates at which different cultural processes operate and affect human society.

The achievements of the *Annales*

The two great achievements of the Annalistes have been an emphasis on viewing human existence at differing time scales, and the recognition that the material component of human behavior has substantial effects over time scales greater than the usual concerns of ethnography, or of the history of attitudes, actions, and intentions. The study of human cultural behavior explained by the *Annales* school (particularly by Braudel) suggests that hierarchies of explanation are not incompatible with studies of being human. What *Annales* lacked and still lacks is a consistent statement about the magnitude of the processes, their effects, the time scales involved, and the relationship between them.

An* Annales *hierarchy of time scales

Lucas has summarized the *Annales* view of time scales in terms of four magnitudes of time, ranked from the minute time of events to the vast slow transformations of environment: (1) events, (2) conjunctures, (3) structures, (4) immobile history (1985: 6–7; further discussion in Knapp, Smith, this volume). Whereas events and conjunctures are the normal concern of history, the level of structures is a notable addition concerned with "the enduring physical, material and eventually mental structures within whose boundaries human individual and collective behavior is confined" (Lucas 1985: 5). Structures are studied over the long term (Braudel's famous *longue durée*) because of their "quality of endurance" (Lucas 1985: 4–5). Beyond the level of structures is the larger scale component of environmental and ecological processes – a topic of fundamental interest in prehistoric archaeology since the 1930s. Immobile history is therefore not a feature of *Annales* insight which is of especial significance to many prehistorians: it is taken for granted and is habitually regarded as dynamic. Curiously, however, the nature of structures and especially the role of the material frame of daily life has not been given the same emphasis in archaeology as it had already gained in *Annales* history by the 1940s and 1950s. In archaeology, material entities were recruited into the definition of cultures in the 1920s as the equivalent of ethnographic entities such as tribes, and were then subsumed into the social reconstructionism promoted by the New Archaeology of the 1960s and 70s. Only with the development of recursive viewpoints in social anthropology/sociology in the 1970s, and its introduction to archaeology in the 1980s (Hodder 1986: 8, 12), has the role of material entities as a potentially interactive component of human behavior become recognizable.

The scale of the material

The emphasis on the role of the enduring material component was advocated by Braudel who, as eulogized by Kinser (1981: 91), gave "material factors an active and even dramaturgical presence nearly unparalleled in previous historiography." He showed that "Things in their simple material existence – or their lack – weigh upon the daily habits of masses of people." In Braudel's view what is richest in humanity – the story of individuals with its quick rhythm – is an entirely ephemeral and "short sighted affair" (Kinser 1981: 69).

The role of the material is usually expressed in terms of a sense of scale, as in Braudel's comments on pre-industrial imperial capitals. Istanbul is said to have had a population of 400,000–700,000 in the sixteenth century AD compared to Cologne with 20,000. Istanbul was a giant which needed every sheep in the Balkans to support it (Braudel 1985: 52). To appreciate the immense scale of the Chinese imperial system, Manchu Peking is said to have had 2 million or more people in it (Braudel 1985: 540). In AD 1669, 43.3 million bags of grain lay in the palace storerooms along with over 1 million loaves of salt (Braudel 1985: 547). This education in scale is occasionally provided in the form of surprising comparisons such as: the luxury liner Queen Elizabeth II could hold 27,000 men in all – the number of soldiers in Cromwell's army (Laslett quoted by Lucas 1985: 52).

The historical achievement has been to show how the magnitude of phenomena and their material nature had an impact on the conditions of social life. One of the most effective expressions of this perception is provided by a historian who, ironically, is not usually described as an Annaliste! John Keegan's stunning evocation of human existence on the three great battlefields of Agincourt, Waterloo, and the Somme is both expressive and analytic (1976). The condition of life is conveyed and its characteristics are explained. He points out that the noise levels and violence of Agincourt were close to the life experience of the combatants, but on the Somme the immensity of the sound and destruction was far outside the normal experience of life, even in the harsh industrial cities of the early twentieth century. Keegan explains how the physical scale of the battlefield, made possible by weapon technologies, interacted with the available communication capacity of the combatants to produce the duration and the disasters of those battles. Even though initially derived from human actions, the resulting material context and the physical processes which engendered it created circumstances with which individuals and social groups had to cope. The material products and processes became an environment with which human intent had to contend and which savagely tested social institutions. The enduring material component of human behavior can be analyzed as an independent variable which exerts selective pressure on social action, even though it had originally derived from that action. Historians already use an analytic perspective which recognizes the large-scale role of the material as a factor which, in the longer term, is not subservient to human intent.

The use of a larger scale and longer term perspective on culture, rather than the short-term view of ethnography, combined with the independent role of the material at that larger scale, offers a valuable status to archaeology. Archaeological theory need not be bound by the premise that the past is somehow inadequate because it is a damaged record of essential information about specific events. The efforts of *Annales* historians demonstrate that a long-term perspective, provided it aims at the kind of expression and analysis achieved by John Keegan, would produce a history of people even though it need never refer to individuals.

As yet such a perspective has not been attained in the normal practice of archaeology. In a discussion of large-scale cultural processes Binford declared that "This level of organization is likely to be the unit upon which evolutionary selection operates, rather than the level of specific events" (1981: 198). But as yet no paradigmatic approach in archaeology has achieved this goal. The difficulty may be that the resulting explanatory approach would be quite unfamiliar. Although Dunnell has argued for the development of a long-term, large-scale perspective, he suspects that "we will not be answering the questions archaeologists have traditionally asked ... One thing is clear: no one will want to know" (1982: 21). Perhaps this offers a clue to the apparently unfashionable status of such a perspective at the present time, when academics are rather insecure and the dialogue within archaeology is chronically unstable.

The problems of an Annaliste approach

The central problem is that the various kinds of time scale proposed by Annalistes have not been precisely defined, nor have their magnitudes been rigorously specified. Three kinds of time are articulated, "geographic, social, individual. An almost immobile history of man's relations with the milieu which surrounds him, ... a slowly rhythmic history, ... [and] a history of short rapid nervous oscillations" (Kinser 1981: 65–6). The hierarchy of time scales possesses no internal consistency, nor does it consist of a hierarchy of processes nested within each other, each operating at its own distinctive rate and scale (as, for instance, is specified in the hierarchy of biological reproduction from DNA to parturition – Salthe 1985). Nor does the hierarchy incorporate a precise relationship between the magnitudes and selective effects of the different levels of process (as, for example, is found in ecological theory – Allen and Starr 1982, and in the recent form of neo-Darwinian evolutionary theory – Eldredge 1985).

Studies of *Annales* have been emphatic that it does not possess "a common and unified concept of the discipline ... It would be vain to search for the traces of a doctrine, or a privileged mode of explanation, in the early *Annales*" (Furet 1983: 390–1). The absence of this integration is apparent in the restricted development of a theoretical linkage between differing time scales. Braudel had to remain vague and general to avoid explaining how "'structure' functions with respect of new elements given causal force such as 'conjuncture'" (Kinser 1981: 89). The *Annales* hierarchy is not one of processes but of different associations at differing scales: for instance between individuals in events, social entities in conjunctures, value systems and material things in "structures," and economies, long-distance movement, and environment in immobile history.

The Annaliste hierarchy lacks the internal definition of scale and the relationship between levels of process which could produce a stable theoretical structure. There is no actual operational linkage between these levels (Clark 1985: 194). Nor is there consistent quantification of the time scales over which each level of the hierarchy is thought to operate or of the rates at which those operations take place. The effect is to permit the proliferation of each category across a wide range of time scales because there is no defined relationship between levels in the hierarchy to hold them in place. Braudel for example defines long duration as almost motionless history (as, for instance, in physical geography) and conjuncture as the history of slow rhythms, perhaps over centuries. Others, such as Le Roy Ladurie, seem to employ long duration for the characteristics of, for example, an economic system or a social formation enduring over several centuries, whereas conjuncture is applied to quicker, medium term rhythms (Lucas 1985: 6). Kinser has commented on the luxuriance of Braudel's development of the term conjuncture which includes "very long," "long," and "short" conjunctures. Furthermore there are "a dozen contexts in which the word is used either programmatically or too vaguely for its referents to be identified" (Kinser 1981: 93). The same applies to the notion of structure. This has been extended "to cover a whole range of phenomena from material structures through to the secret and the unconscious" (Lucas 1985: 4–5), and the *longue durée* is now applied to both highly tangible and completely ephemeral expressions. Geographical frames, biological realities, limits of production, spiritual constants, and mental frameworks can form prisons of the *longue durée* (Braudel 1980: 31). The usage is unstable and over-inclusive. It over-incorporates very different processes and phenomena. As is apparent, the way in which the differing structures endure is very different. The hierarchy is like Kuhn's "paradigm": it expresses the crucially apparent but is unfortunately too malleable to suffice as a standard. We know what is being referred to, but the meaning slips away under careful scrutiny.

For Annalistes the absence of a standard theoretical framework has made integration too difficult in general. As of the mid-1980s, Lucas could contend that Braudel's *La Méditerranée* had been the only real attempt to write an integrated history of the kind envisaged (1985: 8). Instead, Annalistes have vigorously and effectively diversified their interpretative strategies and at the same time have become increasingly specialized. The lack of integrative rigor has allowed luxuriant dispersal across a diverse range of information and an arbitrary emphasis on perspectives from several different time scales. The trend is regrettable but is logically unavoidable. More recent specialist studies have tended toward limited ranges of temporal scale. Although the interests of an individual historian may be quite diverse (e.g., Le Roy Ladurie 1979), overall integration is lacking. The analysis of geoeconomics has diversified but has in each case become more specific (e.g., Le Roy Ladurie 1985), while Le Goff (1985) and Le Roy Ladurie (1981) have elaborated the study of folk culture and its social implication. Yet in the 1950s Braudel argued vigorously that a preference for one scale of history to the exclusion of the others would be undesirable (1980: 34).

Nor have attempts to obtain explanatory frameworks from other disciplines been successful, in part because such frameworks are lacking in other fields but also because the assumptions do not comfortably travel into the different logical domains of another discipline. "In some cases, historians reacted by simply taking over the models appropriate in other disciplines; ... [they] were caught between social science and history in that double jeopardy of scholarly rigour where the models and assumptions of theory were applied in the fundamentally different circumstances of the other" (Lucas 1985: 10). Such a lack of coherence "leads to the unending pursuit of new research topics, turned up by accidents of life" (Furet 1983: 405) – also a succinct statement about archaeology over the past twenty years (Fletcher 1989). What is lacking is a frame of reference that can link the significance of different insights and classes of observation.

Hierarchies of explanation, time perspectivism, and archaeology

The logical problems of the *Annales* temporal hierarchy indicate that care is needed in the development of an equivalent, but explanatory, hierarchy for archaeology. Without some theoretical means of linking the different time scales and defining the rates of process to which they refer, the notion of a time-scaled hierarchy is liable to be overwhelmed both by trivial correlates and by consequent disconnection between differing scales of analysis. Incompletely articulated hierarchies may have an adverse effect on the potential explanatory value to be gained from recognizing processes of differing magnitudes. Until a rigorous scaling hierarchy is recognized *and* defined, the issue of indeterminacy, and the partial connection between differing scales of process cannot be articulated and discussed. The problem needs to be remedied because it produces severe, well-recognized, logical complications. As Holly remarked of the human sciences

(1978: 14): "Too often the languages we employ are either incapable of distinguishing one level from one another, or we use more than one language at a time, thus mixing up scales." Archaeology suffers from this malady. Although the discipline already uses hierarchical arrangements of theory, it does not have a rigorously defined hierarchy of explanation (Bailey 1983; 1987; Gamble 1987; Fletcher 1989).

If differing magnitudes of process are not clearly defined, the utility of recognizing different grades of temporal and spatial detail is not fully apparent. This leads to a suite of logical problems because the search for explanations can be pushed, without constraint, up or down the scale, either reduced to the functioning of the smallest components or viewed as some deterministic derivative of vast, impersonal processes. Instead of accepting that different degrees of detail will suffice for different kinds of enquiry, the discipline is vulnerable to arguments in favor of single standards of necessary or appropriate detail, or to tacit acceptance of that assumption. The particular risk when we are concerned with understanding human beings is an emphasis on a "proper" grade of data quality defined by the detail sought in ethnographic enquiry. In consequence archaeological data are liable to be seen as somehow damaged or inadequate, and therefore in need of reconstitution or renovation to that "proper" standard in order to be useful or meaningful. According to this logic it follows that the task of repairing the archaeological record requires an emphasis on methodologies of data retrieval in order to obtain "better" data, and on taphonomy in order to know what "distortions" have affected the information. A descent into the frustrations of the debate about the "Pompeii premise" is promoted (Binford 1981; Schiffer 1985; discussion by Smith, this volume). By contrast, what should be of concern is the possibility of questions about processes of differing magnitude, questions which can be asked of data that possess differing degrees of detail over various spans of time. Rather than regarding the data as somehow defective and inadequate for the questions we might prefer to ask, we should instead ask whether those questions are inappropriate. We might then try to frame new classes of question that may be answered in contexts where long time depth and gross patterns beyond the familiar ethnographic, or even historical, scale are available.

At present, because of the lack of a coherent, scaled hierarchy of explanation, archaeology and *Annales* are affected by similar patterns of theoretical divergence and the marked development of an emphasis on the small scale. Over the past twenty years, the focus of Annaliste interest has "shifted away from the 'system of systems' towards definable problems in history ... accompanied by the decline of economics and sociology as the inspiring social sciences and the rise of the influence of social anthropology." Furthermore, what has developed is a "newer preoccupation with the arcane, rarely directly stated and often unconscious world of *mentalités*, the world of belief, symbol and cultural patterns" (Lucas 1985: 8).

As a topic of enquiry *mentalité* is valid, but it does not follow that its characteristics or those at any other level of analysis should have explanatory priority and can exclude a hierarchical analysis (Shanks and Tilley 1987a: 120–7). At present archaeology uses widely varied forms of explanation. A shift to theories of intent and individual action is just like a preference for any other logical position within the current spectrum of social theory. *Mentalité*, therefore, cannot be considered an invalid development in archaeology. The conundrum is that theories of intent and action run into problems of assessibility whose implications appal Spaulding (1988) and trouble Renfrew (1982).

Once dissatisfaction arose with the generalizing form of enquiry prevalent in the New Archaeology, the opponents of processualism had to revert to an individual-based humanism: greater generalization was unlikely to seem attractive. Such a reversion, however, presupposes a divergence between different scales of explanation rather than a complementary hierarchical connection. The alternative to the quandary of producing either low-grade generalizations (Flannery's "Mickey Mouse" laws, 1973) or idiosyncratic individualism detached from the data to which it purports to refer, is to develop a workable explanatory hierarchy in which different levels of explanation are not deterministically linked. The value of the "individual action" approach can be acknowledged but its domain of applicability would be delimited, probably to its advantage. Conversely, although large-scale generalization is legitimate, determinism would be obviated and the over-determination of individual action avoided; this also eliminates those forms of adaptationism which explain cultural phenomena as if they are derivatives of response to the environment. Adaptationism is contrary to the essential dynamism of a hierarchy of operational processes (as in the biological theory of evolution) in which each level of process has a selective effect on the smaller scale, faster processes below it in the hierarchy. In such a hierarchy each level of process produces variants according to its own internal mechanisms, not in response to its external, larger scale context (as, for instance, the genetic code produces variants at random relative to the circumstances of the animals carrying it). The variants generated at a given level are the product of a consistently functioning mechanism, but they might not work in the prevailing circumstances. The external environment does not determine what the genetic system produces. Rather it acts as a selective agent that affects the degree to which features generated by the genetic system will be viable and reproduce. Neither determinism nor reductionism is required.

The role of explanatory hierarchies

Relating different scales of process to each other and to different degrees of necessary detail requires a recognition of indeterminacy, the use of methodological uniformitarianism, and a premise that the particular rates of process involved in the hierarchy are potentially explicable. Indeterminacy is required in the relationship between the levels in a hierarchy of processes. Without it deterministic links must follow which allow that all explanation may either be derived reductively from the nature of the smallest scale components of the hierarchy, or else is predetermined by controlling effects produced by macro-scale phenomena. Indeterminacy in the relationship between levels of process allows that each level has its own internal order and dynamics, but is then subject to delimitation over larger spans of time by larger scale processes. If, however, we introduce indeterminacy between levels, some other conceptual device is needed to explain how the different scales of process interrelate to produce the nature of the observed reality. This is done by specifying how the parameters which limit processes that operate on different scales relate to each other, and requires the logic of operational uniformitarianism to tie the hierarchy together. Uniformitarian statements connect the past and the present, and must therefore link phenomena which operate over differing time scales if they are to be logically valid and operationally relevant. The third point is that particular ranges of process rate should be appropriate to different levels in the explanatory hierarchy; otherwise there could be no consistent relationship between levels. Without stability in the relative magnitude of different processes, the scale of their effects could oscillate arbitrarily and explanation could only be contingent and uniquely contextual. If there is to be operational consistency throughout the hierarchy, the different rates of process must, in some fashion, be stable.

Of necessity these propositions have to be discussed in some detail because they are scarcely considered by Annalistes or in current archaeological theory; furthermore, they are subject to considerable ambiguity. This is especially the case for the discussion of uniformitarianism, a topic which has exercised theorists in biology and geology since Lyell's statements concerning uniformitarianism in the nineteenth century (Gould 1965; Simpson 1970).

Indeterminacy and scales of process

As an advocate of macro-scale analysis in evolutionary biology S. J. Gould published a paper in 1986 entitled "Evolution and the triumph of homology, or why history matters." He had no difficulty in arguing that history – in the sense of a succession of unique events – matters in a study of the vast patterns and processes of biological evolution and, moreover, that history is consistent with a "science" of large-scale, long-term processes. A gradation of scales from the micro- to the macro-level is envisaged, in which there is order at each level, generated by processes specific to that level and by the selective constraint of larger scale processes on smaller scale phenomena. Large-scale processes do not determine what will occur at any given level below; rather they affect the consequences which follow from the occurrence of a phenomenon at the lower level in the hierarchy. Uniqueness and large-scale patterns are compatible. The "history *contra* science" dichotomy, whether in archaeology, or in anthropology and history, is founded on dubious assumptions about the significance of uniqueness and the nature of scientific theory. In the study of human behavior, determinacy is not required at the individual level to produce large-scale patterns of behavior, nor does indeterminacy at a given level of detail prevent the occurrence of order on a larger scale.

In a hierarchical structure, large-scale processes cannot be reduced to small-scale ones and small-scale ones are not determined by large-scale ones. There is a critical indeterminacy in the relationship between processes operating at differing magnitudes. This logic of levels of order without determinate relationships between them has become the standard explanatory structure of the sciences, contrary to much misapprehension expressed by humanists. Even in the physical sciences, a reductionist/deterministic universe of the kind envisaged by the eighteenth-century philosopher Laplace, where the future could be absolutely predicted from the known positions of all its components, is no longer a precept of theory (Stewart 1989: 40, 283–5). Since the turn of the century, reductive determinism has been replaced by hierarchies of explanation interlinked by indeterminacy. Medawar has emphasized that "the general trend in the sciences, contrary to popular imagination, is toward hierarchical integration of diverse fields – not just the purported increasing specialisation" (1986: 71–2).

The characteristics of the smallest components of the universe are not precisely determinable and a totally predictable universe is impossible. Bronowski provides an apt illustration (1973: 356–7): no matter how much you improve the "magnification" needed to look at increasingly minute components of matter you still observe fuzziness. Ultimately this is not a failing of the measuring equipment, but is itself a characteristic of reality and the relationship of observers to that reality. We can comprehend reality in terms of differing scales of order which are not absolutely determined by phenomena recognizable at a finer grain of detail.

By contrast a reductionist view holds that the nature of the smallest component sufficiently explains the largest system or is essential for basic understanding. This produces a serious logical quandary for a humanistic, individually oriented viewpoint. Combined with reductionism and a premise of rationality it can lead to a form of determinism wherein cultural forms are specified by rational response to circumstances, thereby mirroring the biological and behavioral determinism of sociobiology, the least effort principle, and optimal foraging. An alternative which avoids such a quandary is to argue for an absence of order or pattern, in order to prevent the mechanistic tyranny which the advocacy of the individual sought to escape. In Braudel's view expressed in the 1950s, the proponents of such views "remain in the grip of an insidious and retrograde humanism no longer capable of providing them with a valid framework for their studies" (1980: 25).

The logic of indeterminacy obviated the uniqueness conundrum more than fifty years ago. It does so precisely on the grounds that unpredictable individual entities aggregate into ordered larger scale patterns. The uncertainty principle in physics (Heisenberg 1959) explains why the conjunction of the position and velocity of a subatomic particle is indeterminate, even though highly ordered atomic and molecular structures derive from the nature of those particles. In the terminology of *Annales*, which itself still lacks a rigorous concept of indeterminacy, all that is required is "the application of the principle that microphenomena are indeterminate whereas macrophenomena are determinate" (Lucas 1985: 5). We need not, therefore, have any logical problem with the co-occurrence of individual, idiosyncratic human beings and large-scale coherent pattern in aggregate human behavior. The supposition that human uniqueness vitiates the claim for analyzable order in human affairs is caught in a logical paradox: it assumes that our individual uniqueness militates against behavioral generalizations. But the contention that our uniqueness either does not aggregate into order, or that the detail of the micro-scale is necessary before generalizations can be made, is now an anomalous view of unique entities. What the proponents of human uniqueness must explain is why their viewpoint of uniqueness is so aberrant.

The conundrum of uniqueness and order is obviated because the levels of a hierarchy are not deterministically or reductively connected. For instance, since external circumstances do not restrict the variety of forms which a system of replication is able to produce, only the internal selection for code coherence within the process (e.g., in the gene code and its replicative procedure) can delimit the possible range of viable forms. As stated earlier, circumstances only delimit the degree to which some of that range of variability can persist. The cultural equivalent is that the variability which a human community produces in its verbal signals, actions, and material expressions cannot be predetermined by the circumstances in which the community exists. If it were predetermined all cultural products would be deterministically fit for their situation and no maladaptive behavior could occur. But human communities may pattern their behavior and act in ways which have a seriously damaging effect on their prospects of survival, as is illustrated by the nutritional and health crises that attended the formation of agricultural economies and growth of urban settlements (Cohen and Armelagos 1984; Cohen 1989).

Whereas the products of cultural replication are not predetermined by external circumstances, the consequences of their existence are delimited at several levels of process. First, they are constrained at the general scale of within-community interaction. Some degree of behavioral coherence and predictability is required in each form of cultural expression, if community life is to be viable (Fletcher 1977; 1981b; 1988). The expressions used in a language, whether verbal or non-verbal, cannot vary arbitrarily without adversely affecting a community's capacity to communicate. Second, the material products of a community are subject to the more familiar, external selective constraint exercised by the larger scale processes of the natural environment. The constraint on the community is not the particulars of its environment, but the parameters of economic and ecological processes. A community can drastically affect the components of its environment, for example by cutting down all the trees in its local region. What selects against a community that carries out such an exercise is the collapse of the ecological balance on which the rest of its economy depends. The existing economy will fail if the energy input–output balance of production is persistently infringed. What the community is able to attempt is not predetermined, but the selective pressures which will operate against its actions define the nature of the outcome (Butzer 1982: 284–5).

Larger scale processes therefore act as the parameters within which the forms produced by smaller scale processes or events can persist. Hierarchies of explanation rule out Lamarckian response as an adequate interpretation of cultural change, because the factors which initiate the existence of cultural phenomena are not causally tied to the factors which define why some of them persist. The same logic rules out stable correspondence between different kinds of cultural expression which replicate and persist at different rates; otherwise the relationship between them would also be determinate. Transient verbal meaning and actions cannot therefore be linked deterministically to the material, spatial framework of a settlement because that framework is replicated far more slowly and in some cases may endure for many years. A hierarchical model in which indeterminacy applies rules out inevitable correspondence between the different kinds of cultural message; such a model allows that the verbal and active component of social life could change relatively rapidly and find itself trapped by a formidably inert, durable material framework which the community might not be able to change.

The role of uniformitarianism

Uniformitarian propositions allow us to connect the past and the present, but the statement that "the present is the key to the past" is not a sufficient explanation of how this is done. The logical procedure can be illustrated by the familiar instance of the significance which we ascribe to fossil remains. A single, securely dated, diagnostic piece of hominid bone can transform our knowledge of the temporal or spatial distribution of our ancestors. That we know nothing from that bone about details of demography or the diurnal movement of the species makes no difference to the value of the major insight it can provide. Scarce data, scattered across a long time span, may be useless for ethnographic reconstruction but highly informative for the study of large-scale processes. The use of differing grades of evidential detail depends upon our theoretical premises. We know that the single piece of bone came from an individual who was a member of a breeding population, not because that is self-evident or repeatedly observable in the present but because we possess an operational uniformitarian model of biological reproductive processes which explains why no other possibility could occur. Though the familiar observation seems obvious, the security of our opinion cannot be based on cumulative examples, since this alone offers no logical guarantee that the next example will conform (O'Hear 1982: 16–25). The models of genetic reproduction and biomechanics which secure our expectations about the relationship between bones and living animals are derivatives of "methodological uniformitarianism" (Gould's terminology, 1965): they are operational uniformitarian propositions. Such propositions provide the specifications for processes or conditions which are consistent in operation through space and time, as for example with the workings of genetic reproduction. Although operationally the same at all times, such processes generate or allow varying products over time (e.g., in the form of different species). Put another way, the processes and operational conditions are the same over time but the substantive products are particular to each period of time and each region.

High-level methodological uniformitarianism can be used to tie together hierarchies of explanation, for instance the role played by the concept of natural selection in the biological theory of evolution. If the hierarchy of explanation is to be useful it has to specify that the parameters of different processual levels are consistently related over time. Natural selection, in its simple sense, is a proposition about an operationally uniform process consequent on the fundamental disparity between the vast capacity of a rapid reproductive system to generate offspring, and the finite capacity of the more slowly produced supply of resources needed to support them. Natural selection defines the selective relationship between circumstances and the genetic mechanism which produces physiological variability. The inevitable consequence is that some offspring do not survive to reproduce. It follows that on the large scale entire species can become extinct, and that the paleontological record will therefore contain evidence of species which need have no direct modern descendant or equivalent (Gould 1989). But these life-forms must still have conformed to the same biomechanical specifications and ecological parameters as apply now: this is what allows us to identify the dinosaurs, analyze their physical structure, and produce assessable models of their behavior.

By contrast, in substantive uniformitarianism either constancy in rate of process or constancy in the occurrence of a phenomenon is assumed (Gould 1987: 120–5).

Gould regards statements of substantive uniformitarianism as logically invalid but testable (1965: 227–8). But an additional, particular, conspicuous variant, used in archaeology, assumes that the associations between material features and active phenomena (such as social relationships) observable in the present are constant and can be retrodicted into the past. The premises of this assumption are not amenable to testing in the archaeological record when the active component of the association, or verbal commentary, is absent because collateral analogies would have to be introduced as proxy indices for the absent data. But those analogies cannot be shown to be secure. Because such associations cannot therefore be tested, archaeologists retrodict them from the present and the recent past into the archaeological record. This device helps us to say something about the past which seems reasonable and plausible but assumes the presence of particular kinds of active behavior. The problem is that an assumption has to be made about the universal uniformity of relationships between the material and the social, when that is precisely the issue which stands in need of appraisal. If in actuality the phenomena and the associations do not remain constant through time, inappropriate uniformities will be imposed on the past, because the material features which survive in the record need not be referents for the proposed active correlates. The lack of a present-day analogue, for instance, would make the recognition of the dinosaurs logically impossible: they would be merged into classes of known animals. Archaeologists cannot securely use substantive, associational uniformitarianism on its own to connect the past and the present.

Methodological uniformitarian statements are also needed in order to gauge how far or in what way particular processes develop. Such statements set the standards by which we connect current empirical evidence to its equivalents in the past. If we are to compare adequately current data with their past equivalents, a consistent set of indices will be required. With such indices current data can be calibrated against the magnitude of their past equivalents. A classic instance of the difference between the effects of substantive and methodological uniformitarian logic occurred in the development of the ^{14}C dating technique. The principles of physics by which one explains the production of ^{14}C are an example of an operational uniformitarian proposition. But the assumption in the 1950s and early 60s (discussed by Renfrew 1979: 57–8, 84–5), namely that the rate of ^{14}C production was constant at the current rate, is an example of an erroneous substantive statement. Although useful in initiating the use of ^{14}C dates, the substantive presumption led to erroneous expectations because, as became apparent, the rate of ^{14}C production actually varies over time and the dates had to be calibrated against other markers of sidereal time.

Extrapolating from short-term contemporary contexts to the long-term contexts of the past requires appropriate uniformitarian statements. This demands care with the use of uniformitarian logic, because very different explanatory implications follow from the two different forms of uniformitarianism. Although Bailey (1983: 174–80) and Gould (Gould and Watson 1982: 365–71) discuss the issue, the distinction between substantive and methodological uniformitarianism is, as yet, poorly defined and rarely noted in archaeology. This is the case, for instance, in Salmon's study of philosophy and archaeology (1982: 79–82), and in Kelley and Hanen's overview of scientific methodology (1988: 263–4). The general ambiguity that follows from neglecting this issue echoes the problems in nineteenth-century geology (S. J. Gould 1965; 1986: 61), and in *Annales* scholarship. Kinser correctly observes a logical flaw in Braudel's use of the terms "structure" and "pattern" (1981: 73), and while his own analysis is rather cumbersome, Kinser at least seeks to express the difference between encompassing statements about processes (immanent but not directly observable structures) and generalizations about phenomena (i.e., observable realities) (1981: 80–3). Braudel's structures are patterns of rhythms and associations of activities, not models for the explanations of those patterns. The ambiguity incorporates a frequent logical error of uniformitarianism, namely the substantivist fallacy that because an association of two phenomena is repeatedly observed there is a constant process which produces that effect. Although not intended to be a scientific correlation, one of Braudel's minor generalizations illustrates the problem: "We can say that the house of the peasant with a hoe, wherever it may be, is almost invariably rectangular and has only one storey" (Braudel 1985: 176). It may be observed that numerous West African hoe cultivators, even those who live in close proximity to urban centers and are definitively peasants, build and reside in curvilinear buildings. Braudel's substantive statement contains a characteristic qualified "probability" – that the association is "almost invariably" the case. Such a qualification obviates any consistent retrodiction to the past while simultaneously trying to claim a meaningful association, as if some definable process were involved.

The serious problem of substantivism is that, although obviously specious in this case, the logical fallacy exists even when the proposed associations seem reasonable, and the constructs are sophisticated. Use of a substantive social/material association to extrapolate social content into the past requires a deterministic relationship; otherwise the analogy has no content and is being preferred arbitrarily in the specific cases to which it is applied. Since this problem exists for what one would suppose was the comparatively simple relationship between people and amounts of residential space, its implications for the analogical extrapolation of more esoteric material–social correlates should be very serious. Retrodicting from residential densities in the contemporary settlements of a region back to the densities in prehistoric sites of the same locality, in an attempt to estimate past community sizes, provides an example. Such associational extrapolations assume what first must be demonstrated, namely that the specifics of cultural pattern have remained constant over time. They also infringe the condition that phenomena which replicate at different rates cannot be deterministically linked. The assumption is logically incompatible with the indeterminacy inherent in a hierarchy of explanation, because a constant correlation is being applied between phenomena which differ in their stability over time. Social intangibles change more rapidly than their enduring material context. We cannot assume that they will remain in the same synchrony all the time. The relationship can change even during the history of any one settlement. In London and Paris, the average residential density of the entire city has changed substantially over the past 900 years (Fletcher 1981a: 113, 115–16). In consequence we have no grounds – other than preference – for choosing to extrapolate back from local densities rather than from estimates derived from the very different residential densities in the settlements of other regions. We cannot assume regional constancy in residential densities. To return to the Braudelian example: on another scale hoe agriculture can obviously persist over long spans of time compared to the rate at which the shape of buildings can be transformed.

Because deterministic substantivism has to be excluded on logical grounds and because it infringes the expectation that different operational levels in a hierarchy function at different rates, hierarchical explanatory structures need to be integrated by operational uniformitarian statements based on methodological principles. These have yet to be rigorously defined for human behavior. Their absence helps to suggest why the development of appropriate hierarchies has so far proved problematic.

Time perspectivism and rates of cultural process

The recognition that particular processes operate at particular rates is necessary if the scale relationship between the different levels in a hierarchy is to be stabilized. Why they operate at those rates rather than at any other may seem self-evident but needs to be explained. By seeking explanations for the different rate of process, one may minimize the possible arguments about whether or not a pattern of oscillations, or a replication rate, or a class of phenomena should be regarded as epiphenomenal. Since the recognition of a hierarchy allows patterning within one scale of process without determinate linkage to other levels, it follows that viewing particular classes of data as epiphenomena depends upon one's scale viewpoint, not on any absolute standard. When genetic codes are being analyzed, the characteristics of an animal's physiology which result from its life experience are incidental epiphenomena. Yet on a larger scale, when viewed from an ecologist's perspective, those physical changes may be crucial markers of a population's short-term adjustment to its environment. In cultural terms, metrical order in the patterning of residential space (Fletcher 1977; 1981b; 1988) could remain stable despite changes in the shape of the buildings constructed. Although the same room sizes and linear distances might be used, a community could change from building round huts to the construction of rectangular buildings (Fletcher 1977: 80–1). Changes in shape would not have the same cultural significance as changes in the tacit spatial message carried by buildings. The former could, at most, only be considered to indicate borrowing, the latter suggesting a far more profound change, perhaps even the replacement of one population by another with a different tacit way of patterning space.

In the absence of an integrated hierarchy of explanation and a set of operational uniformitarian principles of the kind used in biology, differing scales of analysis seem like mutually incompatible intellectual fashions. Debate becomes locked into disputes about which analysis is of greater consequence when in practice they should be viewed as complementary parts of an analytic hierarchy. The persistent disagreements in archaeology in the 1980s about the explanatory status of individual action, cultural group process, behavioral parameters, and environmental factors as regulators of cultural life illustrate the problem (Bailey 1983; Hodder 1984; Binford 1987; Shanks and Tilley 1987a; 1987b; Spaulding 1988).

A hierarchy of explanation which differentiates between different rates of cultural replication and places them in a selectionist framework should help to resolve this issue. Cultural signals are produced in various forms with differing degrees of endurance and differing replication rates: they must therefore be allocated to different hierarchical levels of process. Verbal signals are more rapidly produced and decay fastest. They are also learned early in life and provide a flexible means of expression that can provide rapid adjustment to circumstances, even though the verbal grammar may remain stable. Non-verbal active signals such as proxemics and kinesics take longer to learn and provide a much slower message system, whose signals are more stable over time and whose messages take longer to learn. The somewhat disturbing circumstance can arise in which our body language may be inconsistent with the expressions of intent and meaning which our facility with verbal games can produce. Our slowest cultural message system is material patterning. The ability or the permission to produce culturally acceptable material entities may be deferred until puberty or later. The buildings constructed by a community carry a material message made up of spatial signals. The message provides a predictable milieu for social life, serving as a tacit training device to inculcate into the children of the community its standard spatial pattern. Verbal messages, non-verbal proxemic/kinesic communication, and material messages are three different classes of human signal transmission, whose signals are replicated or sustained at differing rates. Each message system has its individual signal rate and a differing degree of inherent inertia.

In a time perspectivist view material entities – such as buildings – not only have a recursive role in relation to social life (Hodder 1986; Moore 1986; Miller 1987), but they must also be capable of restricting and regulating human action. Although some aspects of our material assemblages, such as containers and small decorative items, can be replicated quite rapidly and change relatively quickly, large entities such as buildings possess far more inertia and might persist for decades or even centuries as a constraint on social change. While the achievement of post-processual structuralists and contextualists has been to show that small items may be very informative about human action and about the political nature of cultural expression (Miller 1987; Shanks and Tilley 1987b), we must now consider the role played by larger material entities that possess more inertia. Even if the potential for a textual analysis of small items is as great as Shanks and Tilley hope, this demonstration cannot be generalized to an argument that the nature of all material entities is sufficiently explicable as a cultural message, by reference to the words associated with it.

As Moore (1986) has shown for built space, the verbal correlates of material space are not direct and there is an inertia to the forms which material space retains as social life changes. Verbal meanings and transient acts such as the disposal of ash may be connected promptly to changing social purposes (Moore 1986: 143–5), but built forms – because they possess more inertia – are far more equivocal in their message. Donley, for example, illustrates on a small scale how social change had to cope with intractable material space in Lamu (1982). The "social" has to negotiate with its substantial material framework by using more transient material entities, such as minor alterations to walls or the addition of new furnishings, to adjust the unyielding built space to new social needs.

The inertia of large material entities can both protect social life and obstruct change. The material fabric of rooms with durable walls serves to mitigate disturbance by the sounds and visual effects of other people's activity. Conversely, old building stock demands a price for any change: it must be bypassed, demolished, or renovated. A contest exists between a community's capacity to avoid or remove old constructions and the amount that has to be cleared away to effect some preferred social change. For example, we are now learning how costly it is to maintain old concrete structures such as bridges, or to renovate nineteenth-century Victorian sewers. Social action does not therefore simply effect material change. Instead it has to negotiate with material contexts of varying degrees of durability that have consequent effects on the outcome, whether in terms of capital cost or the occurrence of social pathologies resulting from behavioral stress (Fletcher 1981a: 98–9).

The role of the partially independent cultural message systems of verbal expression, non-verbal communication, and transient and durable material entities is readily explicable. The spectrum of different signal rates functions as the cultural equivalent of the biological means by which life forms interact, whether successfully or unsuccessfully, with changing circumstances (Bonner 1980: 62–3; Fletcher 1988: 37–8). The value of using several types of messages which change at differing rates is that short-term signals allow prompt expedient adjustment. Progressively slower systems then provide the longer term options which may prove to be enduringly viable in new circumstances. Each level of signal replication also has its price. Fast, ephemeral signals can only refer to their context, they cannot transform it. By contrast durable entities, such as buildings, may provide effective long-term spatial contexts and shelter: they may also be wastefully ineffective and costly to deal with or remove.

Cultural analysis becomes far more interesting when verbal messages, actions, and material signals are viewed as a hierarchy of independent, interacting message systems. If each of the cultural message systems is replicating and changing at its own rate, and is not deterministically regulated by changes in the other message systems, non-correspondence could result between the material component of a community's behavior and its active or verbal cultural expressions. The "social" could cease to mesh with its material context, allowing the possibility that communities may cease to be viable because of behavioral disjunction between (1) their active modes of stating the meaning content of social life and (2) the material milieu with which the people have to cope. A hierarchical time perspective provides archaeology with the freedom to use Annaliste insight on the dramaturgical role of the material frame of social life as an independent variable with its own distinct behavioral impact.

Conclusions

At present archaeology lacks an articulated time scale perspective. It does not possess rigorous definition of rates of cultural process and lacks clarity about uniformitarianism. Although the *Annales* hierarchy will continue to be useful for a variety of enquiries within the purview of historical studies, it is not sufficiently coherent to carry the burden of the enormous ranges of time scale that archaeology must manage. Archaeology, however, has the potential to achieve what *Annales* set out to do. The development of a rigorous time perspective view in archaeology will require a precise definition of indeterminacy appropriate to the study of cultural processes. A suite of operational propositions with a methodological uniformitarian form is needed to link the past with the present and to connect the differing scales of process in the hierarchy. In due course, archaeologists should rigorously specify the various levels in a hierarchy of cultural replication and seek to explain the differing rates at which different kinds of cultural signaling operate and have their effects. The variety of cultural message systems suggests that a rigorous hierarchy of explanation should incorporate more levels than the Annaliste convention, and should include the operational role of the material component of community behavior as a regulator of social life.

Acknowledgments

My interest in the *Annales* historians extends into a murky graduate past and a long, satisfying discourse with Tim Murray. Only recently, in conversation with Bernard Knapp, did I decide to pursue the topic into print: my especial thanks to him for that stimulus and encouragement. Coincidentally, a paper given by Emmanuel Wallerstein on a brief visit to Sydney University further assisted my thoughts, as did a paper by Rhys Jones at the World Archaeological Congress in 1986. My thanks to them both for a perspective on the context of long-term analyses and an example of the problems confronting archaeology.

To Bernard Knapp I am also grateful, despite the pain, for his vigorous form of editing. Daniel Tangri kindly provided a second opinion: my thanks for his help and intellectual company. Greg Wyncoll's critical views on hierarchies of explanation and his advice on developments in biological theory have been much appreciated.

References

Allen, T. F. and T. B. Starr 1982 *Hierarchy: Perspectives for Ecological Complexity*. Chicago: University of Chicago Press.

Bailey, G. N. 1983 Concepts of time in Quaternary prehistory. *Annual Review of Anthropology* 12: 165–92.

1987 Breaking the time barrier. *Archaeological Review from Cambridge* 6: 5–20.

Binford, L. R. 1981 Behavioral archaeology and the "Pompeii premise." *Journal of Anthropological Research* 37: 195–208.

1987 Data, relativism and archaeological science. *Man* 22: 391–404.

Bonner, J. T. 1980 *The Evolution of Culture in Animals*. Princeton: Princeton University Press.

Braudel, F. 1972 *The Mediterranean and the Mediterranean World in the Age of Phillip II*. New York: Harper and Row.

1980 *On History* (translated by S. Matthews). Chicago: University of Chicago Press.

1985 *The Structures of Everyday Life: The Limits of the Possible* (translated by S. Reynolds). London: Fontana Paperbacks.

Bronowski, J. 1973 *The Ascent of Man*. London: British Broadcasting Corporation.

Butzer, K. W. 1982 *Archaeology as Human Ecology*. Cambridge: Cambridge University Press.

Clark, S. 1985 The *Annales* historians, in Q. Skinner, ed., *The Return of Grand Theory in the Human Sciences*, pp. 177–98. Cambridge: Cambridge University Press.

Cohen, M. N. 1989 *Health and the Rise of Civilisation*. New Haven: Yale University Press.

Cohen, M. N. and G. J. Armelagos 1984 *Palaeopathology at the Origins of Agriculture*. New York: Academic Press.

Donley, L. W. 1982 House power: Swahili space and symbolic markers, in I. Hodder, ed., *Symbolic and Structural Archaeology*, pp. 63–72. Cambridge: Cambridge University Press.

Dunnell, R. C. 1982 Science, social science and common sense: the agonizing dilemma of modern archaeology. *Journal of Anthropological Research* 38: 1–25.

Eldredge, N. 1985 *Unfinished Synthesis. Biological Hierarchies and Modern Evolutionary Thought*. New York: Oxford University Press.

Eldredge, N. and S. N. Salthe 1984 Hierarchies and evolution, in R. Dawkins and M. Ridley, eds., *Oxford Surveys of Evolutionary Biology*, volume 1, pp. 182–208. Oxford: Oxford University Press.

Flannery, K. V. 1973 Archaeology with a capital S, in C. L. Redman, ed., *Research and Theory in Current Archaeology*, pp. 47–53. New York: John Wiley and Sons.

Fletcher, R. J. 1977 Settlement studies (micro and semi-micro), in D. L. Clarke, ed., *Settlement Archaeology*, pp. 47–162. London: Academic Press.

1981a People and space: a case study on material behaviour, in I. Hodder, G. Isaac, and N. Hammond, eds., *Pattern of the Past: Studies in Honour of David Clarke*, pp. 97–128. Cambridge: Cambridge University Press.

1981b Space and community behaviour, in B. Lloyd and J. Gay, eds., *Universals of Human Thought: The African evidence*, pp. 71–110. Cambridge: Cambridge University Press.

1988 The messages of material behaviour, in I. Hodder, ed., *The Meanings of Things. Material Culture and Symbolic Expression*, pp. 33–40. One World Archaeology 6. London: Unwin Hyman.

1989 Social theory and archaeology: diversity, paradox and potential, in J. W. Rhoads, ed., *Australian Reviews of Anthropology. Mankind* 19(1): 65–75.

Furet, F. 1983 Beyond the *Annales*. *Journal of Modern History* 55: 389–410.

Gamble, C. 1987 Archaeology, geography and time. *Progress in Human Geography* 11: 227–46.

Gould, S. J. 1965 Is uniformitarianism necessary? *American Journal of Science* 263: 223–8.

1986 Evolution and the triumph of homology, or why history matters. *American Scientist* 74: 60–9.

1987 *Time's Arrow. Time's Cycle. Myth and Metaphor in the Discovery of Geological Time*. Cambridge, MA: Harvard University Press.

1989 *Wonderful Life. The Burgess Shale and the Nature of History*. London: Hutchinson Radius.

Gould, R. A. and M. B. Schiffer (eds.) 1981 *Modern Material Culture: The Archaeology of Us*. New York: Academic Press.

Gould, R. A. and P. J. Watson 1982 A dialogue on the meaning and use of ethnoarchaeological reasoning. *Journal of Anthropological Archaeology* 1: 335–81.

Grene, M. 1987 Hierarchies in biology. *American Scientist* 75: 504–10.

Heisenberg, W. 1959 *Physics and Philosophy: The Revolution in Modern Science*. London: Allen and Unwin.

Hodder, I. A. 1984 Archaeology in 1984. *Antiquity* 58: 25–32.

1986 *Reading the Past*. Cambridge: Cambridge University Press.

1987 The contribution of the long term, in I. A. Hodder, ed., *Archaeology as Long Term History*, pp. 1–8. Cambridge: Cambridge University Press.

Holly, B. P. 1978 The problem of scale in time–space research, in T. Carlstein, D. Parkes, and N. Thrift, eds., *Timing Space and Spacing Time*. Volume 3, *Time and Regional Dynamics*, pp. 2–18. London: Edward Arnold.

Ingold, T. 1986 *Evolution and Social Life*. Cambridge: Cambridge University Press.

Jones, R. 1986 Palaeolithic time scales and rates of cultural change: evidence from Arnhem Land and Tasmania. Paper presented at World Archaeological Congress (Southampton, England, September).

Keegan, J. 1976 *The Face of Battle*. London: Cape.

Kelley, J. H. and M. P. Hanen 1988 *Archaeology and the Methodology of Science*. Albuquerque: University of New Mexico Press.

Kinser, S. 1981 *Annaliste* paradigm? The geohistorical structuralism of Fernand Braudel. *The American Historical Review* 86: 63–105.

Koestler, A. and J. R. Smythies (eds.) 1969 *Beyond Reductionism: New Perspectives in the Life Sciences*. London: Hutchinson.

Le Goff, J. 1985 *Mentalités*: a history of ambiguities, in J. Le Goff and P. Nora, eds., *Constructing the Past: Essays in Historical Methodology*, pp. 167–80. Cambridge: Cambridge University Press.

Le Roy Ladurie, E. 1979 *The Territory of the Historian* (translated by B. and S. Reynolds). Hassocks: Harvester Press.

1981 *Festival at Romans: A People's Uprising at Romans 1579–1580* (translated by M. Feeney). Harmondsworth: Penguin.

1985 The history of climate, in J. Le Goff and P. Nora, eds., *Constructing the Past: Essays in Historical Methodology*, pp. 167–80. Cambridge: Cambridge University Press.

Lewontin, R. C. 1980 Theoretical population genetics in the evolutionary synthesis, in E. Mayr and W. B. Provine, eds., *The Evolutionary Synthesis*, pp. 58–68. Cambridge, MA: Harvard University Press.

Lucas, C. 1985 Introduction, in J. Le Goff and P. Nora, eds., *Constructing the Past: Essays in Historical Methodology*, pp. 1–11. Cambridge: Cambridge University Press.

Medawar, P. 1986 *The Limits of Science*. Oxford: Oxford University Press.

Miller, D. 1987 *Material Culture and Mass Communication*. Oxford: Blackwell.

Moore, L. H. 1986 *Space, Text and Gender*. Cambridge: Cambridge University Press.

O'Hear, A. 1982 *Karl Popper. The Arguments of the Philosophers*, gen. ed. T. Honderich. London: Routledge and Kegan Paul.

Pearson, M. P. 1982 Mortuary practices, society and ideology: an ethnoarchaeological study, in I. Hodder, ed., *Structural and Symbolic Archaeology*, pp. 99–113. Cambridge: Cambridge University Press.

Rathje, W. L. 1979 Modern material culture studies. *Advances in Archaeological Method and Theory* 2: 1–37.

Renfrew, C. 1979 *Before Civilisation: The Radiocarbon Revolution and Prehistoric Europe*. Harmondsworth: Penguin.

1982 Space, time and man. *Transactions of the Institute of British Geographers*, n.s. 6: 257–78.

Salmon, M. H. 1982 *Philosophy and Archaeology*. New York: Academic Press.

Salthe, S. N. 1985 *Evolving Hierarchical Systems: Their Structure and Representation*. New York: Columbia University Press.

Schiffer, M. B. 1985 Is there a "Pompeii premise" in archaeology? *Journal of Anthropological Research* 41: 18–41.

Shanks, M. and C. Tilley 1987a *Social Theory and Archaeology*. Cambridge: Polity Press.

1987b *Re-constructing Archaeology*. Cambridge: Cambridge University Press.

Simpson, G. G. 1970 Uniformitarianism, an inquiry into principle, theory and method in geohistory and biohistory, in M. K. Hecht and W. C. Stiere, eds., *Essays in Evolution and Genetics in Honour of Theodosius Dobzhansky*, pp. 43–96. New York: Appleton.

Spaulding, A. C. 1988 Archaeology and anthropology. *American Anthropologist* 90: 263–71.

Stewart, I. 1989 *Does God Play Dice? The Mathematics of Chaos*. Oxford: Blackwell.

Weitz, S. 1984 *Nonverbal Communication*. New York: Oxford University Press.

Whitelaw, T. 1983 People and space in hunter-gatherer camps: a generalising approach to ethnoarchaeology. *Archaeological Review from Cambridge* 2: 48–66.

PART II
CASE STUDIES

4 Rhythms of change in Postclassic central Mexico: archaeology, ethnohistory, and the Braudelian model

MICHAEL E. SMITH

This paper applies insights from the work of Fernand Braudel to the problem of correlating archaeology and native history in Postclassic central Mexico. Two aspects of Braudel's model of hierarchical temporal rhythms are emphasized. First, Braudel's *theoretical construct* provides a useful framework for conceptualizing past time and processes of change in complex societies. Second, his *empirical findings* on the diverse types of socioeconomic change and their rhythms contribute to the dialectical interaction between changing research questions and chronological refinement. These points are illustrated through an examination of archaeological and native historical data on processes of socioeconomic change in Postclassic central Mexico. Greater attention to temporal rhythms and chronological issues leads to more successful archaeological/historical correlation in central Mexico and thereby helps advance our understanding of processes of change.

Introduction

The Postclassic epoch in highland central Mexico was a time of major social, economic, and political change. Large cities and territorial empires rose and fell, significant demographic changes took place including mass migrations and rapid population increase, the city-state emerged as the dominant political form, and warfare, trade, and alliances became significant forms of interaction between polities. These developments are reflected not only in the archaeological record, but also in native historical chronicles preserved by the Nahuatl dynasties of the Late Postclassic city-states. While the existence of two separate but parallel sources of information on this period provides an excellent opportunity to construct models of change, the full potential of this approach has yet to be realized for a number of reasons. In this chapter, I argue that the application of Braudel's model of hierarchical temporal rhythms contributes greatly to a clarification of the problems and potentials of archaeological/historical correlation in Postclassic central Mexico. This in turn leads to an improved understanding of processes of social change in one of the most important regions of the Precolumbian New World.

A longstanding methodological problem in the joint consideration of Postclassic archaeology and native history is that the two sources of data have been juxtaposed prematurely before either has been sufficiently analyzed on its own terms. Difficulties with this procedure when applied to Bronze Age Greece are outlined by Evans:

> It does seem to me important that in a field in which various kinds of evidence, philological, literary and anthropological, as well as archaeological, are available, they should in one important sense be kept separate. Though comparisons of findings in each must be useful at all stages, it seems to be fatal to mix elements drawn from more than one in elaborating an argument. The kind of information provided by each of them is so distinct that when intermingled they inevitably weaken the reasoning. This must, in fact, be able to stand up first to judgement in terms of the strict logic of its own discipline. (Evans 1974: 17)

Brinkman makes the same point for Mesopotamia, arguing that "disciplinary autonomy does not preclude interdisciplinary work but is a necessary pre-condition for making meaningful such work" (1984: 179).

For Postclassic central Mexico, ethnohistorians working with native history have tended to ignore archaeology (e.g., Calnek 1978; Berdan 1982; Hassig 1985), and when they do incorporate archaeological data, it is often misinterpreted (e.g., Davies 1977: 132–40). Archaeologists on the other hand have always structured their research and interpretations in terms of native history. Historical events are used to gauge the accuracy of archaeological chronologies (e.g., Vaillant 1938; Tolstoy 1958; Sanders, Parsons, and Santley 1979: 457–74), native historical concepts like Toltec, Chichimec or *calpulli* are incorporated into archaeological interpretations (e.g., Sanders, Parsons, and Santley 1979: 137–76; Diehl 1983), and in general the analytical separation between the two types of data is less than it should be. The result is that many "archaeological" interpretations of Postclassic central Mexico are so permeated by historical constructs that their archaeological reliability or accuracy is difficult to judge. One particularly flagrant example is the assignment of historically derived dates to archaeological phases (discussed in Smith 1987a).

It should be noted here that the above discussion deals with the *diachronic* correlation of archaeology and native history. Most attempts to correlate archaeology and ethnohistory in central Mexico have been *synchronic* in orientation, with the goal of reconstructing contact-period social and cultural organization using Spanish descriptions rather than native historical traditions (see Spores 1980 or Charlton 1981 for general discussions). Archaeologists pursuing this latter approach in central Mexico (e.g., Brumfiel 1980; 1985; 1987; Evans 1988; see Smith 1987b) have generally been more explicit and cautious about the analytical separation of archaeological and ethnohistorical data in their work.

Other reasons for the general lack of success in past attempts to correlate archaeology and native history in central Mexico are discussed by Nicholson (1955), Charlton (1981: 155), and Smith (1984; 1987a). First, the degree of refinement of existing archaeological chronologies is not adequate to monitor much of the fast-paced action of the native histories. This relates directly to the hierarchical nature of rhythms of social change in complex societies. Processes that operate over long time-scales (e.g., many demographic or ecological changes) can be monitored with existing archaeological chronologies, while processes of shorter duration (like the wars and dynastic events depicted in Nahuatl native history) require the refinement of archaeological sequences before their material manifestations can be studied (Smith, this volume). Second, earlier archaeologists tended to employ the simplistic notion of a one-to-one association of ceramic types or styles with ethnic groups (Vaillant 1938; Noguera 1963), which more often than not has proved to be inaccurate in Postclassic central Mexico (Smith 1984: 176).

Charlton (1981: 155) suggests a final factor possibly hindering archaeological/ethnohistorical correlation: "the lack of correlation between sociopolitical change and ceramic change." This is a sweeping statement that is open to challenge on both empirical and theoretical grounds (Smith 1983: 15; Knapp *et al.* 1988). Braudel's work suggests that we need to separate "sociopolitical change" into its component processes, some of which have material indicators while others do not, and some of which operate at time scales amenable to archaeological investigation while others do not.

Figure 4.1 Map of central Mexico showing the major Postclassic archaeological sties discussed in the text

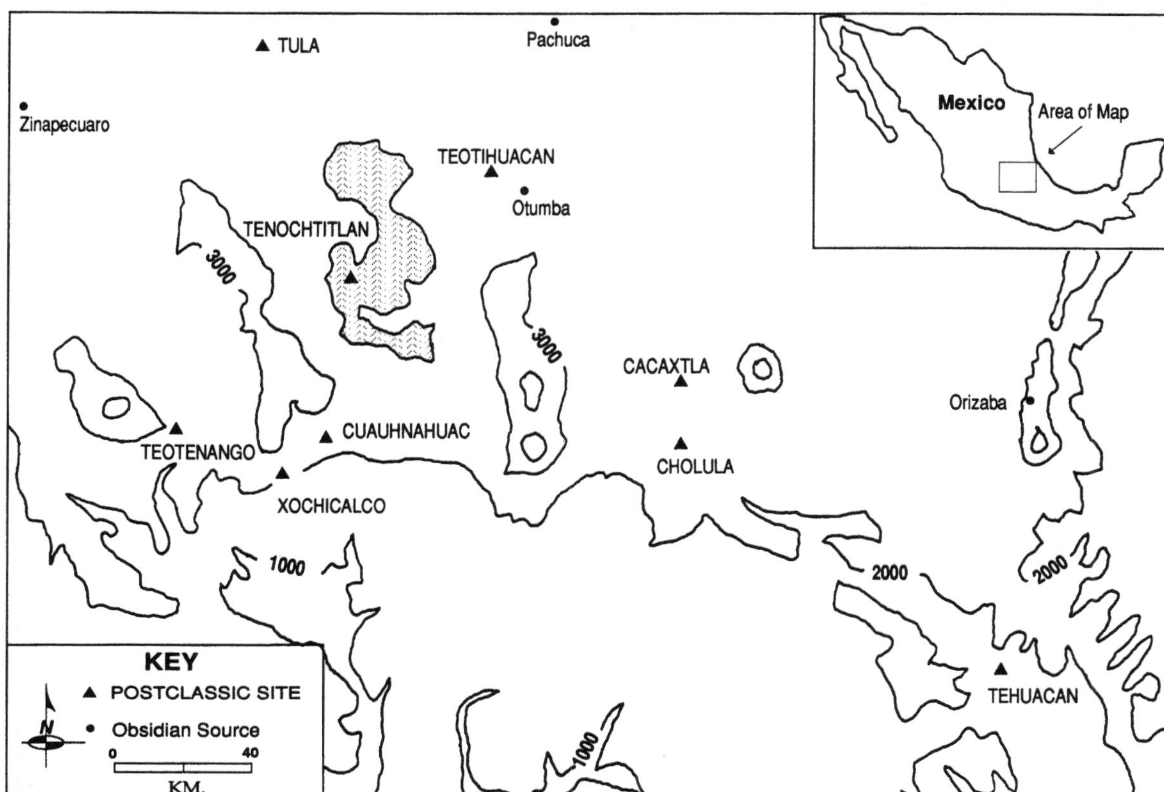

Braudel's model of hierarchical temporal rhythms is discussed in chapters by Knapp, Fletcher, and Smith (this volume; see also Braudel 1972; 1980). In the sections that follow, the various socioeconomic processes documented in the archaeological and historical records for Postclassic central Mexico are discussed in relation to their time scales. Insights from Braudel's work greatly aid the process of archaeological/historical correlation, and lead to a more satisfactory understanding of the rhythms of change that operated in the Precolumbian past.

Central Mexico, as discussed in this chapter, includes the Basin of Mexico and surrounding highland valleys, covering parts of the Mexican states of Mexico, Hidalgo, Puebla, Tlaxcala, Morelos, and Guerrero (Figure 4.1). This area comprised a significant economic and social unit throughout most of the Postclassic epoch in that local populations were in frequent contact with each other and achieved a moderate level of regional interdependence. By the time of the Spanish conquest in 1519, the inhabitants of central Mexico were also linked by a single language (Nahuatl) and a common cultural system, and most were part of a single hegemonic empire. William T. Sanders (1956) was the first scholar to analyze the socioeconomic integration of central Mexico in his formulation of the "Central Mexican Symbiotic Area." Following suggestions made above, the archaeological and native historical records for Postclassic central Mexico are first presented independently, and then brought together for comparison and correlation.

Figure 4.2 Archaeological chronologies for Postclassic central Mexico

Date, A.D.	Period	Basin of Mexico	Tula	Western Morelos	Cuernavaca	Tehuacan	Tlaxcala
1500	**Late Postclassic**	Late Aztec	Palacio	Late Cuauhnahuac	Tecpan	Late Venta Salada	Tlaxcala
1400				Early Cuauhnahuac			
1300	**Middle Postclassic**	Early Aztec	Fuego	Temazcali	Teopanzolco		
1200				Tilancingo			
1100	**Early Postclassic**	Mazapan	Tollan			Early Venta Salada	
1000				Phase H	Not yet defined		Texcalac
900	**Epiclassic**	Coyotlatelco	Corral	Phase G			
800							

Sources:
Basin of Mexico: Sanders, Parsons and Santley (1979: 457–474).
Tula: Diehl (1983: 19).
Western Morelos: Smith (1983); Hirth (1984).
Cuernavaca: Smith (1983).
Tehuacan: MacNeish, Peterson and Flannery (1970: 177–237).
Tlaxcala: García Cook (1976: 64–89).

The archaeological record for Postclassic central Mexico

Chronology

Central Mexican archaeological chronology employs units that were initially designed as developmental stages (Formative, Classic, Postclassic) but now retain a primarily chronological connotation. The Postclassic epoch, from the fall of Teotihuacan to the arrival of Spanish invaders, is often divided into four units known as the Epiclassic, and Early, Middle, and Late Postclassic periods (Figure 4.2).[1] The outlines of this scheme were first established for the Basin of Mexico by George Vaillant (1938); later workers refined and confirmed the sequence (e.g., Tolstoy 1958; Parsons 1966; Sanders, Parsons, and Santley 1979). While these four periods were well established by stratigraphy and ceramic styles, their dating was worked out initially by (questionable) correlation with ethnohistory (see Nicholson 1955 for comment), and surprisingly few chronometric dates have been run on the sequence. Recent radiocarbon dates from nearby areas like Hidalgo and Morelos, whose sequences are closely linked to the Basin of Mexico through cross-ties, tend to support the consensus dating (e.g., Diehl 1983: 57; Norr 1987; Smith and Doershuk n.d.), but there is a clear need for chronometric dating in the Postclassic Basin of Mexico.[2] Outside of the Basin of Mexico, Morelos, and Hidalgo, Postclassic chronologies in central Mexico are less refined, and consist of either hypothetical sequences unsupported by published archaeological data (as in the Toluca Valley or Cholula) or else rough divisions into two periods generally referred to as Early and Late Postclassic (as in Tlaxcala and much of Puebla, including Tehuacan; see Figure 4.2); this situation is discussed further in Smith (1987a).

The Epiclassic period

The period immediately after the breakup of the large Classic polity of Teotihuacan was characterized by warfare and conflict among a number of smaller, though urban, polities throughout the central Mexican highlands. In the Basin of Mexico, total population dropped to two-thirds of its Classic level (Sanders, Parsons, and Santley 1979: 129). Teotihuacan, though much reduced in size and grandeur, remained a major city with a population on the order of 30,000–40,000 (Sanders, Parsons, and Santley 1979: 130). Among the excavated contexts in Epiclassic Teotihuacan is a workshop for the production of obsidian projectile points (Rattray 1987). Population in the rest of the Basin of Mexico was centered on a number of "settlement clusters" (Sanders, Parsons, and Santley 1979: 129–33), with most inhabitants living in large towns and cities. This period witnessed the lowest proportion of rural settlement of any phase in the Prehispanic sequence of the Basin (*ibid.*).

At least three major urban polities rose to prominence in central Mexico outside of the Basin of Mexico following the demise of Teotihuacan. The areas south and west of the Basin were respectively dominated by the large fortified hilltop urban centers of Xochicalco (Hirth 1984) and Teotenango (Piña Chán 1975). Both of these sites have impressive ceremonial and defensive architecture, large dense populations, and iconographic depictions of militarism and conflict (Figure 4.3). A number of obsidian workshops are present at Xochicalco (Sorensen, Hirth, and Ferguson 1981), which was involved in exchange with a number of central and west Mexican supply areas. The site of Cacaxtla in southern Tlaxcala (López de Molina 1981) is best known for its elaborate mural paintings with wide-ranging stylistic influences, including Late Classic Maya art (the Epiclassic period in central Mexico was contemporaneous with the Late Classic period in the Maya lowlands). Again, these paintings emphasize warfare and militarism, and the site is a hilltop urban center with fortifications. Finally, the major site of Cholula in Puebla may or may not have had extraregional politico-military significance in the Epiclassic period (as suggested by Sanders, Parsons, and Santley 1979: 133–4); the published data are unfortunately not sufficiently informative to make a judgment (e.g., Marquina 1970). In summary, the Epiclassic period in central Mexico was a time of large competing urban centers, with no single polity achieving the regional dominance previously held by Teotihuacan. Epiclassic developments in central Mexico and elsewhere in Mesoamerica are reviewed by Webb (1978) and the papers in Diehl (1989).

The Early Postclassic period

Settlement patterns in the Basin of Mexico underwent a major transformation between the Epiclassic and Early Postclassic periods. Whereas the Epiclassic period exhibited one of the highest levels of urbanism in the whole sequence, the Early Postclassic period witnessed the greatest ruralization of settlement, with very few large centers (Sanders, Parsons, and Santley 1979: 138). There is only one large urban settlement in central Mexico at this time: the site of Tula in Hidalgo, just north of the Basin of Mexico (Figure 4.4). Recent research suggests a dense population of around 30,000–40,000 inhabitants (Diehl 1983: 60), and reveals obsidian and other craft workshops, monumental ceremonial architecture, as well as a complex iconography with themes of warfare and militarism (Matos 1974; Diehl 1983; Healan 1986; 1989).

The early Postclassic situation at Cholula is again uncertain; we cannot be sure of its size, organization, or interregional significance. Sanders, Parsons, and Santley (1979: 146–9) suggest that Cholula may have been a political and economic rival of Tula, and they explain a settlement gap in the central Basin of Mexico as a buffer zone between these two major rival polities. However, apart from the uncertainties of Cholula's status, there is little evidence to suggest that Tula had much political or economic influence beyond its local support zone. Tollan phase (Early Postclassic) artifacts and styles from Tula (including architecture) are conspicuous by their absence from contexts outside of the Tula area, and the major Early Postclassic Mesoamerican trade routes generally bypassed Tula and central Mexico (Smith and Heath-Smith 1980). The only evidence which may relate to a possible extension of influence much beyond Tula is that the northern Basin (closest to Tula) represents the only portion of the Basin of Mexico witnessing population growth between the Epiclassic and Early Post-

Figure 4.3 Aerial view of the Epiclassic hilltop city of Xochicalco, Morelos

classic periods (Sanders, Parsons, and Santley 1979: 209–16); in the remainder of the Basin (and overall), population declined at this time. This demographic pattern is echoed in western Morelos, where the number of sites along the Río Chalma dropped between the Epiclassic and Early Postclassic periods (K. Hirth, unpublished data).

The Middle Postclassic period

There is a major discontinuity in settlement location between the Early and Middle Postclassic periods in both the Basin of Mexico (Sanders, Parsons, and Santley 1979: 152) and western Morelos (K. Hirth, unpublished data). At the same time, new bichrome and polychrome ceramic styles were initiated in these areas (and in at least one other part of central Mexico – Malinalco) and continued through the following Late Postclassic period (Figure 4.5). Elsewhere I have interpreted these changes as archaeological evidence for the arrival of new populations in the central Mexican highlands (Smith 1984).

Although a number of Middle Postclassic sites have been excavated in central Mexico (e.g., Tenayuca, Chalco, and Culhuacan in the Basin of Mexico; Teopanzolco [or Cuauhnahuac], Tepozteco, and Tetla in Morelos), most of this work has consisted of limited testing and/or the study of ceremonial architecture; for this reason, we know little about patterns of urban structure or size during this period. Furthermore, there are chronological problems in the surface archaeology of the Middle Postclassic in the Basin of Mexico, where ceramics are difficult to distinguish from Late Postclassic material (see Sanders, Parsons, and Santley 1979: 150–1), making analyses of settlement patterns difficult and less secure than for other periods. Overall, the pattern appears to resemble that of the Early Postclassic, with a high level of ruralization and no large

Figure 4.4 Aerial view of the central ceremonial zone of the Early Postclassic city of Tula, Hidalgo

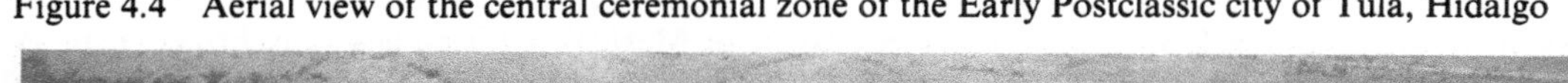

urban centres in the Basin. The Toltec city at Tula was largely abandoned by this time, a situation probably associated with a decline in regional population in the northern Basin of Mexico and the Tula area. This decline is offset by a large settlement buildup in the southern Basin, however. Parsons' recent excavations in the chinampa zone suggest that this population growth was related to the initiation of chinampa construction on a large scale (Parsons *et al.* 1982). The overall trend in the Basin of Mexico and Morelos is for a slight rise in population over Middle Postclassic levels.

The Late Postclassic period

In the Basin of Mexico, two outstanding characteristics of Late Postclassic settlement are a very high population size and density, and an advanced degree of urbanization. Total population increased from 160,000 to 1,000,000, and the proportion of the population living in cities increased from zero to around 35 percent (these trends are discussed further below). The most dramatic example of urbanization is the Aztec capital Tenochtitlan (Figure 4.6), a process analyzed by Rojas (1986). In addition, Texcoco was a large city, and there were five or six smaller urban centers with populations well over 10,000 (Sanders, Parsons, and Santley 1979: 154). Rural population also expanded greatly, and in several areas Late Postclassic settlement is nearly continuous along major strips several km long. This overall population growth was accompanied by major construction projects in both urban ceremonial architecture (e.g., Matos 1988) and agricultural intensification (Parsons *et al.* 1982). The demographic explosion in the Basin of Mexico was mirrored in Morelos (Smith 1991), although there is less evidence for concomitant urban growth in this area.

For the first time in many centuries, a single ceramic

Figure 4.5 Middle Postclassic decorated ceramics from central Mexico. A: Aztec I Black-on-Orange (southern Basin of Mexico); B: Aztec II Black-on-Orange (northern Basin of Mexico); C: Tlahuica Polychrome Type A (Teopanzolco, Morelos); D: Tlahuica Polychrome Type B-4 (Cuexcomate, Morelos); E: Malinalco Polychrome (Malinalco, State of Mexico)

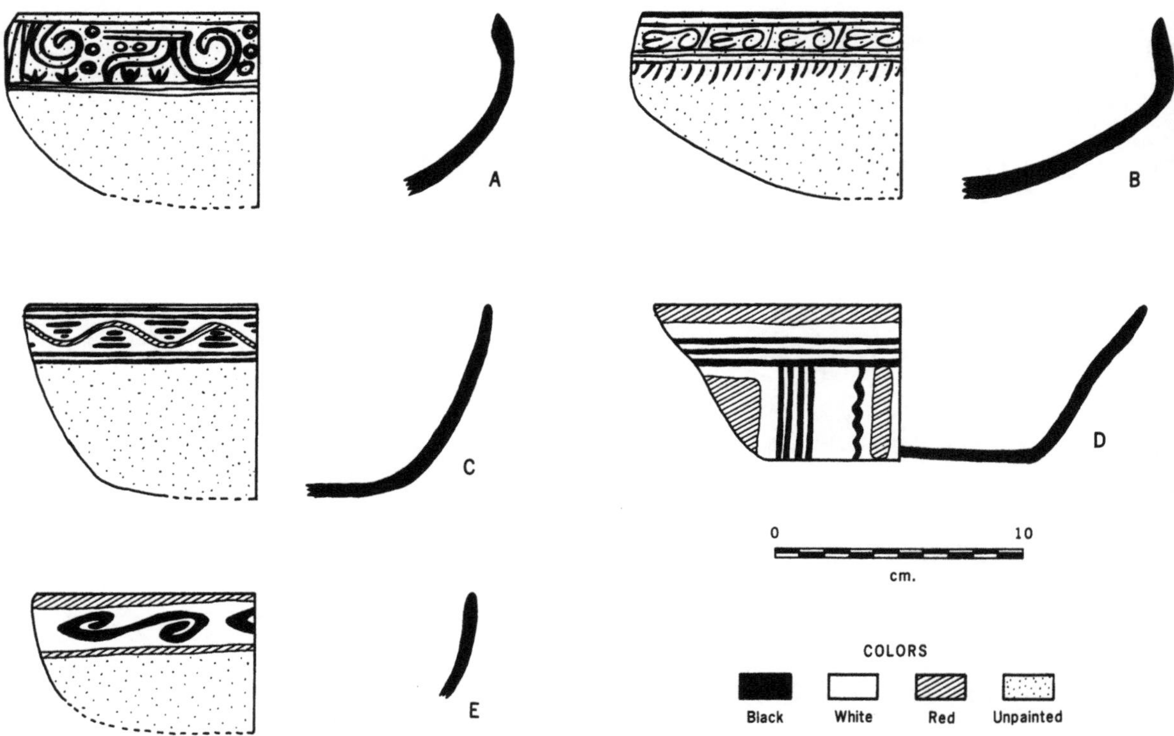

style was predominant throughout the entire Basin of Mexico, suggesting the integration of the Basin into a single exchange system. Aztec tradewares (both ceramics and obsidian) achieved a widespread distribution throughout Mesoamerica, although on a lesser scale than Teotihuacan wares a millennium earlier (Smith 1990). Obsidian tools were manufactured in rural workshops throughout central Mexico (Smith, Sorensen, and Hopke 1984; Brumfiel 1985; 1987; Spence 1985), and there is little evidence of urban lithic production at this time (Figure 4.7). These patterns suggest a period of relative peace and stability, which is supported by a general lack of fortifications or defensible locations at Late Postclassic sites in central Mexico (although there were exceptions like the fortress of Oztuma in Guerrero or Cuauhtochco in Veracruz). Military motifs are moderate elements in Mexican iconography from Tenochtitlan, although they are somewhat rare outside of that context.

Major trends in the Postclassic archaeological record

The Postclassic archaeological record provides a basis for inferring a number of socioeconomic trends, including demography, urbanism, warfare, agricultural intensification, craft production, and long-distance trade orientations. Information on these topics is summarized in Table 4.1. There were two fundamental long-term demographic cycles in the Prehispanic Basin of Mexico. Population grew steadily from the introduction of agriculture through the Classic period of Teotihuacan's dominance (total Basin population of around 250,000 – Sanders, Parsons, and Santley 1979: 186), after which it fell to a low point in the Early Postclassic, only to rise again until the end of the Prehispanic era in the sixteenth century. The Middle to Late Postclassic increase approached a 1 percent annual growth rate, an extremely high rate for a preindustrial context (see Cowgill 1975). In the Late Postclassic, regional population density was

Figure 4.6 Plan of the Aztec Templo Mayor, the central pyramid-temple of the Aztec capital Tenochtitlan (reprinted from Broda, Carrasco, and Matos 1987)

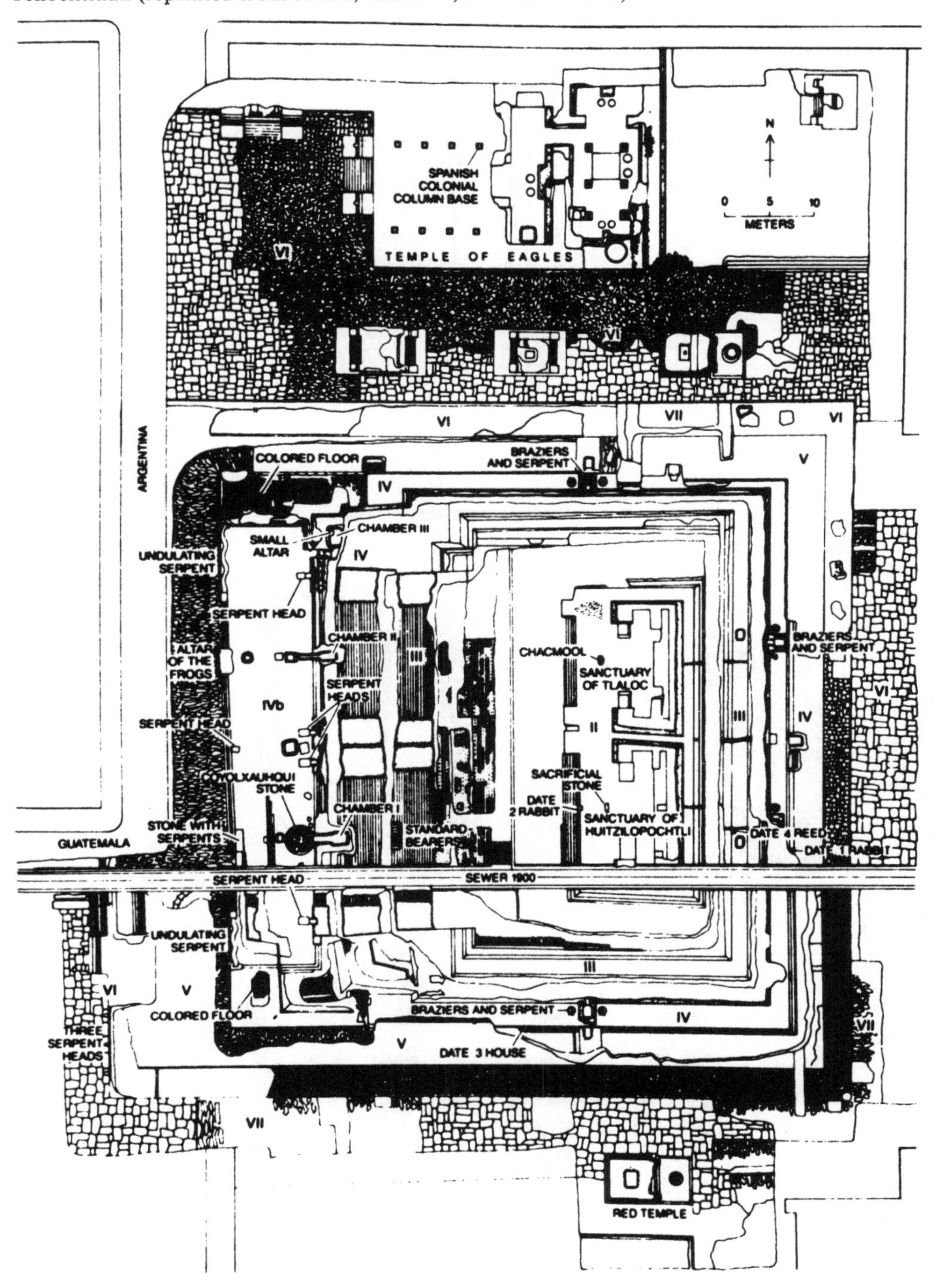

Figure 4.7 Late Postclassic obsidian artifacts manufactured of obsidian from the Puchuca source area, Hidalgo (excavated at the sites of Cuexcomate and Capilco in Morelos by the Postclassic Morelos Archaeological Project)

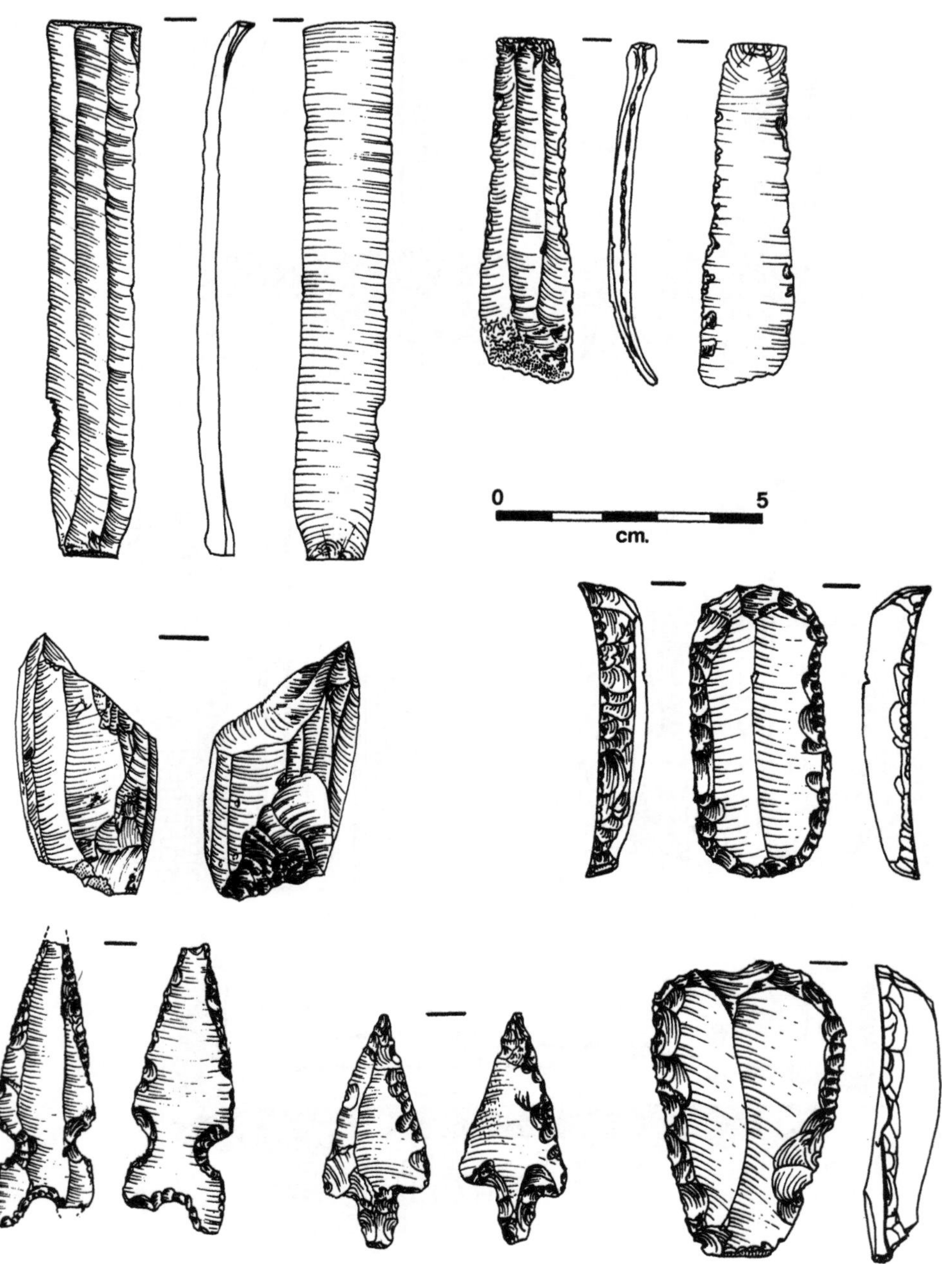

Table 4.1 *Trends in the Postclassic archaeological record*

	Periods			
Variable	Epiclassic	Early Postclassic	Middle Postclassic	Late Postclassic
A Basin of Mexico demography[a]				
Total population	175,000	130,000	160,000	1,000,000
% of population in cities[b]	31	0	0	34
% of population in towns[b]	38	40	29	18
Maximum regional population density	65/km^2	56/km^2	103/km^2	234/km^2
B Central Mexican politico-economic trends[c]				
Settlement orientation	urban <----------	---------- rural ----------	---------->	urban
Primate city	none	Tula	none	Tenochtitlan
Warfare	<----------	---------- common ----------	---------->no data	rare
Agricultural intensification	<----------	---------- low ----------	----------> moderate	high
Textile production	<----------	---------- moderate ----------	---------->	high
Obsidian production	<----------	---------- urban ----------	---------->no data	rural
Trade orientation	<----------	---------- non-nucleated ----------	----------	---------->nucleated

a These data are from Sanders, Parsons, and Santley (1979: 183–219).
b "Cities" refers to supraregional and large regional centers in the Basin of Mexico settlement classification; "towns" refers to small regional centers (Sanders, Parsons, and Santley 1979: 52–60).
c These are subjective judgements whose basis is discussed in the text.

around 150 persons per sq. km overall, with localized areal densities of over 200 persons per sq. km (Table 4.1). Again, this is a very high figure for a preindustrial population.

Urbanization closely followed population levels in the Basin of Mexico (Table 4.1). The Early and Middle Postclassic periods had the lowest populations, distributed in a predominantly rural configuration without large cities. On a wider scale, however, Early Postclassic Tula was a primate city within central Mexico as a whole, although not to the same extent as either Teotihuacan in the Classic or Tenochtitlan in the Late Postclassic. Warfare was significant in site layout and location and iconography in the first half of the Postclassic epoch, although there is less evidence in the two later periods.

There is little evidence for intensive agricultural practicies early in the Postclassic, followed by increasing construction of chinampas, irrigation facilities, hillside terraces, and other agricultural features in the Middle and especially Late Postclassic (Parsons *et al.* 1982; Price 1988). In western Morelos, where Postclassic textile production has been studied in some detail, cotton spinning becomes significant in the Epiclassic period, and then undergoes a major increase in the Late Postclassic (Smith and Hirth 1988); this is in contrast to the Basin of Mexico, where spinning appears to decline between the Early and Late Aztec phases (Brumfiel 1980; 1985; 1987). The macroregional orientation of long-distance trade remained non-nucleated for most of the Postclassic in that no single center controlled a major portion of trade and many important Postclassic trade networks bypassed central Mexico (see Smith and Heath-Smith 1980). The Late Postclassic pattern represents a return to the earlier Classic pattern where one central Mexican city controls a large part of Mesoamerican trade (Smith 1990).

Chronological refinement in Postclassic central Mexico

Before the trends discussed above can be analyzed in greater detail, archaeological chronologies in Postclassic central Mexico need to be refined in a relative sense and dated more accurately in a chronometric sense. Since Parsons' (1966) pioneering work on Aztec chronology, there have been only a few cases of significantly improved chronologies for Postclassic central Mexico. The University of Missouri Tula Project (Diehl 1983) produced a finer Epiclassic/Early Postclassic chronology for that site; the Xochicalco Mapping Project refined the

Classic/Epiclassic sequence in western Morelos (Hirth 1984); and the author's seriation work in western Morelos (Smith 1983; 1987a) produced a finer grained sequence for the post-Xochicalco periods. This latter work illustrates the influence of research goals and temporal rhythms on chronology-building. An Early–Middle–Late Postclassic chronology to match that in the Basin of Mexico was easily derived from test-pit stratigraphy and ceramic crossties. However, an interest in the expansion of the Aztec empire and its local effects led to a major effort in chronological refinement. Quantitative seriation (using multidimensional scaling and discriminant analysis) was applied to ceramic attribute data from excavated secondary refuse deposits, permitting a division of the post-Xochicalco epoch into five phases in place of the prior three. As a result, the pre- and post-imperial periods were separated for the first time in Mesoamerica (see Smith 1983: chapter 4; 1987a).

This example points out again the dialectical nature of chronological refinement (see Smith, this volume). As archaeologists have recovered more data and made more wide-ranging interpretations of the Postclassic archaeological record, the existing chronology that made that work possible has become inadequate for current research interests. Fortunately, several current projects include chronological refinement as an explicit goal – Jeffrey Parsons' excavations in the chinampa zone of the southern Basin of Mexico; Susan Evans' work at rural sites in the Teotihuacan Valley; Thomas Charlton and Deborah Nichols' study of Aztec Otumba; Patricia Plunket's work in southern Puebla, and the author's excavations of rural villages in western Morelos (Smith 1991; Smith and Doershuk n.d.). This work promises to lead to more refined sequences in the Basin of Mexico, Morelos, and Puebla, which would permit consideration of socioeconomic changes on the order of the long- and intermediate-term conjuncture.

Central Mexican ethnohistory

The nature of the sources

The major types of primary sources for central Mexican ethnohistory are native-style pictorial codices, first-hand Spanish accounts of the Aztecs, early colonial compilations, and Spanish administrative records. These may be classified into two broad categories, synchronic and diachronic. Synchronic sources provide a richly detailed picture of central Mexico at the time of Spanish conquest and on into the colonial epoch (e.g., Berdan 1982), while diachronic sources depict several centuries of pre-Spanish history for the polities and peoples of central Mexico (e.g., Carrasco 1971). The focus here is on documentary treatments of historical change before the arrival of the Spanish.

The Nahuatl-speaking peoples of central Mexico had a rudimentary writing system that served two primary purposes: religious and historical. The most common form of historical account combined written documents with oral narrative. The major documents, called "continuous year count annals" by Nicholson (1971), were based upon the Mesoamerican 52-year calendar. They typically have an unbroken sequence of year dates arranged along one side of each page of a screen-fold document (Figure 4.8A). Pictorial glyphs and scenes indicate events that happened in particular years and served as points of departure for oral narrative regarding the events portrayed. The purpose of these annals was to record the occurrence of events significant to the ruling dynasties of the city-states. They tend to focus on ethnic origins and later dynastic history: accessions and deaths of rulers, wars, alliances, and the like. Most of our knowledge of the Nahuatl histories comes from what Nicholson (1971: 48) calls "textual histories." These are descriptions and transcriptions of native chronicles (both written and oral) recorded in Spanish and Nahuatl in the sixteenth century.

Because of the nature of Nahuatl native history, the reliability of information declines as one moves back in time. The 80-year period of the Aztec empire (1438–1519) is well covered while the preceding century has somewhat less information. Prior to the founding of Tenochtitlan in 1345, however, the amount of data and its reliability drop off considerably. Most authorities agree that the earliest historical information that is not completely mythological concerns the Toltecs of the Early Postclassic period.[3]

The chronicle of native history

The major events and processes described in the central Mexican sources are listed in Figure 4.9 along with their most probable dates (I tend to follow Davies' (1973; 1977; 1980) approach to chronology and his specific dates for most events). Native history begins with the Toltecs, a semi-legendary people who purportedly invented the calendar and the technology of craft production. The Toltecs are depicted as wise and good, the greatest artists of Mesoamerica, with many other virtues and positive accomplishments. The Toltecs are also said to have created a large empire centered on a magnificent capital city, Tollan. Not only were some Aztec gods like Quetzalcoatl linked to Toltec culture heroes, but later rulers down through Motecuhzoma Xocoyotzin pos-

Figure 4.8 Native historical documents from central Mexico. A: Historical events between the year of AD 1467 (1 reed) and 1479 (13 reed) as portrayed in a continuous year-count annal, the Codex en Cruz (Dibble 1981); B: Migrations of the Aztlan groups as depicted in the Tira de la Peregrinación (1944)

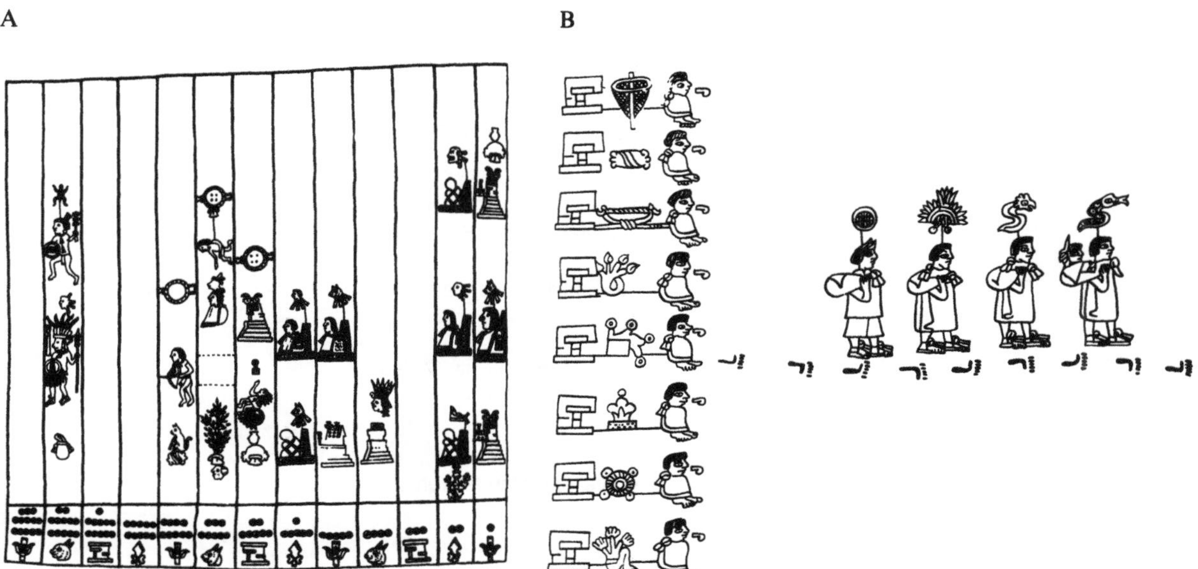

sessed political legitimacy by virtue of their (proclaimed) direct line of descent from the Toltec kings.

Native historical information on the Toltecs is assembled and analyzed by Davies (1977; 1980), who also treats the related problem of the ideological importance of the Toltecs in later times. Davies (1977: 171–5) leaves the dates for the founding of the Toltec capital and empire to the archaeologists (see Diehl 1983), but suggests that AD 900 is not an unreasonable estimate from the fragmentary and conflicting available native dates. The extent of the Toltec "empire" is discussed by a number of authors; Davies (1977: 312–28) and Diehl (1983: 118–21) concur in the inclusion of central and southern Hidalgo, the Basin of Mexico, northern Puebla, and Morelos. The fall of Tollan and the Toltecs, probably at the hands of invading nomads, is dated by Davies to AD 1175.

The next major process depicted in the native historical sources is the arrival in central Mexico of Nahuatl-speaking migrants from the north. These populations reportedly originated in the mythical place of Aztlan in the north and were guided to their eventual homelands in central Mexico by their gods (Figure 4.8B). The historicity and dating of these migrations is covered by Smith (1984). These populations represent the ancestors of the various central Mexican Nahuatl groups of the sixteenth century. The most celebrated immigrant group (due to the source of the majority of the surviving texts) is the Mexica, the last of the Aztlan groups to arrive in central Mexico. Upon their arrival in the Basin of Mexico and the surrounding highland valleys, the settlers proceeded to found city-states and dynasties that quickly obtained links (through marriage) to the Toltec kings (Calnek 1978; 1982).

According to the sources, the thirteenth through early fifteenth centuries was a time of population increase, political expansion, and the growth of social stratification. The various city-states interacted intensively in both peaceful and violent ways: trade, marriage alliances, and elite co-operation were important, and these were accompanied by battles and shifting political alliances. This situation, described by Davies (1973; 1980) and analyzed by Brumfiel (1983), provides an excellent example of the process of "peer polity interaction" (Renfrew and Cherry 1986). The end result of these processes was the development of increasingly powerful and centralized states. The late fourteenth century saw the rise of the Tepanec empire in the western Basin of Mexico, the Acolhua state or empire in the eastern portion of the Basin, and the Cuauhnahuac conquest-state in Morelos to the south (Smith 1986).

Figure 4.9 Ethnohistorical chronology for Postclassic central Mexico

Date, A.D.	Archaeological Period	Historical Event	Historical Date*
	Late Postclassic	Spanish Conquest	1519
1500			
		Aztec Empire Established	1428
1400			
		Tepanec Empire Established	1370
	Middle Postclassic	Tenochtitlan Founded	1345
1300		↑ Growth of City-States and Dynasties ↓	
		Arrival of Aztlan Migrants	ca. 1200-1250
1200			
	Early Postclassic	Fall of Tollan	1175
1100		↑ Toltec Empire ↓	
1000			
	Epiclassic		
900		Toltec Empire Established	ca. 900
800			

*See text for discussion of the dates and chronology.

Table 4.2 *Areas of agreement between archaeology and ethnohistory*

Factor	Process/Event	Agree	Disagree	Not comparable
Demography	Aztlan migrations	X		
	Population growth	X		
Urbanism	Chronology of Tula	X		
	Primate cities	X		
	Founding of Tenochtitlan		X	
	Growth of Tenochtitlan			X
	Rural–urban orientation			X
Economics	Intensive agriculture			X
	Textile production			X
	Obsidian production			X
	Trade orientation			X
	Basin of Mexico market system			X
Political/military	Extent of Aztec empire	X		
	Extent of Toltec empire		X	
	Late Postclassic warfare		X	
	Growth of city-states			X
	Growth of Tepanec empire			X
	Growth of Aztec empire			X

This trajectory of political evolution culminated in the founding of the Aztec or Triple Alliance empire in the wake of the defeat of the Tepanecs by the Mexica and Acolhua in 1428 (Davies 1973). The Aztecs then initiated a process of expansion by conquest so that by 1519 the empire covered most of central and northern Mesoamerica. Late native history is preoccupied with the story of what king conquered which towns in what year, coupled with the nature of the resultant tribute paid to Tenochtitlan.

Diachronic correlation of archaeology and ethnohistory

It should be clear from the above discussions of archaeological and native historical data that there are some cases of agreement, some cases of disagreement, and many examples of non-comparability. When individual processes and events are classified by social category, some patterns begin to emerge (Table 4.2). Demographic processes show the greatest agreement, followed by aspects of urbanism. There is little comparability between the sources of evidence for economic phenomena, while political/military developments present a range of levels of agreement. Some of these patterns are the simple product of the nature of the evidence (e.g., native history has little to say about economics), but others derive from the nature of the phenomena, particularly the temporal rhythms involved in various processes of change. The four categories listed in Table 4.2 are discussed in turn.

Demography

The arrival of the Aztlan migrants is known primarily from native history, and it finds archaeological agreement in changing patterns of settlement locations and ceramic styles (Smith 1984). Postclassic population growth, including the dramatic Middle/Late Postclassic surge, is revealed primarily in the archaeological record through settlement pattern studies. Although there is little explicit or precise information in native history on population levels, the general accounts of political development and migrations suggest steadily increasing populations in the final few Prehispanic centuries (e.g., Davies 1973; 1980). The high level of agreement in demographic questions is due to three factors: (1) demographic phenomena have clear material expressions in the archaeological record; (2) demographic phenomena often have major social impacts which lead to their inclusion in historical accounts; and (3) much demographic change proceeds over long time scales that can be monitored by both archaeology and history.

Urbanism

Radiocarbon dates for the major Early Postclassic occupation of Tula (Diehl 1983: 57) match native historical dates for the florescence of the Toltec capital Tollan. There is further agreement between the sources that both the Early and Late Postclassic periods witnessed large primate cities in central Mexico, while the Epiclassic and Middle Postclassic periods show no such pattern of urban dominance. Beyond the huge cities, however, the rural vs. urban orientation of settlement as documented by regional survey is simply not reflected in Nahuatl native history.

The only significant disagreement concerning cities and urbanism relates to the founding of Tenochtitlan. Davies (1973: 37; 1980: 182) argues convincingly that the traditional historical date for this event (AD 1325) is incorrect and needs to be moved up to 1345. This matches closely the archaeological date for the Early/Late Aztec transition in the Basin of Mexico (Figure 4.9). However, excavations in Mexico City (Tenochtitlan) have turned up significant amounts of Aztec II Black-on-Orange ceramics, an Early Aztec marker (Vega 1979). There are a number of minor archaeological and historical revisions which could resolve this contradiction (e.g., the traditional date for Tenochtitlan is correct after all; the Early/Late Aztec transition is dated too early; there was pre-Mexica settlement at Tenochtitlan; etc.), but they have yet to be adequately explored. The historically documented rapid urban growth of Tenochtitlan (e.g., Lombardo de Ruiz 1973; Rojas 1986) cannot be studied archaeologically because of the logistics of excavating in the center of a modern metropolis, although some aspects of urbanization are reflected in the ceremonial state architecture excavated by the recent Templo Mayor project (Matos 1988).

The agreement between archaeology and ethnohistory on some urban phenomena can be attributed to the same reasons given above for demography – the material expressions of urbanism, the social impact of at least the large cities, and the time spans involved. The disagreement over the founding of Tenochtitlan is a minor issue that will probably be resolved with further research. The two cases of a lack of comparability arise from the logistics of fieldwork in a modern city and the lack of native historical information on all but the largest cities. This is generally a profitable area for joint archaeological–historical analysis, at least partially because the growth and decline of cities and towns often occurs over the relatively long time spans (the longer form of conjuncture) amenable to study by both excavation and surface methods (Braudel 1981). Some recent examples of useful joint archaeological–historical studies of urbanization include Diehl (1983), Redman (1986), Smith (1989), Knapp (1992), and studies in Renfrew and Cherry (1986).

Economics

Analysis of economic change presents a major methodological challenge in Postclassic central Mexico. The lack of economic data for earlier periods in Nahuatl native history makes archaeological–historical correlation irrelevant for long-term changes over the course of the Postclassic epoch. For the final century or two (Late Postclassic period), there are scraps of economic data that permit some changes to be investigated with historical data. For example, we know something of the chronology of the celebrated *pochteca* trade, and there are some examples of early and late imperial tribute quotas from the same area. Furthermore, the founding of the Aztec empire in 1428 is generally acknowledged as a major socio-political turning point in central Mexico, and many economic patterns described in 1519 are believed to be the result of changes brought about by the growth of the empire and concomitant socioeconomic transformations (e.g., Davies 1973; Brumfiel 1983; Smith 1986; Rojas 1986). As an example, the extensive market system that linked the entire Basin of Mexico into a single economy (Smith 1979; Brumfiel 1980; Berdan 1985) could only have developed under the conditions of peace and stability after 1428.

It is tempting to relate these economic changes to the dramatic transformations documented in the archaeological record between the Middle and Late Postclassic periods. For example, the Basin-wide uniformity of Late Aztec ceramic assemblages might appear to relate to the operation of the historically documented market system, or various Early to Late Aztec changes in archaeological markers of production and exchange might seem to be due to historically documented conditions before and after the formation of the empire (Brumfiel 1980; 1985). However at this stage of central Mexican chronology these are not valid correlations because the relevant chronological unit for the archaeological record – the Late Postclassic period – includes nearly equal intervals of time before and after the formation of the empire (see Smith 1987a for comment).

If scholars wish to deal with these issues, archaeological chronologies will have to be refined to the point where we can separate at least the pre- and post-imperial periods. Another stimulus to chronological refinement comes from Braudel's insights into the rhythms of economic change. He shows that many economic

Figure 4.10 Extent of the Aztec empire in 1519 with the locations of late Aztec trade ceramics indicated (see Smith 1990). This map is a preliminary version of the new map of the empire now in preparation by the Dumbarton Oaks Aztec Empire Project. Provincial borders are still subject to revision; the final map will be published in Berdan *et al.* (n.d.).

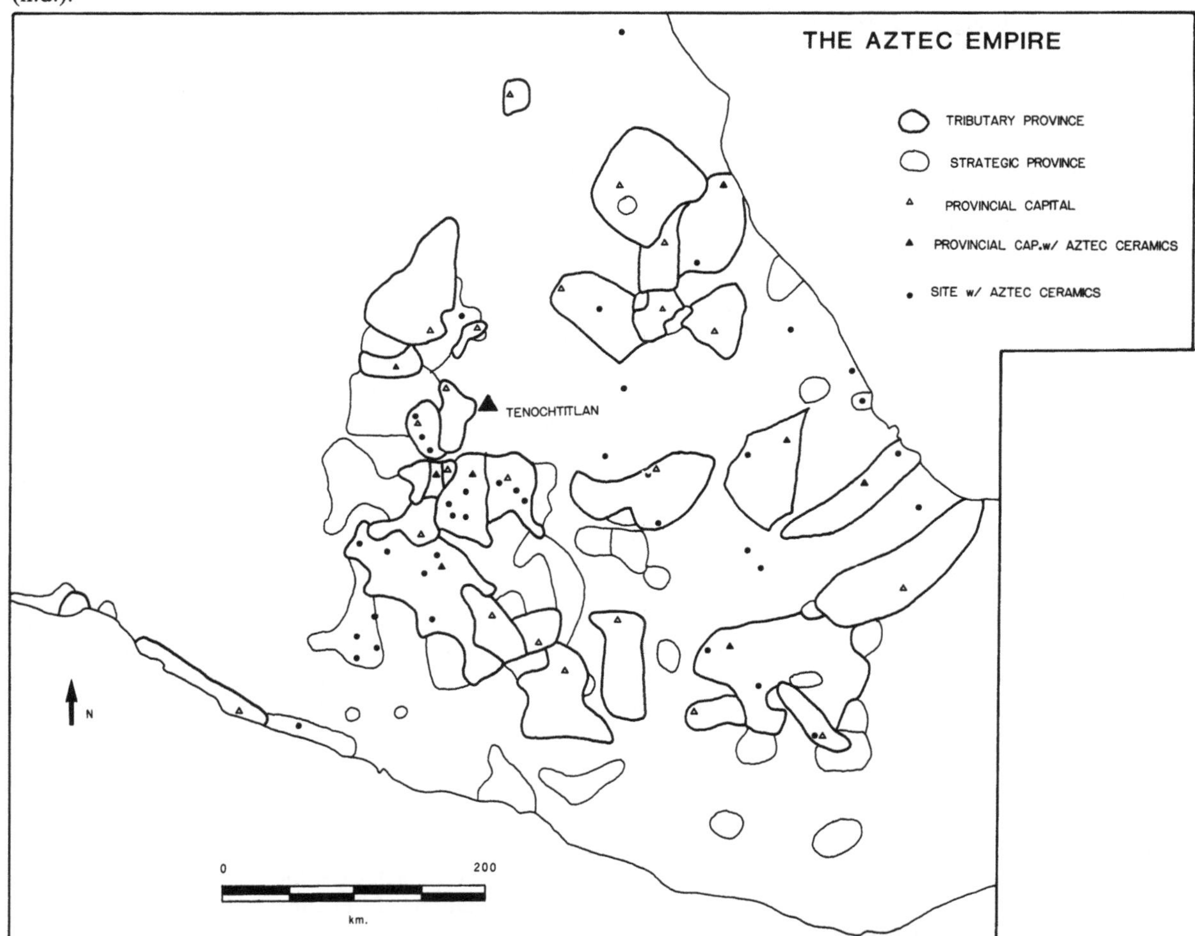

phenomena operate at the level of the conjuncture, which is often a faster paced rhythm than the changes on a 200-year scale revealed by the existing archaeological record. It is entirely possible that the changing Postclassic patterns of production and exchange revealed in the central Mexican archaeological record are spurious in that quantitative means for individual phases can mask cyclical variability of a quite different pattern.

Political and military processes

The geographical extent of large polities is another useful area of archaeological–historical correlation; Braudel includes "the changing dimensions of states and empires" (1972: 899) as an example of his longer conjuncture. For Postclassic central Mexico, we have agreement of sorts on the extent of the Aztec empire and a major disagreement for the Toltec case. As mentioned above, there is no archaeological evidence suggesting any kind of empire or expansive state centered on Tula in the Early Postclassic, while the historical sources attribute a large area to Tollan's domination. My own inclination is to doubt the native history, since so much of the historical information on the Toltecs is clearly mythological and exaggerated. Other archaeologists, however, tend to follow the sources over the archaeological record on this subject (e.g., Diehl 1983; Sanders and Santley 1983; Healan 1989).

The case for the Aztec empire is complex, but existing

archaeological data can be construed to agree with the historical accounts of the empire's extent. The political geography of the empire is currently undergoing revision, and a new map to replace Barlow's (1949) classic version is being produced by the Dumbarton Oaks Aztec Empire Project under the direction of Frances Berdan (Berdan *et al.* n.d.). Aztec expansion did not in most cases lead to the imposition of rulers, cities, garrisons, or colonies in the provinces (Hassig 1985; Smith 1986). However, a map of the distribution of Aztec ceramics outside of the Basin of Mexico coincides relatively well with the new map of the empire (Figure 4.10; see Smith 1990). While it is unlikely that the expansion of the empire led to the spread of the ceramics in question, the parallel distributions imply some link between ceramic trade and Aztec imperialism. Both the archaeologically documented artifact distributions and the historically documented imperial territory are due to the same underlying factor – the economic interest of the Aztecs in particular regions of Mesoamerica (Smith 1990). This is a complex issue, and unfortunately the whole methodological problem of the archaeological analysis of imperialism is rather poorly developed (see Bartel 1980; 1985; Alcock 1989).

There is some disagreement between archaeology and native history on the question of Late Postclassic warfare. The historical sources are full of information on battles, armies, and conquests, and this finds support in one class of archaeological remains – iconographic depictions on the imperial sculpture of Tenochtitlan (Townsend 1979). Militarism and warfare were clearly important aspects of Aztec society in 1519 (Berdan 1982: 105–8; Hassig 1988). However, compared to earlier periods, Late Postclassic sites are not located in defensible positions and do not exhibit defensive features like walls and ditches. While a number of fortresses have been found (e.g., Oztuma, Cuauhtochco; see Berdan *et al.* n.d.), these are the exceptions, located on the margins of central Mexico. It is possible that the native historical sources exaggerated the prevalence and importance of warfare because of their dynastic orientation and propagandistic role in Aztec society (see Smith 1986: 84; Gillespie 1989), or it may be that these patterns increased in intensity throughout the Late Postclassic. In Braudel's scheme (1972: 899), wars tend to operate on the level of the shorter conjuncture, and the growth of militarism may have occurred too quickly to be reflected in architectural patterns at most sites. In any case, by the mid-fifteenth century, most Aztec military activity was carried out on the frontiers of the empire, away from central Mexico (Hassig 1988).

Finally, three political–military processes documented in native history have few relevant archaeological manifestations: the growth of city-states, and the expansion of the Tepanec and Aztec empires. The first is amenable to archaeological analysis, but the emphasis on temples and test pits at Middle Postclassic sites (see above) prevents meaningful conclusions. As suggested above, the problem with the Aztec and Tepanec empires is the rapidity and lateness of their growth; the answer to the lack of comparability is chronological refinement and the development of archaeological methods for analyzing ancient imperialism.

Conclusions

Temporal rhythms in Postclassic central Mexico

The archaeological–ethnohistoric correlations discussed above permit a number of conclusions on the rhythms of social change in Postclassic central Mexico. There were no fundamental upheavals on the scale of Butzer's (1982) adaptive transformation between the fall of Teotihuacan and the arrival of the Spanish. The epoch begins and ends with urban state-level societies and relatively dense populations. However, within this setting, two major long-term trends on the scale of the *longue durée* stand out, both established sometime in the Early Postclassic and continuing through the end of the Prehispanic era. First, the archaeological record reveals an interlocking trend of population growth, agricultural intensification, urbanization, and economic growth. These processes begin slowly in the Early Postclassic and then accelerate at a greater rate in the Middle and Late Postclassic periods (see Table 4.1). In broad terms, this trend bears some resemblance to the "great agrarian cycle" in early modern Languedoc as analyzed by Le Roy Ladurie (1974). In the French case, the cycle also begins with a rural orientation of settlement and low population levels. Rapid population increase and economic growth led to the expansion of settlement and trade, but the limits of agricultural production were soon reached, leading to widespread poverty and general economic recession. The Aztec growth cycle never had a chance to reach maturity and subsequent decline on its own; Cortés arrived in a period of growth and expansion before recession could set in.

A second basic long-term trend is documented primarily in the realm of native history – the growth of the city-state as the dominant political form in central Mexico. City-states may have gotten their start in the wake of Teotihuacan's decline (Hirth 1984), but it is in the context of the fall of Tula and the arrival of the Aztlan migrants that this political form really took root and spread throughout the central Mexican highlands. The subsequent rise of the Tepanec and then Aztec empires did not signal an end to the dominance of city-states, since these loosely integrated empires left local political institutions in place and were built upon a foundation of local independent polities (Hodge 1985; Smith 1986). In Braudel's sense, the city-state represents one of the important and enduring "structures" of Postclassic central Mexico. While archaeology has yet to contribute much to our knowledge of Postclassic city-states (although see Brumfiel 1980; 1983), this is due to the small number of projects that have undertaken extensive excavations with the recovery of socioeconomic and political data as a goal (current work by Thomas Charlton and Deborah Nichols at Otumba will make a major contribution here).

At the level of Braudel's conjunctures, there are a number of such social and economic cycles recorded in both the archaeological and the native historical records for Postclassic central Mexico. The various empires – Toltec (if this was indeed an empire), Tepanec, and Aztec – were relatively short-lived cyclical phenomena (compared to many Old World empires). The Aztec case is similar in at least outline form to the growth of European empires in the sixteenth century which also developed out of a city-state background. According to Braudel (1972: 678, 895–6), economic growth, fueled by population growth, encouraged the growth of territorial states and empires in Europe. Urbanization in post-Teotihuacan central Mexico was another cyclical or conjunctural process. No single city maintained its growth or economic dominance for more than one of the existing archaeological periods, and the rural–urban orientation of settlement in the Basin of Mexico also followed a cyclical trajectory.

The temporal scale of the conjuncture lies at the edge of current archaeological capabilities in central Mexico. The existing chronology is sufficient to document contrasting patterns and the presence of change, but it is not refined to the point where we can analyze adequately the actual processes or events of change. Just how did the urban orientation of the Epiclassic Basin of Mexico evolve into the rural settlement configuration of the Early Postclassic? What socioeconomic changes were associated with the expansion of the Aztec empire? The answers to these and many other important research questions will come only after central Mexican archaeological chronologies are refined beyond their current level of resolution.

The relevance of Braudel

Fernand Braudel's model of hierarchical temporal rhythms helps advance the study of change in Postclassic central Mexico in several ways. Perhaps the most obvious contribution is the framework that Braudel's model provides for the interpretation of various types of sociocultural change. Different processes operate at different temporal scales, and changes at the level of the *longue durée* (e.g., many settlement pattern shifts) should not be viewed as equivalent to changes operating over shorter intervals (e.g., urbanization or the rise and fall of empires). This insight (see also Bailey 1983; 1987) casts doubt on attempts to provide unitary causal explanations for processes as diverse as settlement pattern change, urbanization, and shifts in production and distribution patterns (e.g., Sanders, Parsons, and Santley 1979; Sanders and Santley 1983). Particularly appealing for archaeologists is Braudel's theoretical justification for a strong emphasis on processes and structures of the *longue durée*, a level of time appropriate for the study of much of the data of prehistory.

Another contribution of Braudel's model to studies of Postclassic central Mexico is that it helps account for patterns of agreement, disagreement, and non-comparability between the archaeological and native historical records. The general agreement between the two sources of data on demographic phenomena (see Table 4.2) is due in large part to the relatively long time span over which many demographic processes operate, while much of the disagreement and non-comparability of economic, political, and military matters arises from their shorter temporal rhythms coupled with the relatively coarse grain of Postclassic archaeological chronologies. This observation points out a third important benefit of Braudel's model: it can help archaeologists relate chronology-building to research goals and fieldwork results (Smith, this volume). For central Mexico, existing archaeological chronologies are adequate to study the processes of the *longue durée*, and past emphases on settlement patterns and demography (e.g., Sanders, Parsons, and Santley 1979; Blanton *et al.* 1979) are appropriate for the same end. However, as research goals turn to economic and political changes that typically operate at shorter time scales (e.g., agricultural intensification, state-formation, urbanization, or imperialism; see for example Parsons *et al.* 1982; Brumfiel 1983; 1987; Smith 1986; Matos 1988), archaeologists need to devote more attention to chronological refinement (Smith 1987a).

The relevance of Braudel's model, particularly in relation to the correlation of archaeology and history, extends far beyond Postclassic central Mexico, as other articles in this book show. Few scholars would question the need to consider both archaeological and historical data (where both are available) in the attempt to develop more adequate models and interpretations of the complex societies of the past, and there are many general discussions of this issue in the literature (e.g., Nicholson 1955; 1978; Evans 1974; Spores 1980; Charlton 1981; Adams 1984; Brinkman 1984; Smith 1987a; Deetz 1988; Knapp this volume; 1991; note that most of these discussions are by archaeologists, not historians). However, this case study suggests that we need to go beyond programmatic statements about archaeological data versus historical data and take into account the particular kinds of evidence available. Different classes of archaeological remains as recovered by different methods provide very different kinds of information, and this variability needs to be considered explicitly in attempts to relate archaeology and history. If we compare settlement patterns as revealed by surface reconnaissance, or excavations of different types like test pitting, trenching ceremonial architecture, or clearing residential structures, these operations not only supply different kinds of evidence (Smith 1987b) but also permit varying levels of chronological refinement. A similar situation exists with regard to historical data. Varying kinds of documentary sources not only provide different information, but also permit different levels of temporal control and refinement. A major benefit of Braudel's work is that it forces scholars to confront these issues, thereby leading to more successful correlations of the archaeological and historical records.

Conclusions

The work of Braudel and the wider *Annales* school is not a panacea that will provide instant illumination of the archaeological past, but it does tie in with current concerns in archaeological method and theory (Fletcher and Smith, this volume), and can help advance the study of the past in a number of ways. Explicit attention to the issues raised by Braudel's model of hierarchical temporal rhythms not only helps in the interpretation and explanation of varying sociocultural processes in the Precolumbian past, but it also makes methodological contributions to archaeological research. This paper emphasizes two relevant areas of methodology – chronological refinement and the correlation of archaeology and ethnohistory – but there are others as well (Fletcher and Knapp, this volume). These two relevant aspects of Braudel's model – the explanatory and the methodological – are illustrated by the example of Postclassic central Mexico presented above. This was a setting for the rise and fall of complex state-level societies, and the application of insights from the work of Braudel contributes both to our understanding of the social processes involved and to the resolution of problems in correlating archaeology and ethnohistory.

Notes

1 The author's objections to a recently proposed chronological nomenclature involving horizons and intermediate phases (e.g., Sanders, Parsons, and Santley 1979: 91–3) are discussed in Smith (1987a).

2 Recent obsidian hydration at the Late Aztec/Early Colonial site of Siguatecpan (Susan Evans, personal communication) is a step in the right direction.

3 There is some disagreement over the historical accuracy of Nahuatl native history. Some scholars interpret nearly everything in these accounts as literal history (e.g., Carrasco 1971), while others take the opposite view that mythological elements dominate to the extent that it is nearly impossible to derive historically accurate information from the accounts (e.g., Gillespie 1989). The middle ground followed here assumes that both mythological and historical information are present in Nahuatl native history, and that historical accuracy can be determined by standard methods of source criticism and comparison. For examples of this latter approach, see Nicholson (1971), Davies (1977; 1980), and Smith (1984).

Acknowledgements

I would like to thank Bernard Knapp for the encouragement to write this paper and for helpful comments on earlier drafts. My knowledge and understanding of the archaeological and ethnohistorical records for Postclassic central Mexico have benefited greatly from discussions over the years with Frances Berdan, David Grove, Kenneth Hirth, William Sanders, and many other colleagues. Figures 4.3 and 4.4 are reprinted with permission of the Companía Mexicana de Aerofoto, Mexico City; Figure 4.6 is reprinted with permission of the University of California Press; and Figure 4.8A with permission of the University of Utah Press. Figures 4.5 and 4.10 were drafted by Michael Smith, Figure 4.7 by Fernando Botas. Figures 4.1, 4.2, and 4.9 were prepared by the Loyola University Center for Instructional Design.

References

Adams, R. McC. 1984 Mesopotamian social evolution: old outlooks, new goals, in T. K. Earle, ed., *On the Evolution of Complex Societies: Essays in Honor of Harry Hoijer, 1982*, pp. 79–129. (Other Realities 6.) Malibu: Undena Press.

Alcock, S. E. 1989 Archaeology and imperialism:

Roman expansion and the Greek city. *Journal of Mediterranean Archaeology* 2: 87–135.

Bailey, G. N. 1983 Concepts of time in Quaternary prehistory. *Annual Review of Anthropology* 12: 165–92.

1987 Breaking the time barrier. *Archaeological Review from Cambridge* 6: 5–20.

Barlow, R. H. 1949 The Extent of the Empire of the Culua Mexica. *Ibero-Americana* 28.

Bartel, B. 1980 Colonialism and cultural responses: problems related to Roman provincial analysis. *World Archaeology* 12: 11–26.

1985 Comparative historical archaeology and archaeological theory, in S. L. Dyson, ed., *Comparative Studies in the Archaeology of Colonialism*, pp. 8–37. British Archaeological Reports, International Series 233. Oxford: BAR.

Berdan, F. F. 1982 *The Aztecs of Central Mexico: An Imperial Society*. New York: Holt, Rinehart and Winston.

1985 Markets in the economy of Aztec Mexico, in S. Plattner, ed., *Markets and Marketing*, pp. 339–67. Lanham, MD: University Press of America.

Berdan, F. F., R. E. Blanton, E. H. Boone, M. G. Hodge, M. E. Smith, and E. Umberger *Aztec Imperial Strategies*. (In preparation)

Blanton, R. E., S. Kowalewski, G. Feinman, and J. Appel 1979 *Ancient Mesoamerica: A Comparison of Change in Three Regions*. New York: Cambridge University Press.

Braudel, F. 1972 *The Mediterranean and the Mediterranean World in the Age of Philip II* (translated by Sian Reynolds). 2 vols. New York: Harper and Row.

1980 *On History* (translated by Sarah Matthews). Chicago: University of Chicago Press.

1981 *The Structures of Everyday Life: The Limits of the Possible* (translated by M. Kochan and S. Reynolds). New York: Harper and Row.

Brinkman, J. A. 1984 Settlement surveys and documentary evidence: regional variation and secular trend in Mesopotamian demography. *Journal of Near Eastern Studies* 43: 169–80.

Broda, J., D. Carrasco, and E. Matos 1987 *The Great Temple of Tenochtitlan: Center and Periphery in the Ancient World*. Berkeley: University of California Press.

Brumfiel, E. M. 1980 Specialization, market exchange, and the Aztec state: a view from Huexotla. *Current Anthropology* 21: 459–78.

1983 Aztec state making: ecology, structure, and the origin of the state. *American Anthropologist* 85: 261–84.

1985 The division of labor at Xico: the chipped stone industry, in B. L. Isaac, ed., *Economic Aspects of Prehispanic Highland Mexico*, pp. 245–79. Research in Economic Anthropology, Supplement 2. Greenwich, CT: JAI Press.

1987 Elite and utilitarian crafts in the Aztec state, in E. M. Brumfiel and T. K. Earle, eds., *Specialization, Exchange, and Complex Societies*, pp. 102–18. New York: Cambridge University Press.

Butzer, K. W. 1982 *Archaeology as Human Ecology: Method and Theory for a Contextual Approach*. New York: Cambridge University Press.

Calnek, E. 1978 The city-state in the Basin of Mexico: Late Pre-Hispanic period, in R. P. Schaedel, J. E. Hardoy, and N. S. Kinzer, eds., *Urbanization in the Americas from its Beginnings to the Present*, pp. 463–70. The Hague: Mouton.

1982 Patterns of empire formation in the Valley of Mexico, Late Postclassic period, 1200–1521, in G. A. Collier, R. I. Roslado, and J. D. Wirth, eds., *The Inca and Aztec States, 1400–1800: Anthropology and History*, pp. 43–62. New York: Academic Press.

Carrasco, P. 1971 The peoples of central Mexico and their historical traditions, in G. F. Ekholm and I. Bernal, eds., *Archaeology of Northern Mesoamerica*, pt 2, pp. 459–73. Handbook of Middle American Indians 11. Austin: University of Texas Press.

Charlton, T. H. 1981 Archaeology, ethnohistory, and ethnology: interpretive interfaces. *Advances in Archaeological Method and Theory* 4: 129–76.

Cowgill, G. L. 1975 On causes and consequences of ancient and modern population changes. *American Anthropologist* 77: 505–25.

Davies, N. 1973 *The Aztecs: A History*. New York: G. P. Putnam's Sons.

1977 *The Toltecs Until the Fall of Tula*. Norman: University of Oklahoma Press.

1980 *The Toltec Heritage: from the Fall of Tula to the Rise of Tenochtitlan*. Norman: University of Oklahoma Press.

Deetz, J. 1988 American historical archaeology: methods and results. *Science* 239: 362–7.

Dibble, C. E. (ed.) 1981 *Codex en Cruz*. Salt Lake City: University of Utah Press.

Diehl, R. A. 1983 *Tula: The Toltec Capital of Ancient Mexico*. New York: Thames and Hudson.

(ed.) 1989 *Mesoamerica After the Decline of Teotihuacan*. Washington, DC: Dumbarton Oaks.

Evans, J. D. 1974 The archaeological evidence and its interpretation: some suggested approaches to the problems of the Aegean Bronze Age, in R. A.

Crossland and A. Birchall, eds., *Bronze Age Migrations in the Aegean: Archaeological and Linguistic Problems in Greek Prehistory*, pp. 17–26. Park Ridge, NJ: Noyes Press.

Evans, S. T. 1988 *Excavations at Cihuatecpan: An Aztec Village in the Teotihuacan Valley*. Vanderbilt University Publications in Anthropology 36. Nashville: Vanderbilt University, Department of Anthropology.

García Cook, A. 1976 *El Desarrollo Cultural en el Norte del Valle Poblano: Inferencias*. Instituto Nacional de Antropología e Historia, Departamento de Monumentas Prehispánicos, Serie Arqueología, No. 1. Mexico City.

Gillespie, S. D. 1989 *The Aztec Kings: The Construction of Rulership in Mexican History*. Tucson: University of Arizona Press.

Hassig, R. 1985 *Trade, Tribute, and Transportation: The Sixteenth Century Political Economy of the Valley of Mexico*. Norman: University of Oklahoma Press.

1988 *Aztec Warfare: Imperial Expansion and Political Control*. Norman: University of Oklahoma Press.

Healan, D. M. 1986 Technological and nontechnological aspects of an obsidian workshop excavated at Tula, Hidalgo, in B. L. Isaac, ed., *Economic Aspects of Prehispanic Highland Mexico*, pp. 133–52. Research in Economic Anthropology, Supplement 2. Greenwich, CT: JAI Press.

(ed.) 1989 *Tula of the Toltecs: Excavations and Survey*. Iowa City: University of Iowa Press.

Hirth, K. G. 1984 Xochicalco: urban growth and state formation in central Mexico. *Science* 225: 579–86.

Hodge, M. 1985 *Aztec City-States*. University of Michigan, Museum of Anthropology, Memoirs 18. Ann Arbor.

Knapp A. B. 1992 *Society and Polity at Bronze Age Pella: An* Annales *Perspective*. Sheffield: Sheffield Academic Press.

Knapp, A. B., P. Duerden, R. V. S. Wright, and P. Grave 1988 Ceramic production and social change: archaeometric analysis of Bronze Age pottery from Jordan. *Journal of Mediterranean Archaeology* 1(2): 57–113.

Le Roy Ladurie, E. 1974 *The Peasants of Languedoc* (translated by John Day). Urbana: University of Illinois Press.

Lombardo de Ruiz, S. 1973 *Desarrollo Urbana de Mexico-Tenochtitlan Segun las Fuentes Históricas*. Mexico City: Instituto Nacional de Antropología e Historia.

López de Molina, D. 1981 Un informe preliminar sobre la cronología de Cacaxtla, in E. C. Rattray, J. L. King and C. Díaz Oyarzabal, eds., *Interacción Cultural en México Central*, pp. 169–74. Mexico City: Universidad Nacional Autónoma de México.

MacNeish, R. S., F. A. Peterson, and K. V. Flannery 1970 *The Prehistory of the Tehuacan Valley*. Volume 3, *Ceramics*. Austin: University of Texas Press.

Marquina, I. (ed.) 1970 *Proyecto Cholula*. Instituto Nacional de Antropología e Historia, Série Investigaciones 19. Mexico City.

Matos Moctezuma, E. (ed.) 1974 *Proyecto Tula*. Instituto Nacional de Antropología e Historia, Colección Cien^tífica 15. Mexico City.

1988 *The Great Temple of the Aztecs*. New York: Thames and Husdon.

Nicholson, H. B. 1955 Native historical traditions of nuclear America and the problem of their archaeological correlation. *American Anthropologist* 57: 594–613.

1971 Pre-Hispanic central Mexican historiography, in *Investigaciones Contemporáneos Sobre Historia de México*, pp. 38–81. Mexico City and Austin: El Colegio de México and University of Texas Press.

1978 Western Mesoamerica: A.D. 900–1520, in R. E. Taylor and C. W. Meighan, eds., *Chronologies in New World Archaeology*, pp. 285–329. New York: Academic Press.

Noguera, E. 1963 Correlación de la arqueología y la historia en la porción norte del valle de México. *Anales del Instituto Nacional de Antropología e Historia*, Epoca 6, 15: 39–65.

Norr, L. 1987 The excavation of a Postclassic house at Tetla, in D. C. Grove, ed., *Ancient Chalcatzingo*, pp. 400–8. Austin: University of Texas Press.

Parsons, J. R. 1966 The Aztec ceramic sequence in the Teotihuacan Valley, Mexico. 2 vols. Ph.D. dissertation, Department of Anthropology, University of Michigan. Ann Arbor.

Parsons, J., E. Brumfield, M. Parsons, V. Popper, and M. Taft 1982 Late Prehispanic chinampa agriculture on Lake Chalco–Xochimilco, Mexico: preliminary report. Report submitted to the National Science Foundation.

Piña Chán, R. 1975 *Teotenango: El Antiguo Lugar de la Muralla: Memoria de las Excavaciónes Arqueológicas*. 2 vols. Mexico City: Gobierno del Estado de México, Dirección de Turismo.

Price, T. J. 1988 Investigation of agricultural features at two rural Late Postclassic sites in western Morelos, Mexico. M.A. thesis, Department of Anthropology, University of Georgia.

Rattray, E. C. 1987 La producción y la distribución de obsidiana en el período Coyotlatelco en Teotihuacán, in E. McClung de Tapia and E. Rattray, eds., *Teotihuacán: Nuevos Datos, Nuevas Síntesis, Nuevos Problemas*, pp. 451–63. Mexico City: Universidad Nacional Autónoma de México.

Redman, C. L. 1986 *Qsar es-Seghir: An Archaeological View of Medieval Life*. New York: Academic Press.

Renfrew, C. and J. F. Cherry (eds.) 1986 *Peer Polity Interaction and Socio-Political Change*. Cambridge: Cambridge University Press.

Rojas, J. L. 1986 *México Tenochtitlan: Economía y Sociedad en el Siglo XVI*. Mexico City: Fondo de Cultura Económica.

Sanders, W. T. 1956 The central Mexican symbiotic region, in G. R. Willey, ed., *Prehistoric Settlement Patterns in the New World*, pp. 115–27. Viking Fund Publications in Archaeology 23. New York: Wenner-Gren Foundation for Archaeological Research.

Sanders, W. T., J. R. Parsons, and R. S. Santley 1979 *The Basin of Mexico: Ecological Processes in the Evolution of a Civilization*. New York: Academic Press.

Sanders, W. T. and R. S. Santley 1983 A tale of three cities: energetics and urbanization in Pre-Hispanic central Mexico, in E. Z. Vogt and R. Leventhal, eds., *Prehistoric Settlement Patterns: Essays in Honor of G. R. Willey*, pp. 243–91. Albuquerque: University of New Mexico Press.

Smith, M. E. 1979 The Aztec marketing system and settlement patterns in the valley of Mexico: a central place analysis. *American Antiquity* 44: 110–25.

1983 Postclassic culture change in western Morelos, Mexico: the development and correlation of archaeological and ethnohistorical chronologies. Ph.D. dissertation, Department of Anthropology, University of Illinois.

1984 The Aztlan migrations of the Nahuatl chronicles: myth or history? *Ethnohistory* 31: 153–86.

1986 The role of social stratification in the Aztec empire: a view from the provinces. *American Anthropologist* 88: 70–91.

1987a The expansion of the Aztec empire: a case study in the correlation of diachronic archaeological and ethnohistorical data. *American Antiquity* 52: 37–54.

1987b Archaeology and the Aztec economy: the social scientific use of archaeological data. *Social Science History* 11: 237–59.

1989 Cities, towns and urbanism: comment on Sanders and Webster. *American Anthropologist* 91: 454–60.

1990 Long-distance trade under the Aztec empire: the archaeological evidence. *Ancient Mesoamerica* 1: 153–69.

1991 *Archaeological Excavations at Aztec-Period Rural Sites in Morelos, Mexico*. Volume 1, *Excavations and Architecture*. Memoirs in Latin American Archaeology 4. Pittsburgh: University of Pittsburgh, Department of Anthropology.

Smith, M. E. and J. Doershuk n.d. Late Postclassic chronology in western Morelos, Mexico. Unpublished manuscript.

Smith, M. E. and C. Heath-Smith 1980 Waves of influence in Postclassic Mesoamerica? A critique of the Mixteca–Puebla concept. *Anthropology* 4(2): 15–50.

Smith, M. E. and K. G. Hirth 1988 The development of Pre-Hispanic cotton-spinning technology in western Morelos, Mexico. *Journal of Field Archaeology* 15: 349–58.

Smith, M. E., J. H. Sorensen, and P. K. Hopke 1984 Obsidian exchange in Postclassic central Mexico: new data from Morelos. Paper presented at the 1984 International Symposium on Archaeometry.

Sorensen, J. H., K. G. Hirth, and S. M. Ferguson 1981 Contents of seven obsidian workshops in western Morelos. Paper presented at the Simposio Sobre la Obsidiana en Mesoamérica (Pachuca, Hidalgo).

Spence, M. W. 1985. Specialized production in rural Aztec society: obsidian workshops of the Teotihuacan Valley, in W. J. Folan, ed., *Contributions to the Archaeology and Ethnohistory of Greater Mesoamerica*, pp. 76–125. Carbondale: Southern Illinois University Press.

Spores, R. 1980 New world ethnohistory and archaeology, 1970–1980. *Annual Review of Anthropology* 9: 575–603.

Tira de la Penegrinación 1944 *Tira de la Penegrinación Mexicana*. Mexico City: Libreria Anticuaria G. M. Echaniz.

Tolstoy, P. 1958 Surface survey of the northern Valley of Mexico: the Classic and Post-Classic periods. *American Philosophical Society, Transactions* 48 (5). Philadelphia.

Townsend, R. F. 1979 *State and Cosmos in the Art of Tenochtitlan*. Dumbarton Oaks, Studies in Pre-Columbian Art and Archaeology 20. Washington, DC: Dumbarton Oaks.

Vaillant, G. C. 1938 A correlation of archaeological and historical sequences in the valley of Mexico. *American Anthropologist* 40: 535–73.

Vega Sosa, C. 1979 La cerámica: clasificación y cronología, in C. Vega Sosa, ed., *El Recinto Sagrado de México-Tenochtitlan: Excavaciones 1968–69 y 1975–76*, pp. 37–53. Mexico City: Instituto Nacional de Antropología e Historia.

Webb, M. 1978 The significance of the "epiclassic" period in Mesoamerican prehistory, in D. L. Browman, ed., *Cultural Continuity in Mesoamerica*, pp. 155–78. The Hague: Mouton.

5 Pottery styles and social status in medieval Khurasan

RICHARD W. BULLIET

The growth of cities in the early Islamic period stimulated many new designs of glazed pottery. One major production area was Khurasan – northeast Iran and adjacent parts of Afghanistan and Central Asia. The chronology and variety of pottery styles mirrors the chronology of conversion and the resultant emergence of political-religious factions. On this basis it is argued that factional differences carried social and aesthetic overtones. This study exemplifies the *Annales* technique of wedding material culture to other areas of historical enquiry.

Introduction

What the *Annales* school of historiography means to historians often differs from what it means to archaeologists. At least that is my perception as a historian who has published in *Annales: Economies, Sociétés, Civilisations*. For archaeologists, one attraction of the *Annales* approach may be that it provides a set of hypotheses, or at least rubrics, which enable them to integrate some of their data into a historical framework that is meaningful both to them and to a broader audience.

As a historian, however, I see the *Annales* approach less as a set of ideas than as a revolution in the concept of historical data. Nineteenth-century historiography was broad enough to encompass the precise attentiveness to documents of Leopold von Ranke's disciples, the hazy spiritualism of historians influenced by Georg Friedrich Hegel, and the attempts at scientific analysis of the Marxists. Yet there was comparatively little breadth in defining historical data. Some historians favored government documents and diplomatic correspondence. Others felt that art and literature bespoke the true spirit of past historical epochs. Still others made use of limited amounts of economic and anthropological data.

On the whole, however, historians remained devoted to the idea that the best subjects for historical investigation were those that had just the right amount of data: not too much, not too little. They spoke and still speak of this as "commanding their sources." Historians "commanded their sources" when they had read and understood all of the documents pertaining to a subject and had felt it congeal into a story, a story that the data seemed to tell all by themselves and in just one way. Woe betide the historian who tackled a problem with too little data because the story did not emerge. Likewise, woe to the historian who took on a problem with too much data because he or she would never be able to "command the sources."

With the *Annales* historians appeared a new boldness in defining historical data, and along with it a willingness to resort to theory, often anthropological or sociological, to make sense of data that were too sparse or too abundant. The redefinition of data brought within the historian's ken written materials as diverse as pawnshop records and the dates of Japanese cherry tree blossoming, as well as material remains that had previously been ignored. Historians began to look at archaeology not just as a potential source of art treasures and humbler artifacts that could attest to the taste of princes or commoners, but as a systematic source of data about the material environment which could augment documentary sources and help in the historical interpretation of a given society. The watchword seemed to be "try everything and see what works."

This new approach was particularly attractive to historians working with too little or too much data for traditional analysis. In the case of the early history of Islamicization in the Middle East, both of these conditions obtain at the same time. Little is known from literary sources about how the Middle East became Muslim. Conversion occurred without benefit of missionaries, an organized church, a hallmark of conversion comparable to baptism or, amazingly, without much evidence of interest in the subject on the part of Muslim authors. The entire region of Arab–Muslim dominion from Morocco to Central Asia yields only a handful of anecdotes and statements about religious conversion from the start of the Arab conquests in AD 634 down to the year 1000. Yet over that time span the majority of the population of Middle Eastern lands from Egypt to Iran is generally thought to have converted to the new faith.

In 1979 I published a book entitled *Conversion to Islam in the Medieval Period: An Essay in Quantitative History*. In it I applied modern sociological theories of innovation diffusion to interpreting distinctive patterns in large numbers of personal names extracted from medieval Muslim biographical dictionaries. These data had been available in published form for many years, but previous historians had ignored them because they told no story in and of themselves. They had to be organized, interpreted in light of specific theories, and speculated upon: all things encouraged by the example of the *Annales* historians.

With respect to Iran, the hypothesis put forward on the basis of this exercise in using too much data for conventional historical interpretation was that the growth of the Muslim community followed a logistic curve that started slowly in the seventh and eighth centuries, accelerated to a bandwagon period of Muslim community growth in the ninth century, and slowly tapered off in the tenth century (Figure 5.1).

Since this was presented as a heuristic hypothesis that could probably never be conclusively proven given the paucity of direct evidence, a question subsequently arose as to whether and how it could be used to make other data more understandable. My intention here is to look at pottery remains from the northeastern Iranian region of Khurasan from the vantage point of this postulated conversion timetable to see what conclusions can be drawn about social and religious changes brought about by conversion.

Khurasan: a case study

Khurasan, a region that medieval Muslim geographers considered to stretch from Nishapur in the west to Balkh in the east and from Marv in the north to Herat in the south – in other words, the region of modern northeastern Iran, northwestern Afghanistan, and southern Soviet Turkmenistan – was a major center of political activity in the early Islamic centuries.

Its history in that period is marked by large-scale urbanization. The city of Nishapur, for example, grew from roughly 5,000 in the mid-seventh century to approximately 150,000 by AD 1000 (Bulliet 1976). Unlike some large cities farther west – such as Aleppo and Damascus – that were much larger at the time of the rise of Islam, the cities of Khurasan seem to have had only small non-Muslim communities. In view of this, and of the fact that the most rapid urban growth in Khurasan seems to occur in the ninth and tenth centuries when the putative timetable of conversion to Islam indicates the greatest growth in the Muslim community, it seems reasonable to hypothesize – in the absence of

Figure 5.1 Schematic graph of the progress of conversion to Islam in Iran

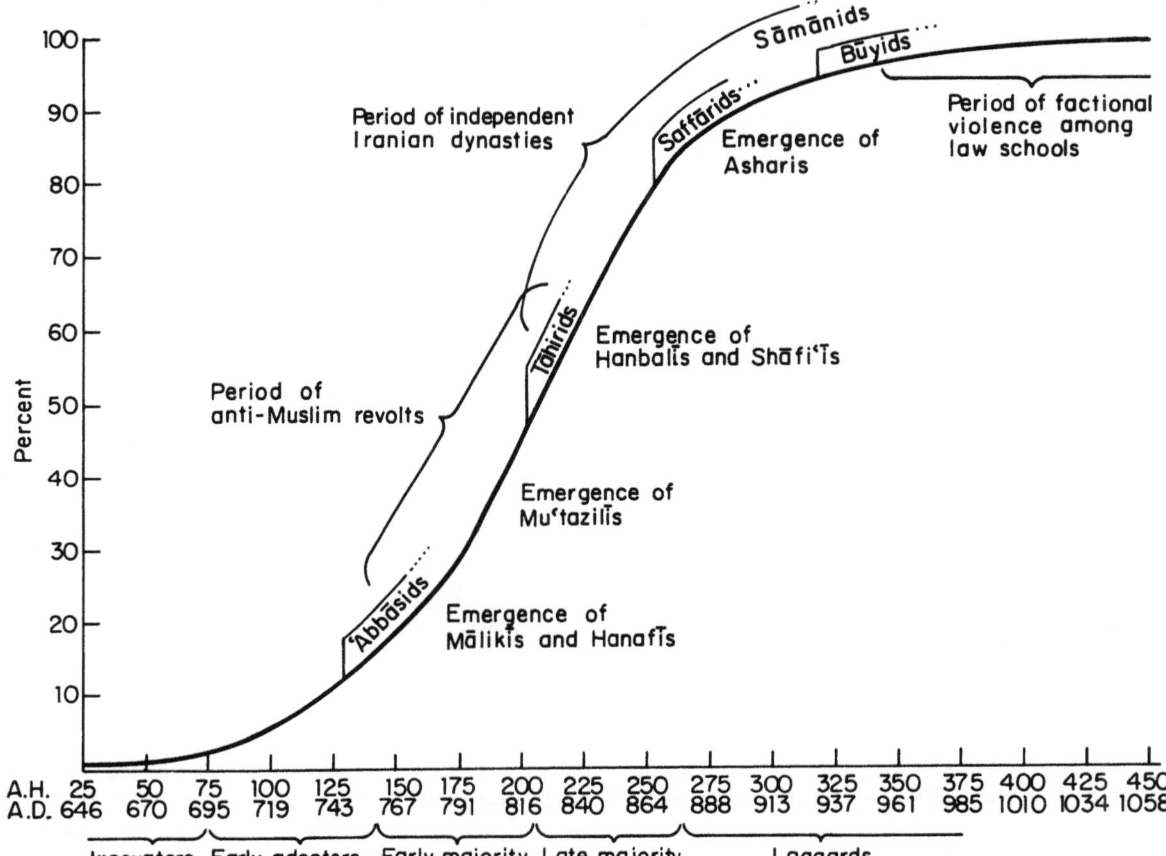

much evidence that the overall Iranian population expanded greatly in that period – that rural–urban migration associated with conversion played a major role in this growth. There were probably both push and pull aspects to this migration: converts feeling compelled to move from predominantly non-Muslim communities to escape ostracism brought on by their change in religion; other people being drawn by the richness and opportunities in the burgeoning Muslim governing centers and converting to Islam to become part of the dominant community there.

The only extensive and well-published archaeological materials pertaining to the cities of Khurasan are those stemming from the pre-World War II Metropolitan Museum of Art expedition to Nishapur. Charles Wilkinson, a member of the expedition, brought out several volumes, including one on pottery (*Nishapur: Pottery of the Early Islamic Period* n.d.), and the Metropolitan has an extensive display of its findings. Nevertheless, the expedition was not carried out systematically, and there were no useful stratigraphic findings. In Wilkinson's book the pottery remains are grouped stylistically with only rough chronological distinctions between those from comparatively early sites, that is, before roughly AD 1000, and those from later sites. For present purposes, it is the earlier pottery assemblage that must draw our attention, but it is noteworthy that around the twelfth century most of the earlier styles fade away, and a new assemblage making extensive use of newly developed turquoise glazes becomes dominant.

Even though there has been little archaeological work done on the immediately pre-Islamic period in Khurasan, and the excavations at Nishapur were too spotty to uncover a pre-Islamic settlement there, it is generally assumed that pre-Islamic pottery was mostly unglazed or glazed in a monochrome green. The pottery of early

Figure 5.2 Slip-painted, Black-on-White ware from Nishapur

Figure 5.3 "Imitation Chinese" four-color, splash-painted ware from Nishapur

Islamic Nishapur, by contrast, displays an enormous range of styles, design motifs, and techniques attesting to the striking creativity and skill of the city's population. It is apparent, therefore, that a largely new industry came into being in the context of early Islamic urbanization in Khurasan.

A puzzling anomaly appears, however, when one delves in detail into the pottery inventory of Nishapur. The best known style, featuring black and occasionally red calligraphy painted on a white slip and then covered with a transparent glaze (Wilkinson's categories 3 and 4), is virtually indistinguishable from pottery made in the same period at Samarqand over 500 miles to the east along the fabled Silk Route (Figure 5.2). A very similar slip-painted ware seems to have been made at Jurjan, to the northwest of Nishapur, as well (Kiani 1984: 42).

A second popular style, found at other sites as well, seems to imitate the four-color splash-painted pottery of China (Wilkinson's category 2), though specialists disagree on its exact stylistic provenance (Figure 5.3). It will be referred to hereafter as "imitation Chinese" ware.

A third style, however, a buff-colored ware painted with rather stylized floral and animal motifs and, much more rarely, elaborate scenes of riders at the hunt or other recreations such as dancing and wine-drinking, and even some Christian motifs, is exclusive to Nishapur (Wilkinson's category 1) (Figure 5.4). It has not shown up in Samarqand (Wilkinson n.d.: 3), and an analogous technique at Jurjan features distinctly different motifs, mostly large birds and animals (Kiani 1984: 44). It would appear, therefore, that the market for pottery in the burgeoning Islamic cities of the northeast was somehow segmented or stratified. The evidence indicates that local potters catered to some tastes that might be considered cosmopolitan, in so far as they were shared by buyers in fairly distant cities, and to others that seem to have been essentially local.

Another factor emerges from a study of the social context: the cities of Khurasan, and the northeast generally, are reported by contemporary chroniclers and geographers to have been riven by factional violence and struggle during the tenth, eleventh, and twelfth centuries AD (Bulliet 1972: 28–46; 1979: 43–63). This factional discord has long been a mysterious phenomenon because, despite the fact that the descriptions of the contending parties differ from city to city, frequently

Figure 5.4 Polychrome buff-painted ware from Nishapur

referring to geographical sections of a city, the most recurrent element in references to them is legal philosophy. Sunni Islam had and still has several different schools of thought regarding how law should be derived from sacred text and prophetic example. These different attitudes toward law yield slightly different results in practical terms, but ever since the thirteenth century Sunni Muslims have agreed that these differences are minor and no impediment to mutual recognition and respect.

The sources seem to suggest, therefore, that for 300 years gangs rioted in the streets and killed one another exclusively over legal differences that produced virtually no discord for the succeeding 600 years. The implausibility of this interpretation is reinforced by the fact that even during the period of strife members of the different factions studied under the same teachers and jointly participated in urban affairs. But families adhering to one faction seem not to have intermarried with members of the other faction.

In an early book, *The Patricians of Nishapur* (1972), I argued that the differences between the factions were only nominally legal and that the real differences lay in overall attitudes toward religion and toward the appropriate role of religion in shaping social institutions. I roughly categorized the major factional cleavage as being, most simply stated, "elitist" versus "populist." In my subsequent book on conversion (Bulliet 1979) I suggested further that this division was rooted in the social consequences of conversion, and accompanying urbanization.

The "elitist" group, by this interpretation, was composed of the descendants of comparatively early converts to Islam who persisted in supporting the legal, theological, and spiritual traditions that were dominant at the time of their ancestors' conversion. This group, therefore, held attitudes originating in the eighth and early ninth centuries when Islam was the religion of a small, but dominant, minority of the population. Their rivals were the descendants of later converts to Islam, including many from families that had constituted the powerful rural aristocracy of pre-Islamic Iran, who entered the faith during the bandwagon period of the late ninth or tenth centuries. They adhered to later developing legal and theological attitudes and saw Islam as a more universal and populist faith, their purpose in this being, in part, to reattain, as Muslims, the social eminence they had enjoyed as non-Muslims but now found precluded by the elite stratum of Muslims belonging to families who had converted earlier.

A difficulty with these formulations has been that they are hard to conceptualize in other than ideological and political terms. Was the daily behavior of the "elitist" faction, for example, in any way different from that of the "populist" faction? No documentary evidence seems to have survived to answer this question and help pin down the quotidian distinction between these groups. I should like to argue, however, that the differences in the pottery styles and their peculiar geographic distribution may speak to this issue upon which the written documents remain mute.

The evidence of pottery

The Metropolitan expedition to Nishapur fairly thoroughly excavated several locations in the vast site (Wilkinson 1937; 1938). The main feature of the ruins is a large mound that is certainly the remains of the pre-Islamic walled inner city and adjoining citadel described in medieval sources. It is now called Tepe Alp Arslan. Accounts of the early development of the city after the Arab conquest in the mid-seventh century indicate that villages closest to the pre-existing walled city received Arab settlement first and coalesced to form an outer city (Bulliet 1976). The main mosque was initially in the inner city but was rebuilt in a larger form in the outer city in the ninth century to accommodate the growing population. The main markets were also in the outer city, as was the seat of government.

Figure 5.5 Map of Nishapure showing approximate locations of excavated sites

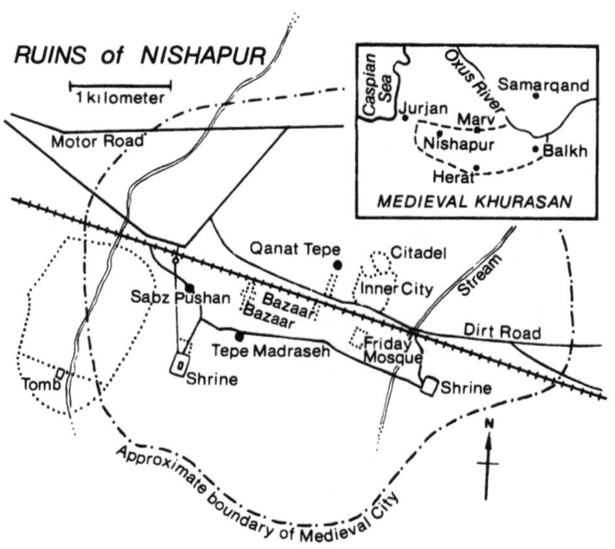

The primary excavations undertaken by the expedition were of mounds designated Qanat Tepe, Tepe Madraseh, and Sabz Pushan. None of these locations is still identifiable on the ground, but the expedition's sketch map (Figure 5.5) indicates that the first was about 200 m from the western wall of the inner city and the others some 2 km to the southwest and a little over 0.5 km from each other.

All three sites yielded coins from the eighth through the thirteenth century (Wilkinson n.d.: xxx–xxxiv), but pre-ninth-century coins were more abundant at Qanat Tepe (85%) than at Tepe Madraseh (67%) or Sabz Pushan (59%). No pre-Islamic coins or coins of the early eighth century were found at Tepe Madraseh although small numbers of both appeared at the other two sites. Out of 579 Islamic coins assigned dates prior to the thirteenth century, 269 are from the late eighth century, and 234 are from the ninth or early tenth centuries. This fairly reflects the main period of urban construction at Nishapur. No two coins were found together, and most of the coins were of low value and heavily worn. Judging from the coin evidence and the site's proximity to the walled inner city, Qanat Tepe would seem to be an older site than the other two, and the total absence of coins of the earliest period at Tepe Madraseh suggests that it was the latest site.

Wilkinson's conclusion on the basis of architecture and building ornament, that Tepe Madraseh was originally built in the middle of the ninth century by the locally based Tahirid dynasty, would reinforce this conclusion with respect to that site (Wilkinson n.d.: xxxi–xxxii).

This hypothesis – that Qanat Tepe is the earliest and Tepe Madraseh the latest of the sites – takes on importance when one looks at the pottery remains. In *Nishapur: Pottery of the Early Islamic Period*, Wilkinson maintains that all of the early pottery styles are intermixed and that no significant difference can be made out between one site and another. Having personally studied the ruins in the mid-1960s, thirty years after the Metropolitan expedition, I can easily understand his unwillingness to make fine distinctions in pottery distribution. Farmers have plowed the ruins and dug into them for centuries, and the landscape is littered with millions of potsherds. Nevertheless, Wilkinson's monograph catalogues the major whole vessels and significant fragments unearthed by the excavation; and despite the fact that the city was obviously a large and bustling center for a long period of time, the distribution of vessels among these three sites is distinctly irregular.

Mention was made earlier of a buff-colored ware painted with floral, animal, ritual, and "recreational" scenes that was apparently local to Nishapur (Wilkinson's category 1: Figure 5.4). Of the items of this ware in Wilkinson's monograph, 56% come from Tepe Madraseh, 16% from Sabz Pushan, and 8% from Qanat Tepe. Turning to the "imitation Chinese" splash ware (Wilkinson's category 2: Figure 5.3), 34% come from Tepe Madraseh, 39% from Sabz Pushan, and 9% from Qanat Tepe. And the famous Nishapuri black-on-white slip-painted dishes (Wilkinson's categories 3 and 4: Figure 5.2) break down into 26% from Tepe Madraseh, 35% from Sabz Pushan, and 19% from Qanat Tepe.

Given our earlier hypothesis that Qanat Tepe is an older site than the other two and Tepe Madraseh a younger site, it appears likely that buff-painted ware became popular later than the other two wares. As Wilkinson has asserted, there is clearly a simultaneity of styles. What is indicated is not the replacement of one style by another, but a distinct growth in popularity of the buff-painted ware in the ninth and tenth centuries.

If the preceding judgments about chronology are correct, it seems likely that the segmentation of the pottery market described at the outset is in part chronologically based. Slip-painted ware, which was also made in Samarqand and Jurjan, is much better represented at the earliest site than the other two wares. The similarly cosmopolitan "imitation Chinese" ware was also more abundant at the earlier sites. By contrast, the buff-

Table 5.1. *Distribution of Nishapuri pottery styles*

	Sites			
Ware	Qanat Tepe	Sabz Pushan	Tepe Madraseh	Other sites[a]
Buff-painted	8%	16%	56%	20%
"Imitation Chinese"	9%	39%	34%	18%
Slip-painted	19%	35%	26%	20%

[a] Less productive excavations were made in other parts of the ruins

painted ware was not only distinctively local but also late. Yet ironically it is the later period, when the buff-painted ware is most popular, that sees some of the strongest communications linkages between Nishapur and the cities on the road to Samarqand (Bulliet 1970).

A plausible explanation for this distribution pattern is the factional division of the city already discussed. The earlier Muslims and their descendants tended to be inclined toward one type of pottery, and the faction made up of later converts and their descendants favored another type. The late ninth-century turning point indicated by the coins and by Wilkinson's suggested dating of Tepe Madraseh coincides with the development of the large group of later converts.

If the factions possibly illuminate the pottery, what can the pottery tell us about the factions? Leaving aside the "imitation Chinese" ware as ideologically neutral (except for its cosmopolitan character), the slip-painted ware heavily emphasizes Arabic calligraphy, never using the Persian language. The calligraphy is often beautifully executed, but it is extremely difficult to read. Many of the inscriptions that can be read consist of proverbs, but some are repeated simple phrases like "blessing." They are not Quran quotations or notably religious in tone.

This seems quite in keeping with our description of the earlier evolving faction in Nishapur as "elitist." Arabic was not the spoken tongue of the population, and only the most educated people could have hoped to read the ostentatious calligraphy. Prior to the ninth century, Muslims constituted a ruling elite dominating a vast population of non-Muslims. Politically they strove for unity under the government of the caliph, and court styles radiated eastward and westward from Baghdad. Indeed, the slip-painted ware of Nishapur and Samarqand may well derive from an effort to imitate the pottery styles of Iraq. Socially, Arab blood lineage or tribal affiliation imparted a certain cachet, as indicated by the abundance of preserved genealogies going back to real or imagined tribal roots.

The buff-painted ware, on the other hand, bespeaks a recrudescence of Persian visual motifs, some of them well attested in the Sassanian period (third to seventh centuries AD). Prior to the mid-ninth century, Iranians who converted to Islam seem to have been disinclined to favor Persian styles or to use the Persian language for elevated purposes. Persian personal names are almost entirely avoided by Iranian Muslims until the eleventh century. The hypothesized late popularity of buff-painted ware would coincide, however, with the revival of Persian in Arabic script as a literary language at local courts, including that at Nishapur. The visual motifs on the pottery not only reflect Persian tradition but, in some cases, as in the hunting scenes, speak specifically to the worldview of the petty aristocracy who were prominent in Nishapur's "populist" faction.

As for the localization of the style in a single city, this too would be in keeping with the fragmentation of political power and development of urban patriciates with strong local identities during the tenth century. Unlike members of the "elitist" faction, the "populists" thought of Islam as the religion of all of the people of Nishapur and of Khurasan, rather than as the religion of a far-flung Arabizing ruling class. Popular local motifs rather than impenetrable Arabic inscriptions describe their taste and symbolize their attitude toward Islam and society.

It is also noteworthy that, unlike the slip-painted ware, the buff-painted ware is predominantly made up of deep bowls. Assuming these wares were used for food, this might indicate that the factions also had dietary differences. Possibly the "populists" favored the medieval equivalent of Iranian dishes like *ash* and *ab gusht* that are now considered traditional and that have the consistency of soup while the "elitists" adhered more to an Arab style of cuisine using more flat plates and small sauce dishes.

In sum, then, what appeared at first glance to be utterly unrelated bodies of data, literary and onomastic, on the one hand, and archaeological, on the other, suggest mutually reinforcing and even explanatory conclusions when interpreted in light of one another. The societal change that accompanied the progress of religious conversion in Khurasan appears to have gone beyond doctrine and affected the fabric of everyday social intercourse and popular taste. The history of style in modern western culture – comparison of the types of people who prefer "modern" to "traditional" styles in housing and furniture, for example – would suggest that this is not too surprising a conclusion, but the social correlates of style in medieval Islam have, as yet, scarcely been explored.

Conclusion

As mentioned at the outset, the term *Annales* historiography conjures up different meanings for different scholars. For some it stands for a structure of ideas; for others it connotes freedom from artificial disciplinary boundaries. Historians of Islam are blessed with a rich and abundant literary record, but cursed by a near absence of official documents, financial records, and the like. Consequently, the thrust of traditional historiography has been in the intellectual and cultural direction where a historian might hope to command adequate sources to come to firm conclusions.

Besides presenting only a partial history of past Muslim societies, however, this approach has encountered concrete difficulties in explaining such phenomena as religious conversion and persistent violent factionalism. The need for a complementary social history has long been felt, but the paucity and intractability of potential sources has seemed to dictate that this should be an unmet need. Only within the simultaneous freedom to explore non-traditional sources, including non-literary artifacts, and encouragement to resort to theory characteristic of the *Annales* school is it possible to break new ground.

The case study presented above has resulted in possible lines for further research rather than firm conclusions. Given this point of departure, it may become possible, on the one hand, to substantiate from more traditional literary sources a clear differentiation between the life-styles of the various factions of medieval Iranian Muslims or, on the other, to explain better some of the artifact assemblages from different archaeological sites. In either case, what we finally grasp will result from the extension of our reach encouraged by the *Annales* approach to the past.

Acknowledgement

I am most grateful for the helpful comments of Dr. Julian Raby.

References

Bulliet, R. W. 1970 A quantitative approach to medieval Muslim biographical dictionaries. *Journal of the Economic and Social History of the Orient* 13: 195–211.

1972 *The Patricians of Nishapur*. Cambridge, MA: Harvard University Press.

1976 Medieval Nishapur: a topographic and demographic reconstruction. *Studia Iranica* 5: 67–89.

1979 *Conversion to Islam in the Medieval Period: An Essay in Quantitative History*. Cambridge, MA: Harvard University Press.

Kiani, M. Y. 1984 *The Islamic City of Gurgan*. Berlin: Dietrich Reimer Verlag.

Wilkinson, C. K. 1937 The Iranian Expedition, 1936. *Bulletin of the Metropolitan Museum of Art* 32, section II: 3–22.

1938 The Iranian Expedition, 1937. *Bulletin of the Metropolitan Museum of Art* 33.

n.d. *Nishapur: Pottery of the Early Islamic Period*. New York: Metropolitan Museum of Art.

6 Independence and imperialism: politico-economic structures in the Bronze Age Levant

A. BERNARD KNAPP

Archaeological and documentary evidence from the southern Levant's Middle and Late Bronze Ages (2000/1900–1200 BC) reveal two latent geopolitical structures. Documentary evidence relevant to the North Jordan and Jezreel Valleys (in the modern-day states of Jordan and Israel, respectively) is discussed as one independent data source. Archaeological material from the same region, and particularly from the North Jordan Valley site of Pella, is presented as a separate, independent data source. An *Annales* framework facilitates reciprocal examination of these two streams of evidence, and makes it possible to offer new perspectives on politico-economic factors that affected independent and imperial polities in the North Jordan, Jezreel, and Beth Shan Valleys between about 1700 and 1200 BC.

Introduction

The study of change through time and space is basic not only to archaeology, but to history, anthropology, and geography. *Annales* historians have emphasized that the recognition of change in patterned human activity on any level may indicate a break in customs, ideas, or technologies. For archaeologists, the challenge is to identify and isolate such patterned changes and to relate them to sociocultural continuity or discontinuity. The conditions of change may be generated within or without society; in many cases, similar factors promote both stability and change, complexity and collapse. Whereas "prime-mover" explanations of sociocultural change once focused on diffusion and immigration, invasion or conquest, the environment, and – most often – on trade and population growth or decline, today explanations of social complexity or collapse draw upon a multivariate mix of social, politico-economic, spatial, and eco-environmental factors (McGuire 1983; Brumfiel and Earle 1987; Trigger 1989: 329–57; Knapp 1990).

The *Annales* approach allocates equal emphasis to processes of continuity or discontinuity in both material and written media. Such an approach presumes that archaeological and documentary data are as much contrastive or contradictory as they are complementary. The purpose of this study is neither to delineate or defend the *Annales*, nor to demonstrate how an *Annales* approach might be tested against the available archaeological record. Instead the goal is to marshal a diverse range of relevant data, and to reconsider it within an appropriate theoretical framework in order to facilitate and increase understanding of sociocultural continuity and change in one protohistoric society. The correlative relationship between short-term event and long-term structure is examined in order to consider "moments" of change in light of sociocultural pattern and process evident in both archaeological and documentary data. The intended result is not so much "historical science" (Gould 1986) as an interdisciplinary *human science*, which should restore some equilibrium amongst relevant material, documentary, and behavioral variables.

As a result of long-standing and deep-seated biases toward the written word in the study of the past, the documentary-rich, complex, Bronze Age societies of the western Asiatic Old World exemplify well a situation in which textual data resources dominate socio-historical or politico-economic interpretations of change, almost always at the expense of material data resources (see the current debate between Dever 1990 and Hoffmeier 1989; 1990). The present study seeks to redress that imbalance in some small measure by examining from another perspective archaeological and documentary data related to the rise and collapse of social complexity in the Middle–Late Bronze Ages (MB, LB) in the southern Levant. The more episodic documentary evidence (cuneiform, hieroglyphic, or hieratic) relevant to the North Jordan and Jezreel Valleys forms one source of information; contemporary, more cyclical and patterned archaeological data from the same region (particularly from Pella in the North Jordan Valley) form another, independent source. The *Annales* framework compels a dialogue between these material and documentary data, provides an account of Levantine social complexity and collapse that moves reciprocally back and forth between distinctive data sets, and establishes successive hypotheses that guide and reorient the direction of the discussion. New perspective is thereby gained on politico-economic factors that affected both independent and imperial polities in the southern Levant between about 1700 and 1200 BC.

The dilemma of interpretation

To state the problem, it is necessary in the first instance to present a composite picture derived from both the archaeological and documentary data. These separate streams of evidence are then teased apart and summarized, both for analytical purposes and in order to delineate what each may contribute, individually and reciprocally, to a fuller understanding of development and decline in the protohistoric Levant.

Between about 2200 and 1200 BC, the geopolitical structure of the southern Levant underwent three transformations:

1 2200–1900 BC (EB IV–MB I): following the urban collapse at the end of the Early Bronze Age, a system of decentralized villages characterized by small-scale farming and/or pastoral subsistence strategies;
2 1900–1600 BC (MB IIA–B–C): an unprecedented phase of urban redevelopment with powerful, localized, Canaanite-dominated city-states characterized by specialized industrial and agricultural production, and integrated regionally on the economic level;
3 1600–1200 BC (LB I–II): Egyptian New Kingdom exploitation and domination of quasi-independent city-state polities, characterized by imperial management of (reduced) local production and exchange, and by imperial manipulation of interregional exchange passing through the southern Levant.

The onus of the present paper is to consider in diachronic perspective, from both preceding and succeeding temporal viewpoints, a well-documented political event (expulsion of the *Hyksos* from the Egyptian Delta by the pharaoh Ahmose – see below) that helped to precipitate the major politico-economic transformation between the strongly centralized polities of the MB and the imperially dominated city-states of the LB (between the structures described in (2) and (3) above). In so doing, it is also possible to consider several other factors that affected the transition from a structure of strong, independent city-state rule to one of Egyptian overlordship, if not ownership. In addition, it is possible to assess, toward narrower, culture-historical ends, the origins of and motivation for the most significant politico-economic outcome of that transformation: the long-term Egyptian presence in the southern Levant (Bienkowski 1989a; Hoffmeier 1989; Knapp 1989a; Dever 1990).

The MB urbanization process and the eventual demise of urbanism, as reflected in the material and documentary records of the North Jordan and Jezreel Valleys, often receive contradictory interpretations. The archaeological record itself has spawned diverse, if not diametrically opposed views (Bienkowski 1989a). A time of crisis during the LB Age, adumbrated by archaeological remains, need not preclude widespread wealth, implicit in both archaeological and documentary evidence. In general, but by no means exclusively, textual records often detail elite situations, whereas archaeological data frequently stem from humbler circumstances. To confront the dilemma of interpreting these two distinct data sources, however, it is necessary to go beyond such practical observations.

Two basic steps taken in a recent monographic case study attempt to move toward resolution of this dilemma (Knapp 1992):

1 to develop a systematic, quantitative approach (including pottery seriation) to archaeological data, supplemented by pottery provenance studies, in order to consider diachronic developments in the local and regional economies of the Bronze Age southern Levant;
2 to utilize an *Annales*-based socio-political framework in order to consider individually and reciprocally short-term events (typically documentary) and longer-term processes (typically archaeological).

The first step provides better understanding of the relationship amongst internal production, interregional exchange, and international relations. The second step makes more explicit and more reliable the interpretation of time, place, and social reality in the protohistoric Levant. The *Annales* approach, furthermore, facilitates recursive evaluation of the synchronic and diachronic, and necessitates a dialogue between data and theory.

The development and history of *Annales* scholarship and the relationship of geohistorical concepts to the study of archaeology has been discussed in detail elsewhere (Lewthwaite 1987; 1988; Knapp 1992; Knapp, Smith, this volume). Amongst the diverse trends that typify Annaliste scholarship today, Le Roy Ladurie's (1979) "structural" mode of analysis (*structure–event–structure*) may help to break down the fact-bound, event-oriented study of Levantine protohistory and history, and to facilitate its reinterpretation in light of the more cyclical facets of Levantine archaeology (see also Marfoe 1987).

Le Roy Ladurie's "structuralism" is more a universal property of knowledge than a particular variety of Lévi-Straussian anthropology (cf. Tilley 1989; *contra* Little and Shackel 1989: 496): its specific aim is to look beyond the surface appearance of cultural phenomena in order to isolate interrelated variables that may have been instrumental in sociocultural transformation (Le Roy Ladurie 1981: 5; Clark 1985: 187). More particularly, Le Roy Ladurie has suggested that it is heuristically advantageous to begin from a structure empirically evident (i.e., in this case, Egyptian imperialism in the LB southern Levant), then move back in time to consider at least one "traumatic event" that helped to establish the structure (Ahmose's expulsion of the *Hyksos*), and finally try to situate that event within the (prior) structure that prevailed at the time of its occurrence (Canaan's centralized urban polities). Subsequently, the analytical process refocuses on the event, in order to assess in more depth its significance as an instrument of innovation, modification, or homeostasis (Le Roy Ladurie 1979: 113–31). Although this type of structural analysis strives to uncover pattern rather than to define an event-oriented, narrative "reality" (Clark 1985: 188), in the present case the analysis not only helps to evaluate the nature of the long-term Egyptian presence in the southern Levant, but also demands close reflection on the events which precipitated that presence.

Before the utility of an *Annales* framework for assessing problems inherent in a material-documentary analysis of protohistoric southern Levantine society is considered, a summary of both aspects of evidence is presented.

Archaeological and documentary data

Detailed presentation of both data-resource sets is available elsewhere (Knapp *et al.* 1988; Knapp 1992): the following, therefore, serves only as a summary recapitulation.

Archaeological data (Table 6.1)

Fieldwork at Pella and other Jordan Valley sites (e.g., Tell el-Hayyat, Tell Ikhtanu, Khirbet Iskander – Figures 6.1, 6.2) provides clear evidence for renewed Middle Bronze (MB) urban activity following the Early Bronze (EB) collapse (Dever 1985a; Falconer 1987a; 1989; Richard 1987; Esse 1989: 89–93; Finkelstein 1989; Prag 1989). Whereas surface finds at Pella indicate occupation of the site early in the MB (MB IIA), stratigraphic excavations in MB IIB/C levels demonstrate that the site

Figure 6.1 The southern Levant, with regions, rivers, and Middle–Late Bronze Age sites mentioned in the text

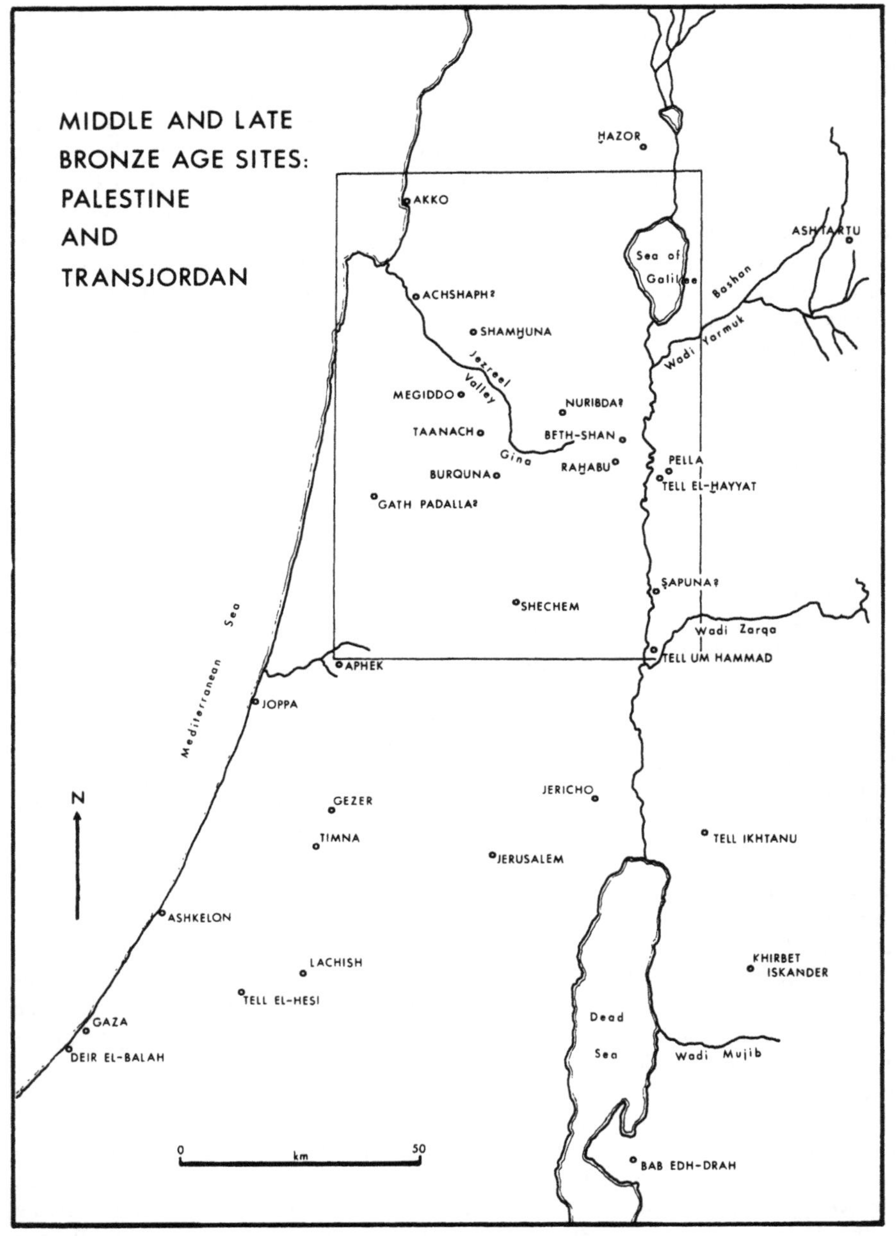

Figure 6.2 Jezreel Valley sites and geographic features mentioned in the text (inset of Fig. 6.1)

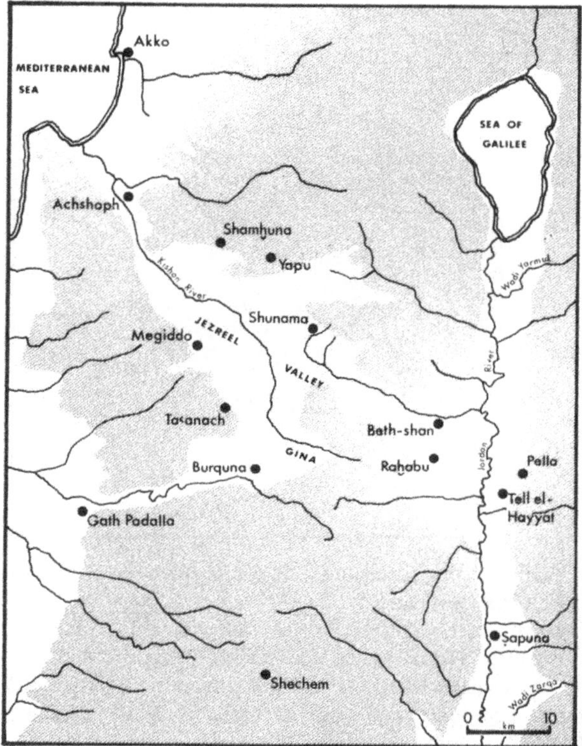

Figure 6.3 General topographic map of *Khirbet Fahl* ("mound" of Pella) and vicinity

Table 6.1. *Basic chronological guidelines, Middle and Late Bronze Age, southern Levant (historical dates)*

EB IV–MB I		
2200–1900 BC	MB IIA	1900–1800 BC
	MB IIB	1800–1700/1650 BC
MB II A–B–C	MB IIC	1700/1650–1600 BC
1900–1600 BC	LB IA	1600–1475 BC
	LB IB	1475–1400 BC
LB I–II	LB IIA	1400–1325 BC
1600–1200 BC	LB IIB	1325–1200 BC

had become a flourishing urban center by that time (McNicoll *et al.* 1982; 1991; Potts *et al.* 1985). Both Middle and Late Bronze materials have been recovered from stratigraphic excavations on Khirbet Fahl (Pella's main tell) and from a series of tombs to its south and east (Figure 6.3). The collective finds – ceramic, metal, sphragistic, stone, glass, terracotta, and exotic (ivory, alabaster, two cuneiform tablets) – demonstrate Pella's prestigious geopolitical position, and point to its international contacts during the seventeenth to fifteenth centuries BC (Potts *et al.* 1985: 196–202; Potts 1986; Leonard 1987; Knapp 1992).

The abundance of intact fine wares – Chocolate-on-White (CW) and White Slip (WS) – from the tombs, and in sherd form on the tell, suggests that Pella, or some site in the vicinity, served as a center of ceramic production or distribution in the North Jordan and Jezreel Valleys. Detailed elemental and mineralogical studies of plain and fine wares in the North Jordan and Baq'ah Valleys, using PIXE-PIGME (Proton-Induced X-Ray/Gamma-Ray Emission Analysis) and NAA (Neutron Activation Analysis), revealed a contrast between local and plain wares, on the one hand, and fine wares (WS, WS Painted, CW) on the other (McGovern 1986; Falconer 1987a; 1987b; Knapp *et al.* 1988). Production percentages of Pella's fine and plain wares (including those analyzed chemically) indicate that the latter were manufactured at a constant rate through time (MB II–LB II, and predominated (by a 5:1 ratio) over fine ware production or use (Figure 6.4a–c). More to the point, however, are figures on the diachronic manufacture of fine wares: during the seventeenth to fifteenth centuries BC, fine ware production or use comprised about 20 percent of the overall sample; by the thirteenth century BC, it had fallen to 5 percent.[1] Architectural remains and other materials from stratified LB II levels (about 1400–1200 BC) also suggest less intensive occupation and a more parochial material culture (Potts *et al.* 1985: 201–2; Potts and Smith 1991). Some LB tomb groups,[2] nonetheless,

Figure 6.4 Production percentages of fine wares, plain wares, and imports at Middle–Late Bronze Age Pella in Jordan

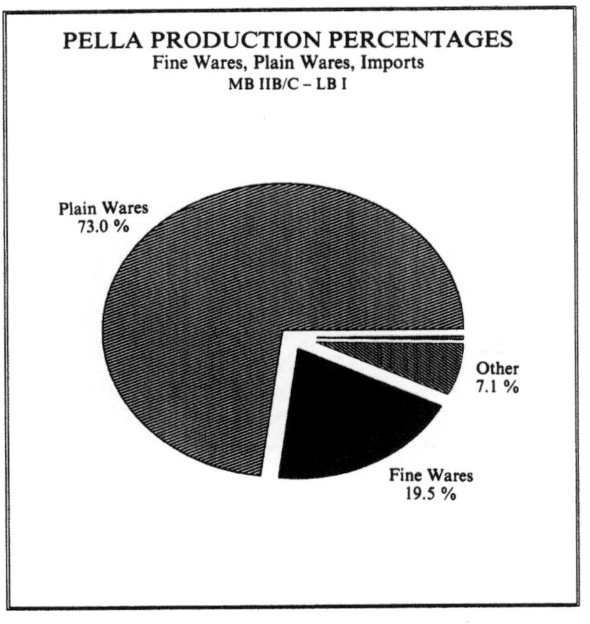

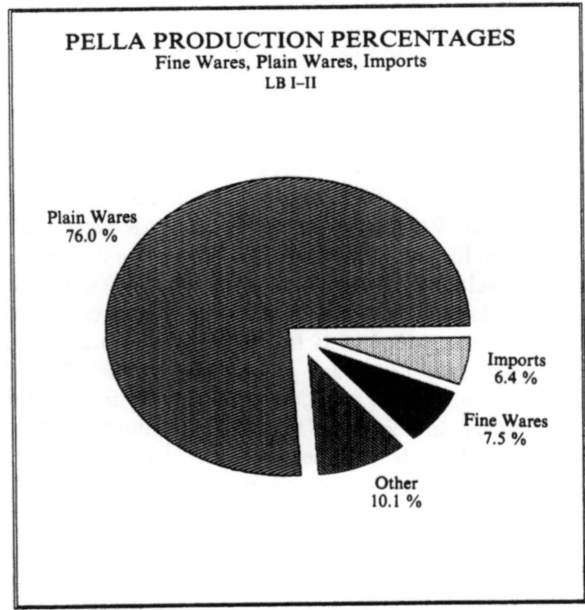

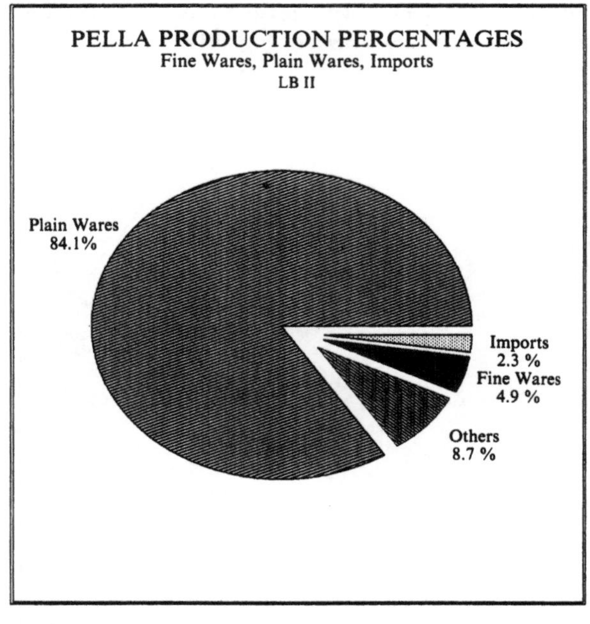

reveal ongoing economic contacts with the eastern Mediterranean world.

In sum: archaeological data from excavations at Pella portray a well-defended MB urban center with widespread eastern Mediterranean and western Asiatic contacts, not least with Egypt (MB "*Hyksos*" scarabs; MB/LB scarabs, ceramics, alabaster unguent flasks). Whereas this trend continued into LB I (about 1600–1400 BC), LB II remains have thus far proved more intractable, a situation echoed at other LB II sites in the southern Levant (Weinstein 1981; Gonen 1984; Bienkowski 1987; McGovern 1987; Dever 1990). The scenario offered by contemporary Syro-Palestinian archaeology nonetheless seems more impressionistic than realistic. At Pella, foreign contacts receded somewhat through time, but they never disappeared. Egyptian presence, in fact, is a constant and intensifying factor, and one that deserves notice because it occurs in a somewhat remote sector of the Egyptian interaction sphere (Bienkowski 1989a; Knapp 1989a). Although Hoffmeier (1989), from his text-dominated standpoint, seems only vaguely aware of the full extent of Egyptian influence in the southern Levant, documentary evidence provides key insights into the Egyptian presence, and into the nature of politico-economic contacts in the southern Levantine MB/LB periods (Knapp 1989a; 1992).

Documentary data

To present a synthetic overview of the relevant textual evidence for the MB–LB southern Levant is far beyond the scope of this study. It must be reiterated, therefore, that the summary comments which follow are based entirely on a thorough study of all primary documentary materials, and on assessment of a wide range of secondary literature that treats those materials (Knapp 1992).

Only hinted at in the Execration Texts of the eighteenth century BC (Posener 1940; Albright 1941), by the time of the sixteenth/fifteenth century BC campaigns of the Tuthmosids there began in earnest a pharaonic preoccupation with the area of the Jezreel and Beth Shan Valleys, and their eastward extension into the North Jordan Valley. Tuthmosis III established troop garrisons and administrative centers in the southern Levant (e.g., at sites such as Megiddo or Beth Shan – on Beth Shan as a Tuthmosid center, see Na'aman 1977: 173 n. 7; 1981: 177–8) to contain local political interference or social unrest; the occasional breakdown of that setup might precipitate the presence of pharaoh and the Egyptian army (e.g., Amenhotep II, Seti I). To ensure agricultural production on the lands surrounding Egyptian administrative centers, and so to provide a grain harvest adequate to feed Egyptian administrators and troops (if not to furnish part of the required annual "tribute" for the temple at Karnak), pharaoh imposed corvée duties (Sethe 1906: IV:744:3–8; Redford 1985: 193, 201 nn. 6–9 for further references; Bienkowski 1987: 50).

The official, albeit somewhat irregular exaction of "tribute" (Bleiberg 1981; 1984) began under Tuthmosis III centered on exploitation of some of the most fertile lands in the southern Levant. Amarna-period documents (early fourteenth century BC: see Figure 6.5) also indicate that eighteenth-Dynasty pharaohs (i.e., during the sixteenth to thirteenth centuries BC) coveted the agriculturally rich North Jordan, Beth Shan, and Jezreel Valleys for strategic as well as economic reasons. Whereas focal administrative centers were maintained by Egyptian officials and troops, local residents provided labor, and local (Amarna-era) rulers were occasionally responsible for crop production on crown lands. Nonetheless, the independence and territorial hegemony of some local rulers must have been responsible for the recurrent socio-political upheaval that plagued the entire region (Kemp 1978: 54–5). Documentary evidence again shows that periodic revolt was widespread in the North Jordan Valley from the eighteenth, fourteenth, and thirteenth centuries BC (Knapp 1992).

Figure 6.5 Late Bronze Age social, economic, and political trends (based on diplomatic correspondence – the cuneiform tablets found at Amarna in Egypt – between the Egyptian pharaoh and the rulers of southern Levantine city-states)

	SOCIO-POLITICAL						ECONOMIC		
Trends & Patterns → / Sites & Areas ↓	Egyptian ownership of towns areas, fortresses	Egyptian officials active / resident in S. Palestine	Egyptian garrisons and troops in S. Palestine	Local fields managed/cultivated for Pharaoh	Local rulers control more than one domain	Local insurrection — Apiru / Garu	Tribute/trade items Southern Palestine to Egypt	Egypta. messengers travel in Southern Palestine	Trade caravans travel in Southern Palestine
Achshaph	367	367	367						
Ashtartu	364				364	256		364	
Beth Shan	[289]		289						
Damascus					250				
Gath			290	[249]					
Gath-Padalla					25·				
Gaza		254 289 TT 6	289 TT 6						
Gezer			290	[249]	289			250	
Gina (S. Jezreel)	365 [250] TT 2	250							
Hazor	227 228					148			
Jerusalem	289		287			366	287 288		
Jezreel (SW)	250								
Megiddo	243 [245]	234 238 TT5	234 244 TT5,6	250 365	365	243 246	242 244		
Pella		256			256	256			255
Rahabu		TT2						TT2	
Rubutu	[289]								
Shamhuna							224		
Shechem	[253]				250 252	254 289	254	250	
Shunama	250 [365]								
Sapuna	273 274					273 274			
Ta'nnach		TT2	TT3,5, 6,7	TT2	TT2		248 TT5	TT2	
Yapu (Yafo ?)	Granaries 294								
Yarimuta	Granaries 85 105								
Canaan/General	306	148 249					64 266 301 309 313-14 323 327 331		226 264 245?316?

Geographic lists establish that New Kingdom (i.e., sixteenth to twelfth centuries BC) Egyptians had nearly precise knowledge of local transport and communication routes (Redford 1982a; 1982b). It seems clear, furthermore, that early eighteenth-Dynasty (about 1500–1400 BC) activity in Palestine was designed not only to control strategic military or mercantile routes along or near the coastal plain, but also to disrupt local, inter-polity relationships in the south or in the central highlands (Ahituv 1978: 105; Weinstein 1981: 10–15; Redford 1985: 196). It will be argued below that the southern Levant functioned as a critical land link in Egypt's trade, transport, and communications with the rest of western Asia. Although it remains difficult to define precisely the mechanisms that characterized Egyptian control over the southern terminus and links of western Asiatic interregional trade, Egyptian "commissioners" and local south Levantine rulers both operated in the politico-economic context of empire.

In sum: Egypt, in order to maintain its extensive commercial and diplomatic relations, had to ensure that its products and personnel could pass unimpeded through the southern Levant to other territories in western Asia or the eastern Mediterranean. Local disruptions to this major transport and communication system occasionally required an Egyptian show of force. Egyptian intentions and efforts in the North Jordan and Jezreel Valleys, therefore, aimed to control or limit access to an interregional trade system, to exploit the agricultural productivity of a diversified southern Levantine economy, and to neutralize local rulers who continually jockeyed for power and autonomy.

This brief recapitulation of the relevant archaeological and textual data (presented *in extenso* in Knapp 1992, Chapters 3, 4) conforms in most respects to standard interpretations of southern Levantine culture-history (e.g., Dever 1987; Finkelstein 1988; Leonard 1989). To move the argument forward, it is necessary to re-examine that evidence in a more detailed, discontinuous narration of cultural complexity and collapse, mindful of the limitations and uniqueness of the two data sets, but at the same time with a predisposition to engage them recursively in an attempt to delineate two divergent politico-economic structures that operated in the Bronze Age of the southern Levant.

Complexity and collapse in the southern Levant

> One trend that transcends all these diverse approaches [to state formation] is an increasing interest in truly integrated archaeological and ethnohistoric studies. Such studies allow the assessment of the rules of ethnicity, ideology, and the fine details of sociopolitical processes, which are difficult to assess unambiguously for the earlier civilizations known solely from archaeological research. Both the later imperial phases of the early civilizations and the more recent examples of primary and secondary state formation are increasingly the object of research by anthropological archaeologists and ethnohistorians together. (Wright 1986: 395)

One prominent view of early second-millennium BC Syro-Palestinian protohistory, based chiefly on documentary evidence, maintains that Middle Kingdom Egypt (conventional dates 1991–1786 BC) dominated, or at least exerted considerable influence in, southern and coastal Levant (Hayes 1971: 503–4; 1973a: 45–6; Posener 1971: 537–50; Kempinski 1983: 227–9; cf. Weinstein 1975; 1981; Dever 1987: 171–2; 1990: 77–8; Teissier 1990: 71 is more ambivalent; see Bienkowski 1986: 130–1 for a convenient summary of the problem). Increasing acceptance of an MB IIA (post-1900 BC) construction date for the elaborate defensive and civic structures typical of many MB Levantine sites poses formidable problems with the concept of Egyptian hegemony at that time. In fact, several lines of evidence make it more parsimonious to conclude that a resurgent Canaanite (urban-sedentary) polity, gradually recrystallized after the EB collapse, must have sponsored these massive public constructions (Kempinski 1983: 12–13; Dever 1985b: 72–4; 1987; Finkelstein 1989: 133–4).

The ethnicity of these Canaanite groups and their precise power relationships within and beyond the southern Levant present formidable problems of interpretation and offer a major challenge to Syro-Palestinian archaeologists and historians specializing in the study of the MB–LB transitional period (around 1600 BC). It is suggested (indeed Dever now *insists* – 1990: 78) that the immediate predecessors of the *Hyksos* Dynasty in Egypt were southern Palestinian rulers who took advantage of political disintegration in seventeenth-century BC Egypt to extend their influence southwest into a region with which they had close, long-standing contact. The *Hyksos*, in other words, comprised (1) Semitic-speaking Canaanite groups who migrated directly from southern Palestine into the Egyptian Delta, and (2) other Canaanite elements already settled in the Delta.

The traditional view (based on Manetho, an Egyptian priest of the Hellenistic period – preserved in Josephus) regards the *Hyksos* as hostile invaders who persecuted the Egyptian population (Hayes 1973b: 183–5; Kempinski 1985: 129–30). This tradition was propagated by early eighteenth-Dynasty pharaohs anxious to eradicate any memory of foreign domination, and perpetuated by modern scholarship bound to documentary evidence (e.g., Hoffmeier 1989; 1990). One result of this text-based focus was to downplay the importance of the fortified MB city-states of the Levant, and to overlook another apparent factor: parts of northeastern Egypt had succumbed to an increasingly sophisticated and politically powerful group of Canaanites from the southern Levant.

Had Egypt, on the contrary, dominated the southern Levant, it is difficult to understand how it would have tolerated either the erection of massive defensive walls around MB centers or the development of power relations that such construction entails. Some confirmation of this viewpoint comes from what, only a decade ago, might have seemed a most unlikely source: fieldwork in the Egyptian Nile Delta. At Tell el-Maskhuta in the Wadi Tumeilat (MacDonald 1980; Holladay 1982; 1983), and especially at nearby Tell ed-Dab'a on the Pelusiac branch of the Nile (Bietak 1979; 1984a), excavations have demonstrated an overwhelming Canaanite component and thus a significant Canaanite influence in Egypt throughout the nineteenth to seventeenth centuries BC.

At Tell ed-Dab'a, the MB IIA settlement already revealed significant Canaanite influence; by MB IIB/C, the material culture had become overwhelmingly Canaanite in character (Bietak 1984a; 1979; Dever 1985b: 74–6; 1987: 172–4). Although the temporal disparity resulting from Bietak's use of an ultra-low chronology remains to be resolved (Bietak 1984a: 476–7; 1987; 1989, and Table 1; Dever 1985b: 74–6; 1990: 80 n. 14), the relative sequence is more significant for the present discussion. During MB IIA, Egyptian power in the eastern Delta began to decline; by MB IIB, Canaanites ("Pre-*Hyksos* Asiatics") had established themselves in the Delta; during MB IIB/C the fifteenth-Dynasty *Hyksos* (Canaanites/Amorites) had secured a power base in the eastern Delta, and extended it south into Egypt proper (Giveon 1983; Bietak 1984b; Kempinski 1985; Dever 1990: 78).

Until Canaanite material culture was revealed by excavations in the eastern Delta, it was difficult to challenge conventional wisdom, and inappropriate to question some of its inherent contradictions: e.g., who were these *Hyksos*? How could they have penetrated Egyptian defenses, or built fortified urban centers in a land dominated by Egypt (except *after* the fall of the powerful twelfth-Dynasty pharaohs)? Whatever may be the sociopolitical implications of this Canaanite presence in the Egyptian Delta during the early second millennium BC, the successful rise of Egypt's seventeenth Dynasty at the end of the MB (late seventeenth or early sixteenth century BC) irrevocably changed the tenor of politico-economic relationships in the southeastern Mediterranean. Further assessment of long-term patterns provides insight into what lay behind the disruptive episodes at the end of the MB period.

In contrast to the viewpoint of Egyptian Middle Kingdom domination, it would appear that local Canaanite rulers held sway in the MB Levant, just as their forebears had done in the third millennium BC (Marfoe 1987: 31–4), and as their Phoenician successors would do – albeit over a much reduced land base – in the first millennium BC (Bietak 1985: 215). The questions that now assume prominence are: How did the early eighteenth-Dynasty pharaohs disrupt the long-term structure of Canaanite rule? Is any structural realignment evident, or is LB Age history simply a series of disconnected, episodic convulsions as the documentary evidence – particularly the Amarna Letters – might suggest?

Recall the archaeological situation in the southern Levant: strongly fortified, apparently independent centers (e.g., Pella, Beth-Shan, Megiddo) dominated the MB IIB/C geopolitical landscape. Material evidence indicates that these polities invested considerable energy to maintain their own integrity as well as that of the surrounding hinterlands. These heavily fortified centers must be regarded as independent Canaanite settlements, perhaps in economic (Knapp *et al.* 1988) as much as in military competition (Bienkowski 1986: 128; 1989b: 176). Dever has argued, plausibly but inconclusively, that such Canaanite centers may have functioned at least on one level in support of their *Hyksos* brethren in the eastern Nile Delta; they would have served as "backup systems" designed to launch counteroffensive campaigns against the early eighteenth-Dynasty pharaohs (1985b: 73). These powerful Theban dynasts, however, not only succeeded in expelling the *Hyksos* from Egypt, they also pursued them into southern Palestine and triumphantly destroyed local enemy "bases." In so doing, the Egyptians laid the foundations of a southern Levantine tributary state that lasted for 300 years.

Careful reconsideration of the *Hyksos* expulsion (by the Pharaoh Ahmose) amplifies the proposed structural framework and lends further credence to the socio-historical reconstruction. The view which relies chiefly on documentary evidence maintains that the post-expulsion campaigns sought only to reinstate lost Egyptian hegemony in the southern Levant. Indeed, Ahmose's early sixteenth-century BC forays into southern Palestine (and into parts of the central and northern highlands? – Weinstein 1981: 2–4) were destructive enough to remove future threats from southernmost Canaan, perhaps even to preclude future rehabilitation of the area into a viable politico-economic branch of the Egyptian state. Tuthmosis III's early fifteenth-century BC campaigns at many coastal or near-coastal sites, however, are argued to have been less severe, probably carried out in order to establish a tributary state in the southern Levant and to secure a trade and communications link through this region (Weinstein 1981: 1–15). What Ahmose initiated for reasons of security, in other words, Tuthmosis III finalized for economic motives.

Weinstein's analysis of the distribution of *Hyksos*

royal-name scarabs provides another way to examine these events: multiple finds of imperial scarabs at sites in southern and inland Palestine ('Ajjul, Gezer, Jericho, Lachish, etc. – Weinstein 1981: 9 Table 1) suggests close political links between these centers and that of the ruling *Hyksos* dynasty at Avaris (Tell ed-Dab'a). Most such centers were annihilated by Ahmose (Weinstein 1981: 8–10). With regard to Pella, recovery of at least two *Hyksos* imperial scarabs (Richards 1985) might also suggest close links with the Egyptian Delta rulers, but Pella suffered no MB IIC/LB I destruction as Weinstein's scenario would predict (further discussion in Knapp 1992; cf. Hoffmeier 1989: 189–90).

Because the Pella scarabs and other Egyptian material (ceramics, alabaster flasks) can, at this stage of excavation, only be assigned broadly to the MB IIC/LB I era, an early sixteenth-century BC Egyptian presence or influence in the North Jordan Valley is only a supposition. Maintenance of vigorous ceramic production and architectural sophistication into the LB I period (Potts *et al.* 1985; Potts and Smith 1991) indicates that Pella, like its counterparts in the Jezreel Valley (Megiddo and Ta'annach), avoided early Egyptian attempts at domination (Lapp 1964: 7–8, 14–16; Seger 1975; cf. Weinstein 1981: 11; Dever 1985b: 80). Whereas Hazor is more problematic, it too seems to reveal little material evidence of Egyptian presence at this date (Bienkowski 1987: 54). Like several other strategic urban centers in the Jezreel Valley, the Galilee, and along the coastal plain, Pella may have maintained some degree of independence, even in the wake of Tuthmosis III's fifteenth-century BC campaigns.

Documentary evidence establishes a further refinement of this scenario: the Tuthmosis campaigns in the southern Levant sought to secure the area's agricultural resources and diverse tribute, and to establish permanent control over strategic interregional trade routes that traversed the area. Egypt's military and administrative policy thus shifted from one of offense and confrontation under Ahmose to one of defense, domination, and exploitation under Tuthmosis III. This shift, which occurred over almost a 70-year time span, signaled the stabilization of a new politico-economic structure in the southern Levant: the Egyptian-dominated vassal states of the Late Bronze Age.

Archaeological and documentary data alike bear witness to Egyptian domination and exploitation. The typical absence of city walls around LB centers even provides negative evidence (Gonen 1987: 98). Through Egyptian intermediaries, imperial authority guided local rulers. Yet the apparent independence and territorial control of rulers in Shechem, Tyre, or Damascus suggest that the southern Levant was partially incorporated and partially independent, with power balanced precariously rather than channeled rigidly into a hierarchical structure (Na'aman 1981: 184). The mutual (linguistic) incomprehensibility apparent in the correspondence between pharaoh and vassal (elegantly demonstrated by Liverani 1983: 49–53) suggests that Egypt's abstract, passive domination remained effective even in the face of concrete resistance from the Syro-Palestinian kingdoms. Pharaonic control of strategic military, communication, and commercial interests in the area inevitably provoked local unrest and prompted interference from local polities, a situation corroborated by the written evidence (already noted above).

During the course of the LB II period (about 1400–1200 BC), another structural change developed in the wake of widespread social "deviation" (Kinser 1981: 95 n. 82), fostered by disaffected rural (*Kharu*, *'Apiru*, *Shasu*) and urban (*ḫupšu*) elements. These "peasant" movements (Halligan 1983: 18, 23) shattered the elusive politico-economic stability so intrinsic to the Egyptian imperial structure. Campaigns to the North Jordan and Jezreel Valleys by nineteenth-Dynasty pharaohs (Seti I and Ramesses II) suggest that seditious activity peaked during the thirteenth century BC. Widespread material evidence for renewed Egyptian presence throughout Palestine suggests that Egyptian domination took its greatest toll on local polities and their erratic economies at this time (Ahituv 1978; Weinstein 1981: 22; Oren 1984; Beck and Kochavi 1985).

The decline of the LB II city-state system and the demise of Egyptian patronage and domination was characterized by an economic shift toward pastoral subsistence strategies, and by a demographic shift away from areas of state control (Stager 1985a: 85–6; McGovern 1987; Finkelstein 1989: 132). The intensification of centrifugal tendencies that had handicapped Egyptian domination throughout the LB Age (Zaccagnini 1984: 19) led to another, decentralized structure of local domination, as farmers and pastoralists alike gravitated toward the highlands that formed an obstacle as well as a refuge, "a frontier of freedom" from imperial or other centralized control (Braudel 1972: 39; Stager 1985b: 5; Liverani 1987: 70).

Political structures and political power: an *Annales* perspective

Egyptian presence in the North Jordan and Jezreel Valleys first becomes visible materially toward the end of the MB Age, and remains prominent in the archaeo-

Figure 6.6 Settlement hierarchies in the Middle Bronze Age southern Levant

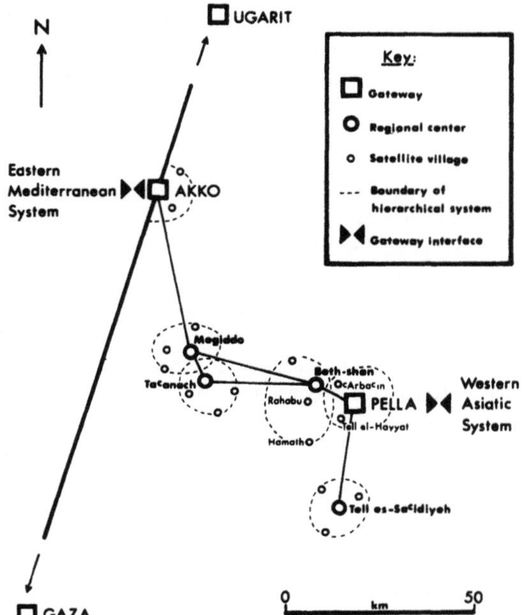

Figure 6.7 Schematic representation of interregional interaction spheres in Late Bronze Age western Asia

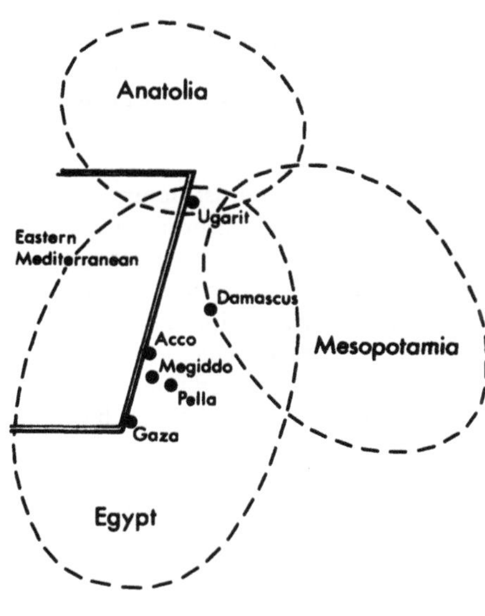

logical and documentary record throughout the LB Age. The Canaanite origins of the *Hyksos* Dynasty that ruled Egypt late in the MB era (Giveon 1981; 1983; Bietak 1984b; Kempinski 1985) had a major bearing on Levanto-Egyptian interrelations. Whilst the nature of the association between the *Hyksos* kings and the MB southern Levantine princes remains unknown, it is clear that the expulsion of the *Hyksos* undermined the predominant structure of localized rule, and operated as the "matrix-event" for the new structure of Egyptian-dominated, urban- or palace-based centers of the LB Age. Egyptian involvement became inseparable from this new structure, which was stabilized by Tuthmosis III's conciliatory administrative and military policy toward the southern Levant.

Whereas the independent Levantine polities of the MB functioned in a context of political co-operation and economic competition (Figure 6.6), Egyptian domination limited such interaction during the LB, as Egyptian officials co-opted economic gains in order to support and maintain the imperial structure (Figure 6.7). During both eras, however, power relations dictated that agricultural wealth and luxury items flow into the urban centers. During the MB, some wealth remained in peripheral areas in order to support the economic structure; during the LB, Egyptian imperial demands may have exceeded the productive capacities of all but the most resilient, self-sustaining urban centers.

The documentary witnesses or material traces of imperial facilities and installations provide a measure of the degree of Egyptian control exercised within the southern Levant (Knapp 1992). The basic core–periphery relationship involved more than a simple redirection of produce and resources. Depending upon pre-existing political structures, the consolidation of provincial territories into an imperial administrative structure, and the transfer of material wealth and information, involves a substantial imperial cost (Cherry 1987: 166–7; Schreiber 1987: 266–7). Although archaeological indicators are lacking, documentary evidence reveals that Egypt maintained its new territories through parsimonious placement of administrative centers and garrisons, and through strategic military exercises (Weinstein 1981: 12–15; Knapp 1992).

Whereas some LB urban polities remained stable or even flourished under Egyptian hegemony, many village polities disappeared from the geopolitical landscape. On the one hand, the archaeological record reveals an apparent collapse: village sites were abandoned and some urban centers declined or contracted in size. On the other hand, written evidence alludes to a certain wealth and prosperity, denoted in the archaeological record of other urban centers. The socio-political perspective adopted in this study makes it feasible to reconcile such apparent contradictions, and in addition helps to endorse conclusions derived from the macroscopic, long-term view of settlement and survey work in Palestine (Gophna and Beck 1981; Broshi and Gophna 1986; Finkelstein 1988: 27–117; Gophna and Portugali 1988).

The politico-economic infrastructure of fifteenth-century BC Palestine and Transjordan became destabilized as a result of Tuthmosis III's campaigns. Whereas Egypt had maintained a low imperial profile during the fifteenth century BC, archaeological and written evidence alike imply – at least *prima facie* – that Egyptian control had slackened throughout the fourteenth century BC. An imperial bureaucracy, however, may find it more cost-effective to develop and manipulate local authority than to undertake a massive politico-economic reorganization and to build an elaborate imperial superstructure on that base (Schreiber 1987; similarly Liverani 1987: 66–7). The Amarna Letters in fact reveal that many local southern Levantine kings had become dependent on imperial support, and that local heirs-apparent, often raised or held captive in Egypt, were indoctrinated with imperial propaganda. In other words, contrary to any apparent pharaonic lack of interest in the southern Levant during the fourteenth century BC, the Egyptian imperial structure had become so firmly entrenched that the last eighteenth-Dynasty pharaohs could ignore both local subsistence concerns and endless calls for military aid (Liverani 1983). Local insurrection in distant sectors of the periphery (e.g., the North Jordan Valley), however, illustrates a more complex pattern of decentralized social tendencies.

If the Egyptian political hierarchy was almost imperceptible during the fourteenth century BC, the centrifugal stresses of the thirteenth century BC required a higher profile, and gave impulse to an intensified Egyptian occupation of the entire southern Levant (Weinstein 1981: 17–22; Oren 1984). This renewed and forceful Egyptian presence exacerbated a tense social situation, and worsened relations between Egyptian-sponsored urban elites and dispossessed social elements (*ḫupšu*, *Shasu*, *ʿApiru*). As rural areas and non-irrigated lands were abandoned, the impact of semi-nomadic elements persisted or increased (Liverani 1987: 69–70). Contemporary economic and demographic disruptions in the eastern Mediterranean hastened local collapse (Shrimpton 1987; Knapp 1989b), and prompted the downfall of the Egyptian imperial structure in the southern Levant. The short-term maximization strategies of urban polities had been critical for the maintenance of the imperial order. Without the surplus production provided by the periphery, and with the disruption in the flow of elite wealth, the established power structure collapsed as its economic base crumbled.

Conclusion

During the Middle Bronze Age, the internal momentum of urbanization accelerated politico-economic intensification; during the Late Bronze Age, the external impact (and associated costs) of Egyptian imperial policy hastened a process of destabilization and collapse. A microscopic view of local production and transformation combined with a macroscopic view of regional pattern and process thus helps to illustrate the dialectic of event and structure in the movement of (proto-)history (Terray 1977: 298–9). The coexistence and interrelationship of events ultimately shapes a structure which at least partially constrains social response and political action.

In protohistoric archaeology generally, where emphasis often falls on certain events at the expense of the processes that generated them or the structures that delimited them, a dichotomy is apparent between process and change (Hodges 1987: 32). If socio-political events are viewed as points of articulation with economic or ideological structures, they may serve analytically as intersections that reveal changes in the configuration of material or historical pattern. Events, in any case, are not historical facts, only heuristic reconstructions, like structures or *conjonctures*.

Future research in this direction should revolve around redefinition of long-term politico-economic processes (or the "time-slices" therein) within changing ecological and technological contexts, when contrasting or complementary socio-historical structures succeeded one another in the politically turbulent cycles that typified early agrarian societies (Adams 1978: 334). In this study, the dialogue between archaeological and documentary data, recast in an *Annales* framework, offers a tentative reconstruction of politico-economic patterns and historical events in the southern Levantine Middle–Late Bronze Ages. It should serve as an invitation to Syro-Palestinian archaeologists and historians to reconsider the spatio-temporal boundaries of their data, and to examine how sociocultural systems arise, collapse, and are transformed into new systems.

Notes

1 The sample under discussion is represented by over 2,200 diagnostic sherds and whole vessels that comprise Pella's ceramic type-series. This material was excavated between 1979 and 1986 and probably represents no more than one-sixth of Pella's entire Bronze Age ceramic corpus. As both the type-series and the corpus grow with continued excavation, the relative proportion of material assigned to the type-series will obviously decrease; methodological issues involved in the use of this sample were noted in Knapp 1987: 14–17, and are discussed in more detail in Knapp 1992.

2 Late Bronze I/II tomb deposits, stored in Jerash since 1967, have now been catalogued and photographed by Stephen Bourke (Department of Archaeology, University of Sydney). I am grateful to Mr. Bourke for allowing me to consult and mention his preliminary catalogue. Cypriot imports include 1 Base-Ring 'I' (BR) jug, 13 BR 'II' jugs, 1 BR 'II' wishbone-handled bowl, 1 Monochrome jug, 1 White Slip II bowl, and 2 White Shaved juglets. Mycenaean imports of LH IIIA2/B date include 2 stirrup jars, 1 cup, 1 piriform amphora, and 1 amphoroid jar.

Acknowledgments

Research upon which this article is based was carried out whilst the author held a three-year research fellowship in the Department of Archaeology, University of Sydney, funded by the Ministry of Science and Technology, Commonwealth Government of Australia. I am grateful to both institutions for that support. I also thank my wife, Christina Sumner, for drawing Figures 6.6 and 6.7, and for reproducing Figures 6.1–6.3. I am also grateful to Piotr Bienkowski for his critical comments; further commentary from the New Directions Editorial Board prompted reorganization of this chapter.

References

Adams, R. McC. 1978 Strategies of maximization, stability, and resilience in Mesopotamian society, settlement, and agriculture. *Proceedings of the American Philosophical Society* 122: 329–35.

Ahituv, S. 1978 Economic factors in the Egyptian conquest of Canaan. *Israel Exploration Journal* 28: 93–105.

Albright, W. F. 1941 New Egyptian data on Palestine in the Patriarchal age. *Bulletin of the American Schools of Oriental Research* 81: 16–21.

Beck, P. and M. Kochavi 1985 A dated assemblage of the late 13th century B.C.E. from the Egyptian residency at Aphek. *Tel Aviv* 12: 29–42.

Bienkowski, P. 1986 *Jericho in the Late Bronze Age*. Warminster: Aris and Phillips.

1987 The role of Hazor in the Late Bronze Age. *Palestine Exploration Quarterly* 119: 50–61.

1989a Prosperity and decline in LBA Canaan: a reply to Liebowitz and Knapp. *Bulletin of the American Schools of Oriental Research* 275: 59–63.

1989b The division of MB IIB–C in Palestine. *Levant* 21: 169–79.

Bietak, M. 1979 Avaris and Pirammese: archaeological exploration in the eastern Nile Delta. *Proceedings of the British Academy* 45: 225–89.

1984a Problems of Middle Bronze Age chronologies: new evidence from Egypt. *American Journal of Archaeology* 88: 471–85.

1984b Zum Konigreich des *'3-zh-r'* Nehesi. *Studien zur Altägyptischen Kultur* 11: 59–75.

1985 Respondent: "Israel's neighbors in the Iron Age in the light of archaeological research," in J. Amitai, ed., *Biblical Archaeology Today*, pp. 215–19. Jerusalem: Israel Exploration Society.

1987 Remarks about the chronology of the Middle Bronze Age culture in the light of excavations at Tell el-Dab'a, in P. Åström, ed., *High, Middle or Low?* vol. 1, p. 56. Studies in Mediterranean Archaeology, Pocketbook 56. Göteborg: P. Åström's Förlag.

1989 The Middle Bronze Age of the Levant: a new approach to relative and absolute chronology, in P. Åström, ed., *High, Middle or Low?*, volume 3, pp. 78–120. Studies in Mediterranean Archaeology, Pocketbook 80. Göteborg: P. Åström's Förlag.

Bleiberg, E. L. 1981 Commodity exchange in the Annals of Thutmose III. *Journal of the Society for the Study of Egyptian Antiquities* 11: 107–11.

1984 The king's privy purse during the New Kingdom: an examination of *INW*. *Journal of the American Research Center in Egypt* 21: 155–67.

Braudel, F. 1972 *The Mediterranean and the Mediterranean World in the Age of Phillip II*, volume 1. New York: Harper and Row.

Broshi, M. and R. Gophna 1986 Middle Bronze Age II Palestine: its settlements and population. *Bulletin of the American Schools of Oriental Research* 261: 73–93.

Brumfiel, E. M. and T. K. Earle 1987 Specialization, exchange, and complex societies: an introduction, in E. M. Brumfiel and T. K. Earle, eds., *Specialization, Exchange, and Complex Societies*, pp. 1–9. Cambridge: Cambridge University Press.

Cherry, J. F. 1987 Power in space: archaeological and geographical studies of the state, in J. M. Wagstaff, ed., *Landscape and Culture: Geographical and Archaeological Perspectives*, pp. 146–72. Oxford: Blackwell.

Clark, S. 1985 The *Annales* historians, in Q. Skinner, ed., *The Return of Grand Theory in the Social Sciences*, pp. 177–98. Cambridge: Cambridge University Press.

Dever, W. G. 1985a From the end of the Early Bronze Age to the beginning of the Middle Bronze, in J. Amitai, ed., *Biblical Archaeology Today*, pp. 113–35. Jerusalem: Israel Exploration Society.

1985b Relations between Syria-Palestine and Egypt in the Hyksos period, in J. Tubb, ed., *Palestine in the Bronze and Iron Ages: Papers in Honour of Olga Tufnell*, pp. 69–87. Institute of Archaeology, University of London, Occasional Paper 11. London.

1987 The Middle Bronze Age: the zenith of the urban Canaanite era. *Biblical Archaeologist* 50: 148–77.

1990 "Hyksos," Egyptian destructions, and the end of the Palestinian Middle Bronze Age. *Levant* 22: 75–81.

Esse, D. L. 1989 Secondary state formation and collapse in Early Bronze Age Palestine, in P. de Miroschedji, ed., *L'Urbanisation de la Palestine à l'Age du Bronze Ancien*, pp. 81–96. British Archaeological Reports, International Series 527(i). Oxford: BAR.

Falconer, S. 1987a Village pottery production and exchange: a Jordan Valley perspective, in J. Berry and A. Hadidi, eds., *Studies in the History and Archaeology of Jordan* 3: 251–9. London: Routledge and Kegan Paul.

1987b Heartland of villages: reconsidering early urbanism in the southern Levant. Unpublished Ph.D. dissertation, University of Arizona, Tucson.

1989 Bronze Age village life in the Jordan Valley: archaeological investigations at Tell el-Hayyat and Tell Abu en-Ni'aj. *National Geographic Research* 5: 335–47.

Finkelstein, I. 1988 *The Archaeology of the Israelite Settlement*. Jerusalem: Israel Exploration Society.

1989 Further observations on the socio-demographic structure of the Intermediate Bronze Age. *Levant* 21: 129–40.

Giveon, R. 1981 Ya'aqob-Har. *Göttinger Miszellen* 44: 17–19.

1983 The Hyksos in the south, in M. Görg, ed., *Fontes Atque Pontes: Eine Festgabe für H. Brunner*, pp. 155–61. Ägypten und Altes Testament 5. Wiesbaden: Harrassowitz.

Gonen, R. 1984 Urban Canaan in the Late Bronze period. *Bulletin of the American Schools of Oriental Research* 253: 61–73.

1987 Megiddo in the Late Bronze Age – another reassessment. *Levant* 19: 83–100.

Gophna, R. and P. Beck 1981 The rural aspect of the settlement pattern of the coastal plain in the Middle Bronze Age II. *Tel Aviv* 8: 45–80.

Gophna, R. and Y. Portugali 1988 Settlement and demographic processes in Israel's coastal plain from the Chalcolithic to the Middle Bronze Age. *Bulletin of the American Schools of Oriental Research* 269: 11–28.

Gould, S. J. 1986 Evolution and the triumph of homology, or why History matters. *American Scientist* 74: 60–9.

Halligan, J. M. 1983 The role of the peasant in the Amarna period, in D. N. Freedman and D. F. Graf, eds., *Palestine in Transition*, pp. 15–24. Sheffield: Almond Press.

Hayes, W. C. 1971 The Middle Kingdom in Egypt, in I. E. S. Edwards, C. J. Gadd, and N. G. L. Hammond, eds., *Cambridge Ancient History*, volume 1, part 2, pp. 464–531. Cambridge: Cambridge University Press.

1973a Egypt: from the death of Ammenemes III to Seqenenre II, in I. E. S. Edwards, C. J. Gadd, and N. G. L. Hammond, eds., *Cambridge Ancient History*, volume 2, part 1, pp. 42–76. Cambridge: Cambridge University Press.

1973b Chronology I: Egypt – to the end of the Twentieth Dynasty, in I. E. S. Edwards, C. J. Gadd, and N. G. L. Hammond, eds., *Cambridge Ancient History*, volume 1, part 1, pp. 173–93. Cambridge: Cambridge University Press.

Hodges, R. 1987 Spatial models, anthropology and archaeology, in M. Wagstaff, ed., *Landscape and Culture: Geographical and Archaeological Perspectives*, pp. 118–33. Oxford: Blackwell.

Hoffmeier, J. K. 1989 Reconsidering Egypt's part in the termination of the Middle Bronze Age in Palestine. *Levant* 21: 181–94.

1990 Some thoughts on Dever's "'Hyksos', Egyptian destructions and the end of the Palestinian Middle Bronze Age," *Levant* 22: 83–9.

Holladay, J. S. 1982 *Cities of the Delta III: Tell el-Maskhuta. Preliminary Report on the Wadi Tumilat Project, 1978–1979.* ARCE Report 6. Malibu: Undena.

1983 An 'Asiatic' Middle Bronze Age farming village in Egypt. *Royal Ontario Museum Archaeological Newsletter* 214: 1–4.

Kemp, B. J. 1978 Imperialism and empire in New Kingdom Egypt (*c.* 1575–1087 B.C.), in P. D. A. Garnsey and C. R. Whittaker, eds., *Imperialism in the Ancient World*, pp. 7–57. Cambridge: Cambridge University Press.

Kempsinski, A. 1983 *Syrien und Palästina (Kanaan) in der letzten Phase der Mittelbronze IIB Zeit (1650–1570 v.Chr.).* Ägypten und Altes Testament 4. Wiesbaden: Harrassowitz.

1985 Some observations on the Hyksos (XVth) Dynasty and its Canaanite Origins, in S. I. Groll, ed., *Pharaonic Egypt*, pp. 129–37. Jerusalem: Magnes Press.

Kinser, S. 1981 Annaliste paradigm? The geohistorical structuralism of Fernand Braudel. *American Historical Review* 86: 63–105.

Knapp, A. B. 1987 Pots, PIXE, and data processing at Pella in Jordan. *Bulletin of the American Schools of Oriental Research* 266: 1–30.

1989a Independence, imperialism, and the Egyptian factor. *Bulletin of the American Schools of Oriental Research* 275: 64–8.

1989b Copper production and Mediterranean trade: the view from Cyprus. *Opuscula Atheniensia* 18: 109–16.

1990 Paradise gained and paradise lost: intensification, specialization, complexity and collapse. *Asian Perspectives* 28: 179–214.

1992 *Society and Polity at Bronze Age Pella: An* Annales *Perspective*. Sheffield: Sheffield Academic Press.

Knapp, A. B., P. Duerden, R. V. S. Wright, and P. Grave 1988 Ceramic production and social change: archaeometric analyses of Bronze Age pottery from Jordan. *Journal of Mediterranean Archaeology* 1(2): 57–113.

Lapp, P. W. 1964 The 1963 excavations at Ta'annek. *Bulletin of the American Schools of Oriental Research* 173: 4–44.

Le Roy Ladurie, E. 1979 *The Territory of the Historian.* Chicago: University of Chicago Press.

1981 *The Mind and Method of the Historian.* Brighton: Harvester Press.

Leonard, A., Jr. 1987 The significance of the Mycenaean pottery found east of the Jordan, in J. Berry and A. Hadidi, eds., *Studies in the History and Archaeology of Jordan* 3: 261–6. London: Routledge.

1989 Archaeological sources for the history of Palestine. The Late Bronze Age. *Biblical Archaeologist* 52: 4–39.

Lewthwaite, J. 1987 The Braudelian Beaker: a Chalcolithic conjoncture in western Mediterranean prehistory, in W. H. Waldren and R. C. Kennard, eds., *Bell Beakers of the Western Mediterranean*, pp. 31–60. British Archaeological Reports, International Series 331. Oxford: BAR.

1988 Trial by durée: a review of historical-geographical concepts relevant to the archaeology of settlement on Corsica and Sardinia, in J. L. Bintliff, D. Davidson, and E. Grant, eds., *Conceptual Issues in Environmental Archaeology*, pp. 161–86. Edinburgh: Edinburgh University Press.

Little, B. J. and P. A. Shackel 1989 Scales of historical anthropology: an archaeology of Colonial Anglo-America. *Antiquity* 63: 495–509.

Liverani, M. 1983 Political lexicon and political ideologies in the Amarna Letters. *Berytus* 31: 41–56.

1987 The collapse of the Near Eastern regional system at the end of the Bronze Age: the case of Syria, in M. J. Rowlands, M. T. Larsen, and K. Kristiansen, eds., *Centre and Periphery in the Ancient World*, pp. 66–73. Cambridge: Cambridge University Press.

MacDonald, B. 1980 Excavations at Tell el-Maskhuta. *Biblical Archaeologist* 43: 49–59.

McGovern, P. 1986 *The Late Bronze and Early Iron Ages of Central Transjordan: The Baq'ah Valley Project, 1977–1981.* University Museum Monograph 65. Philadelphia: University Museum.

1987 Central Transjordan in the Late Bronze and Early Iron Ages: an alternative hypothesis of socioeconomic transformation and collapse, in J. Berry and A. Hadidi, eds., *Studies in the History and Archaeology of Jordan* 3: 267–73. London: Routledge and Kegan Paul.

McGuire, R. H. 1983 Breaking down cultural complexity: inequality and heterogeneity, in M. B. Schiffer, ed., *Advances in Archaeological Method and Theory* 6: 91–141. New York: Academic Press.

McNicoll, A., R. H. Smith, and J. B. Hennessy 1982 *Pella In Jordan* 1. Canberra: Australian National Gallery.

McNicoll, A., R. H. Smith, P. Watson, and S. Gordon (eds.) 1991 *Pella In Jordan* 2. Mediterranean Archaeology, Supplementary Volume 2. Sydney: Department of Archaeology, University of Sydney.

Marfoe, L. 1987 Cedar forest to silver mountain: social change and the development of long-distance trade in early Near Eastern societies, in M. Rowlands, M. Larsen, and K. Kristiansen, eds., *Centre and Periphery in the Ancient World*, pp. 25–35. Cambridge: Cambridge University Press.

Na'aman, N. 1977 Yeno'am. *Tel Aviv* 4: 168–77.

1981 Economic aspects of the Egyptian occupation of Canaan. *Israel Exploration Journal* 31: 172–85.

Oren, E. 1984 "Governor's Residencies" in Canaan under the New Kingdom: a case study of Egyptian administration. *Journal of the Society for the Study of Egyptian Antiquities* 14: 37–56.

Posener, G. 1940 *Princes et pays d'Asie et de Nubie: Textes hiératique sur des figurines d'envoûtement du Moyen Empire*. Brussels: Fondation Egyptologique Reine Elisabeth.

1971 Syria and Palestine, 2160–1780 B.C. – relations with Egypt, in I. E. S. Edwards, C. J. Gadd, and N. G. L. Hammond, eds., *Cambridge Ancient History*, volume 1, part 2, pp. 532–58. Cambridge: Cambridge University Press.

Potts, T. F. 1986 An ivory-decorated box from Pella (Jordan). *Antiquity* 60: 217–19.

Potts, T. F., S. M. Colledge, and P. C. Edwards 1985 Preliminary report on a sixth season of excavations by the University of Sydney at Pella in Jordan. *Annual of the Department of Antiquities, Jordan* 29: 181–210.

Potts, T. F. and R. H. Smith 1991 The Middle and Late Bronze Ages, in A. W. McNicoll *et al.*, eds., *Pella in Jordan* 2. Mediterranean Archaeology, Supplementary Volume 2. Sydney: Department of Archaeology, University of Sydney.

Prag, K. 1989 Preliminary report on the excavations at Tel Iktanu, Jordan. *Levant* 21: 33–45.

Redford, D. B. 1982a Contact between Egypt and Jordan in the New Kingdom: some comments on sources, in A. Hadidi, ed., *Studies in the Archaeology and History of Jordan* 1: 115–20. Amman: Department of Antiquities.

1982b A Bronze Age itinerary in Transjordan. *Journal of the Society for the Study of Egyptian Antiquities* 12: 55–74.

1985 The relations between Egypt and Israel from El-Amarna to the Babylonian conquest, in J. Amitai, ed., *Biblical Archaeology Today*, pp. 192–205. Jerusalem: Israel Exploration Society.

Richard, S. 1987 The Early Bronze Age: the rise and collapse of urbanism. *Biblical Archaeologist* 50: 22–43.

Richards, F. 1985 Scarab seals found in Jordan in the late MBA and early LBA. Unpublished B.A. Honours thesis, Department of Archaeology, University of Sydney.

Schreiber, K. J. 1987 Conquest and consolidation: a comparison of the Wari and Inka occupation of a highland Peruvian valley. *American Antiquity* 52: 266–84.

Seger, J. D. 1975 The MBII fortifications at Shechem and Gezer: a Hyksos perspective. *Eretz Israel* 12: 34*–45*. Jerusalem: Israel Exploration Society.

Sethe, K. 1906 *Urkunden des Ägyptischen Altertums* I–IV. Leipzig: Akademie Verlag.

Shrimpton, G. 1987 Regional drought and the economic decline of Mycenae. *Classical Views* 6: 137–76.

Stager, L. 1985a Respondent: "Archaeology, History and Bible; the Israelite settlement in Canaan: a case study," in J. Amitai, ed., *Biblical Archaeology Today*, pp. 83–7. Jerusalem: Israel Exploration Society.

1985b The archaeology of the family in ancient Israel. *Bulletin of the American Schools of Oriental Research* 260: 1–35.

Teissier, B. 1990 The seal impression Alalakh 194: a new aspect of Egypto-Levantine relations in the Middle Kingdom. *Levant* 22: 65–73.

Terray, E. 1977 Event, structure and history: the formation of the Abron kingdom of Gyaman (1700–1780), in J. Friedman and M. J. Rowlands, eds., *The Evolution of Social Systems*, pp. 279–301. London: Duckworth.

Tilley, C. 1989 Claude Lévi-Strauss: structuralism and beyond, in C. Tilley, ed., *Reading Material Culture: Structuralism, Hermeneutics, and Poststructuralism*, pp. 3–81. Oxford: Blackwell.

Trigger, B. G. 1989 *A History of Archaeological Thought*. Cambridge: Cambridge University Press.

Weinstein, J. 1975 Egyptian relations with Palestine in the Middle Kingdom. *Bulletin of the American Schools of Oriental Research* 217: 1–16.

1981 The Egyptian empire in Palestine: a reassessment. *Bulletin of the American Schools of Oriental Research* 241: 1–28.

Wright, H. T. 1986 The evolution of civilizations, in D. J. Meltzer, D. D. Fowler, and J. A. Sabloff, eds., *American Archaeology Past and Future*, pp. 323–65. Washington: Smithsonian Institution.

Zaccagnini, C. 1984 L'ambiente palestinese nella documentazione extrabiblica del Tardo Bronzo. *Rivista Biblica* 32: 13–27.

7 Braudel and North American archaeology: an example from the Northern Plains

PHILIP DUKE

Little attention has been paid thus far to explaining either the different rates of cultural change in the archaeological record of the Northern Plains of North America or the epistemological relationship between the prehistoric and historic pasts of the area. These two problems are examined by combining Braudel's conception of time with more recent Annaliste explications of the relationship between structure and event. With specific reference to the later prehistoric and early historic record of southern Alberta, Canada, structures of *mentalité* are defined in prehistoric processing and procurement activities and traced into historic period gender relationships. Geographical structures are identified in subsistence activities. These structures were transformed through a recursive relationship with human action, manifested in specific events: the adoption of the bow and arrow and ceramics, and the arrival of European cultures. By denying the existence of the prehistoric and historic pasts as epistemologically separate entities, archaeology may be used to amplify specific ethnographic and historical studies, rather than the other way around, as is usually the case.

Introduction

It has long been recognized that temporal change in the archaeological record of the Northern Plains of North America was, with few exceptions, predominantly slow and sporadic. This feature has set the tone for all archaeological research in the area but has, in the process, generated two research strategies which have hindered understanding of the past. The first strategy is based on the view that human cultures in the region are highly adapted to their local environments with little need for change. Although adaptation does explain certain features of cultural behavior, it leaves unanswered the specific question of why some artifacts in the region show more temporal change and/or greater embellishment than others (see Burnham [1973] and Sahlins [1976] for general critiques of adaptation).

The second research strategy, which has created a more insidious problem, arose from a comparison by archaeologists of the apparently slow tempo of change in prehistoric societies with the more rapid cultural changes of the historic period. Consequently, a classic Lévi-Straussian division was created in Northern Plains archaeology in which the prehistoric past was peopled by "cold" societies studied by archaeologists and the succeeding historic period was peopled by "hot" societies studied by ethnographers and historians. To all intents and purposes, the past has, therefore, been created as two separate worlds, prehistoric and historic/ethnographic. The primary relationship between the two, as far as archaeologists are concerned, is analogical, and this has reinforced their separation. Differences between the historic and prehistoric pasts, however, should not be overstated. The prehistoric/historic interface gains any paramount epistemological significance it might have over other periods of cultural change only because of its concerns and contacts with our own society (Fabian 1983). Furthermore, stressing the paramount importance of the change from the prehistoric to the historic period may inadvertently keep alive the nineteenth-century conception of the division between primitive and advanced (Young 1988).

In adopting such a posture toward the past, archaeologists have allowed their discipline to remain subordinate to ethnography: any intellectual "traffic" between the two has been predominantly one-way. This has been reified institutionally by subsuming archaeology within the wider field of anthropology. One specific result of this is that North American archaeologists have overlooked the important contribution which their discipline's reliance on the long term can make to studies of the short term, the latter reliant on documentary- or informant-based sources. So far, the opportunity has been lost to create models of the past which, while acknowledging the different data of prehistory and history/ethnography, analyze these data sets within a framework complementary to both. If this situation is to be rectified, and archaeology is to make a more independent contribution to historical and ethnographic understanding, it must adopt models which are suited to its own data and apply these models to other types of data.

In this chapter, I propose an explanation of why certain artifacts in the Northern Plains show more temporal change and embellishment than others and, in so doing, I hope to break down the barrier between the prehistoric and historic pasts as epistemologically separate entities. My arguments will be based on an examination of the processes of long-term continuity and change in the Northern Plains from the viewpoint of certain *Annales* conceptions of time and change. They will recognize the long-term nature of archaeological data and, in emphasizing the continuity between prehistory and history, will move the study of the past toward a single ontology (see Duke 1991).

For the sake of argument, discussion is restricted to the cultures of southern Alberta, Canada, the extreme northwestern tip of the Northern Plains, during the past 2,000 years of prehistory and early history. This particular area creates problems of analysis not found in other case studies in this volume. Most significantly, it does not have a long documentary history. Thus, in using a model which attempts to reconcile both material culture and ethnohistoric evidence, these data sets are regarded as essentially sequential, rather than as contemporary and complementary to each other. This problem, however, should be recognized as a problem of data, not of epistemology. Because many of the explanations offered depart radically from those common in southern Alberta archaeology, they must be regarded as tentative. Nevertheless, they provide a potentially powerful way of explaining the data.

The contribution of *Annales*

Despite the many contributions which *Annales* thinking can make to archaeological interpretation, two specific elements characterize the present analysis. The first is the notion of time itself. For a discipline so concerned with the past, archaeology has given surprisingly little serious attention to time as a theoretical and culturally specific concept: Bailey (1983) and Shanks and Tilley (1987: 118–36) are exceptions, and they approach the phenomenon, respectively, from methodological and ideological perspectives (see also Knapp and Smith, this volume). However, the notion of time was addressed consistently by Fernand Braudel in both his seminal discussion of Mediterranean society (1949, English translation 1972/1973) and in many later writings. Braudel argued that historical phenomena operate on different temporal scales and that, depending on the scale, their impact on societies and individuals differs. He categorized historical phenomena into three time scales of *courte, moyenne*, and *longue durée*, which are, to a large degree, situational and operate as scales along a continuum (Knapp, this volume). As Braudel himself emphasized, these temporal models "are valid for as long as the reality with which they are working" (Braudel 1980: 44–5). Braudel's emphasis on geographical structures has been replaced in later Annaliste writings by an emphasis on structures of *mentalité*, concerned with notions of ideology and symbolism within a specific cultural context. The implications of *mentalité* for the analysis of structural change will be considered later.

An immediate benefit to archaeology of such a temporal model is, firstly, that it reasserts the value of the long term, a concept first stressed in archaeology by the palaeoeconomic school (Higgs and Jarman 1975) but one which never became popular in North America. Secondly, Braudelian concepts of time introduce the notion that certain phenomena have different rhythms of change, and that these rhythms have different effects on society and the individuals in it. In adapting Braudel's model for archaeological use (note that it is a model *for*, rather than a model *of*) in the present study, analysis is restricted to a consideration of structure and event, avoiding conjunctures (*moyenne durée*). This decision recognizes the practical problems of temporal resolution in the archaeological record, but keeps untouched the important relationship between short-term events and long-term structures.

The second element of *Annales* thinking incorporated into this study concerns the notion of structural change. This can occur in two ways. First, structures can "clash" with other structures so that some are overwhelmed and temporarily subdued (Braudel 1980). Secondly, the impact of individual human action can affect structural change. Both types of change may be recognized in events, which serve as etically defined "thresholds" of change that allow us to analyze the precise processes by which change occurred.

Although Braudel seemingly rejected short-term events as unimportant phenomena, there is some evidence that he was not completely hostile to them, as some critics would suggest (for example, Beales 1981). And whereas Braudel rejected history as merely a sequence of events peopled by famous individuals, he stated that "I am by no means the sworn enemy of the event" (Braudel 1973: 901), and referred on a number of occasions to the relationship between structure and event as analogous to an hourglass (Braudel 1973; 1980). Later *Annales* historians have regarded the event as an important explanatory concept with an equal relationship to structure (Stoianovich 1976; Le Roy Ladurie 1979; Clark 1985: 196), a shift which brings them much closer to earlier positions held by Febvre and Bloch (Clark 1985: 182).

This shift amongst later Annalistes is paralleled by recent developments in post-processual archaeology, which questions the notion of passivity and determinism in at least certain areas of human behavior (Hodder 1985). Rather than seeing basic organizational structures as inevitably deterministic, post-processual archaeology recognizes the recursive relationship between structure and human action, as individuals negotiate their everyday existence. This relationship, and the encapsulation of change within continuity that it implies, has recently been investigated from an explicitly archaeological viewpoint by Hodder (1987a; 1987b). He accurately describes artifact change, for instance, as "the stream of continual variability and change as one artifact type is transformed into another" (1987b: 2). Thus, change is recognized as important to the continued existence of long-term structures and is seen, in the words of a commentator on *Annales* thinking, "as part of a process of structuring, destructuring, and restructuring" (Stoianovich 1976: 38).

In this study, the event is defined by its relationship to structure, not just by its length of time. It constitutes a marker of transition (Abrams 1982: 195), and serves as a point of analysis of changing structural configurations. Clearly such events need not have been consciously recognized by their participants – and in this they differ fundamentally from the "events" of contemporary mass media. Rather they serve as etic reconstructions enabling us to understand social processes and individual action.

If these notions of time are combined with the structure–event model, we have a powerful tool for explaining processes of change. In the following pages I attempt to show how this tool contributes to an understanding of why only certain artifacts on the Northern Plains show much temporal variation. This discussion is then expanded to consider other aspects of human behavior in the study area, namely the ways in which long-term structural continuity contributed to processes through which gender relationships were transformed by the impact of European culture on aboriginal society, and the ways in which the long-term structure of specific economic subsistence practices of aboriginal society was affected not just by changes in the environment but also by human action.

Figure 7.1 Map of Alberta showing archaeological sites and natural features mentioned in the text

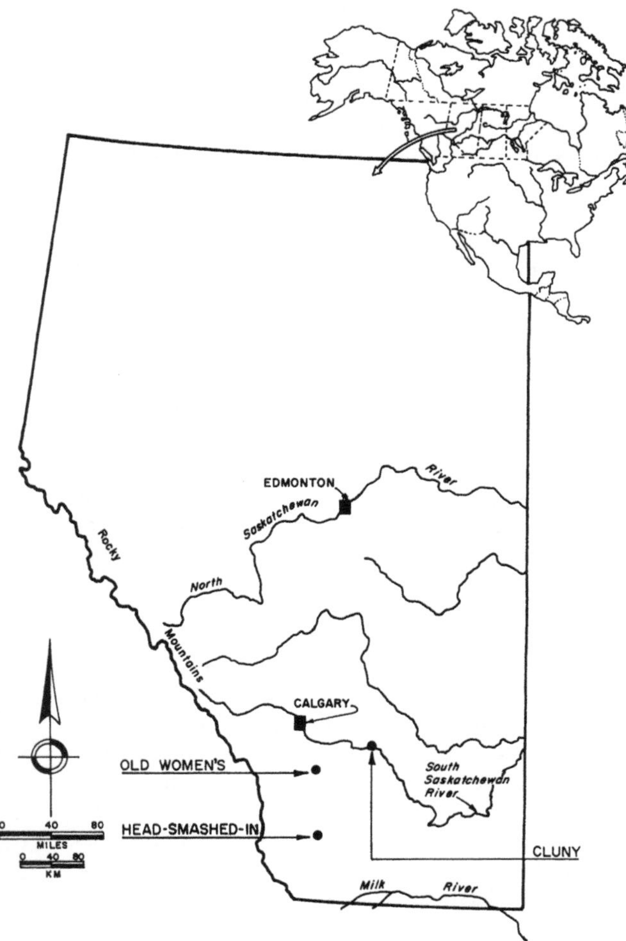

Southern Alberta: a case

The natural environment

Southern Alberta, apart from its mountainous western edge, occupies the extreme northwestern portion of the North American Plains grasslands and is characterized by a relatively flat topography and a generally treeless environment. It has low precipitation, low mean annual temperatures and short growing seasons (Sanderson 1948). The Saskatchewan River system is the area's major aquifer (Figure 7.1).

Prior to European contact, the animal most numerous, and most important to aboriginal culture, was the American buffalo or bison (*Bison bison bison*), a herd animal which weighed up to 1,000 kg. Other fauna included the wapiti (*Cervus elaphus*), deer (*Odocoileus* spp.), pronghorn antelope (*Antilocapra americana*), bear (*Ursus* sp), coyote (*Canis latrans*), swift fox (*Vulpes velox*), bobcat (*Lynx rufus*), beaver (*Castor canadensis*), and muskrat (*Ondatra zibethicus*). European immigration caused the near extinction, or radically altered the distribution, of many of these animals. A variety of resident and migratory birds still inhabit the area.

Grasses are the most important floral component of southern Alberta. Their specific distributions depend on local climate and moisture: xeric grasses have an especially high frequency in the southeastern part of the province, with more mesic types found at higher elevations and along the western and northern edges of the Plains (Morgan 1980). The seasonally varying nutritional content of the grasses helped to determine the seasonal movements of the bison (Morgan 1980). Various shrubs and trees such as willow and cottonwood are found along water-courses.

Paleoclimatic research has identified short-term climatic changes in North America during the last two thousand years (Baerreis and Bryson 1965; Bryson and Wendland 1967). Pending specific studies in southern Alberta, however, descriptions of paleoclimate in the area must remain tentative, although there is a high probability that at least some of these episodes affected southern Alberta (Figure 7.2). Such climatic changes as did occur would have been quantitative, involving the density and frequency of different grass types and thus the fitness of many of the animals inhabiting the area.

Cultural setting: the historic Blackfoot

The historic period begins in southern Alberta in the second half of the eighteenth century when Canadian trappers made contact with aboriginal groups (Ray 1974), although for some time prior to this European goods and horses had circulated through the area. During this time, southern Alberta was exploited by several different tribal groups: the Blackfoot, Cree, Assiniboine, Gros Ventres, Kutenai, Sarcee, Shoshone, and Crow, of which the Blackfoot were the area's primary occupants. Throughout the nineteenth century, both Canadian and American settlers moved west and increasingly threatened Blackfoot territory. The result was that by the final quarter of that century, the Blackfoot had lost their independence and had been relocated on reservations in southern Alberta and northern Montana (Ewers 1958).

The exact length of time the Blackfoot occupied southern Alberta is still undetermined (Byrne 1973; Brink 1986), although their occupation certainly extends some distance into prehistory. Furthermore, although

Figure 7.2 Cultural and paleoenvironmental sequence of southern Alberta. Dates are only approximate.

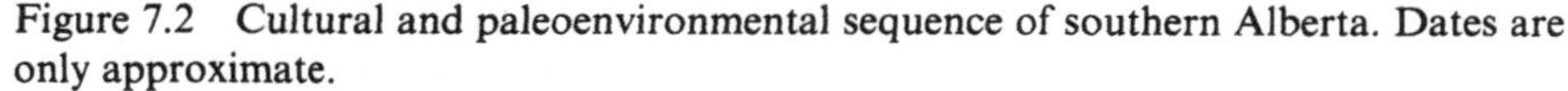

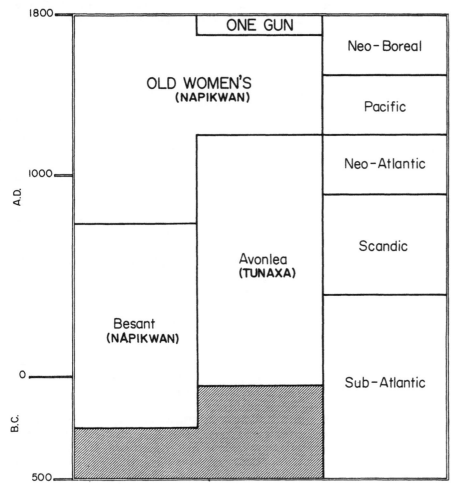

they have existed as a separate linguistic group for a considerable time (Kroeber 1939), it is not at all clear that they existed during the prehistoric period as a separate political-ethnic group in a manner similar to that of the historic period. Indeed, their historical political separateness from other tribes may have been the result of European pressure, rather than a long-term condition.

The Blackfoot are well documented in rich ethnographies (e.g., Wissler 1911; Ewers 1958). The band was the primary social and subsistence unit and varied in size and membership (Dempsey 1982), although tribal solidarity beyond the band was encouraged by pan-tribal societies that fulfilled various policing and judicial roles. The Blackfoot are formally characterized as egalitarian, but the effects of the fur trade and the acquisition of the horse created social rankings, a shift to individualism from communalism, and changes in the status of females throughout the historic period (Lewis 1942; Ewers 1955; Klein 1983).

The Blackfoot relied on the bison for food, clothing, tipi (lodge) covers, utensils, and many other artifacts (McHugh 1974), and used techniques like driving the animals *en masse* over cliffs or into specially constructed timber pounds. The use of such communal techniques lessened, however, as the acquisition of the horse encouraged the killing of individual animals by mounted warriors. Other animals, such as deer and antelope, were taken in smaller numbers for specific purposes such as clothing (Wissler 1910; Ewers 1958). Vegetable foods were utilized to some degree, mainly for medicine and as dietary supplements. Native tobacco (*Nicotiana attenuata*) was grown until European-cured leaves became available through trading (Lowie 1954: 26).

The Blackfoot used the tipi for their domestic living structure. This was a portable, skin- (later canvas-) covered, circular, four-poled structure. The availability of European goods caused a rapid loss of traditional Blackfoot material culture, but the few studies available (e.g., Wissler 1910) suggest that their material culture was largely indistinguishable from that of other tribes of the Northern Plains region.

The prehistoric record

The recency of archaeological investigations in the province means that the vast majority of work is still culture-historical in nature. Because of its morphological changes through time and space, the most useful artifact for understanding the prehistoric culture-history of southern Alberta is the stone projectile point. Other stone tools include shaped and unworked awls, knives, scrapers, and chopping tools. Ceramics were introduced to southern Alberta about 1,500 years ago. Bone tools, both formed and unformed, are also found.

Because of their long stratigraphic sequences invaluable for culture-historical studies, the most important sites in southern Alberta are the large, communal kill-sites. The two most important of these are Head-Smashed-In, with a use sequence going from the historic period back to about 3500 BC (Reeves 1978), and Old Women's Jump, dating back about 2,000 years (Forbis 1962). Both are located in the southwestern part of the province (Figure 7.1). Habitation sites comprise hearths, cooking pits, and lithic and bone debris indicative of a wide range of domestic activities. Stone circles are interpreted as the remains of a domestic structure essentially identical to the historic Plains tipi (Kehoe 1958). Some stone circles, particularly those lacking artifacts, may have been used for other specialized purposes. Rock art panels, in both pictographic and petroglyphic form, are occasionally found on suitable cliff faces. Isolated finds, usually of stone tools or debitage, are nearly ubiquitous, but their archaeological implications are limited.

The culture-history employed in this study relies heavily on that presented in Reeves' 1970 doctoral dissertation (1983). It is acknowledged that relying on only one authority simplifies the current debate on the area's culture-history. The last 2,000 years of prehistory in southern Alberta are characterized by two separate cultural traditions, each comprising sequential phases (Figure 7.2). The *Tunaxa* Tradition is indigenous to southern Alberta and dates back to about 2000 BC. The terminal phase of this tradition is the Avonlea, which dates from approximately AD 200 to 1200; it marks the first use of the bow and arrow in southern Alberta. Overlapping the Avonlea Phase is the Besant Phase, the initial phase of the intrusive *Napikwan* Tradition, which is thought to represent an immigration from the northeastern edge of the Plains. The Besant Phase dates from approximately 200 BC to AD 750. Increasing contact between participants of the Avonlea and Besant Phases resulted in the appearance of the Old Women's Phase in the eighth century, although the Avonlea Phase continued as an independent entity for another 400 to 500 years. In the middle of the eighteenth century, the One Gun Phase is recognized. This has been widely interpreted as an immigration into the area, based on differences in pottery as well as on a unique fortified structure at the Cluny site (Byrne 1973; Forbis 1977). The One Gun Phase was rapidly assimilated into the Old Women's Phase.

The material cultures of these four phases have much in common. Major differences are found in projectile point types and in other items of material culture such as ceramics. Avonlea arrow points, distinguished by their thinness, symmetry, and meticulous body flaking, represent a climax in the quality of point manufacture on the Northern Plains (Kehoe and McCorquodale 1961: 184). The Besant atlatl dart point has a more varied shape. The quality of Besant flaking is far lower generally than that of Avonlea points, both in the techniques of flake removal and point symmetry. About AD 450 the Besant point was replaced by the Samantha Side-Notched, an arrow point which, while identical in shape to the Besant atlatl dart, is smaller. Besant sites prior to AD 450 are further characterized by a high frequency of Knife River Flint, a silicified wood imported from quarries in North Dakota. Points of the Old Women's Phase comprise a variety of temporally seriated arrow forms (Forbis 1962). These point types are not temporally exclusive. At Old Women's Jump, for example, different types are found in the same components. The early point types of the Old Women's Phase are very similar to Samantha Side-Notched points. Through time, however, the side-notching of Old Women's Phase points becomes more marked, and there is an increase in their symmetry and quality of flaking which approaches those on Avonlea points.

Pottery in all phases is unpainted, and decoration consists mainly of impressions from a variety of materials.

The ceramic component of the Avonlea Phase in southern Alberta has been classified by Byrne (1973) as the early variant of the Saskatchewan Basin Complex (AD 150/250–1150). As yet Besant pottery in the province has not been formally classified. Ceramics of the Old Women's Phase belong to the late variant of the Saskatchewan Basin Complex (Byrne 1973: 354). The ceramics of the One Gun Phase belong to the Cluny Complex (Byrne 1973).

Other items of material culture show much less qualitative variation. Although Reeves (1983) used a wide variety of artifacts to define phases on the Northern Plains, it remains the case that sites cannot be phase-assigned without diagnostic points or ceramics: other items simply do not show the variation necessary for this type of segregation.

In summary, therefore, the archaeological record of southern Alberta shows little radical change. The major qualitative changes occur in projectile points and ceramics. One way of explaining this phenomenon requires the division of the material culture into two major categories: procurement, represented in the archaeological record by projectile points; and processing, represented by tools such as scrapers, awls, chopping tools, and ceramics. These categories are based on a generalized analogy from historic groups of the area, including the Blackfoot, where these two sets of tasks correspond to a sexual division of labor. Such a categorization also has validity in other areas: a similar contextual model is employed by Sinclair (1988), for example, in his analysis of Upper Paleolithic tool assemblages in France.

Procurement and processing as long-term structures

In this section, tools of procurement and processing are examined as components of long-term structures of *mentalité*, and it is argued that they not only reflect economic behavior, but also operate as symbols in the field of human action and social negotiation. Change in these tools cannot be due solely to an assumed teleological need for greater efficiency; it must also be explained within its specific historical context. The structures of procurement and processing have a long-term "flow" to them, and cross-cut the temporal boundaries defined by traditional culture-history. Despite their long-term nature, these structures are not immune to the impact of other structures or individual action. All artifacts have many layers of symbolic meaning: the meanings adduced in this study are only one of many potential sets.

Procurement

Tools of procurement, specifically projectile points, constitute a long-term structure, manifested archaeologically by the intense investment of time and effort made in Avonlea points and in the later varieties of the Old Women's Phase, particularly those which appear after AD 1200, when the Avonlea Phase as an independent cultural system begins to break down. This structure, however, did not originate in the Avonlea Phase; indeed, the investment of effort and care in flaking can be traced back to the preceding Pelican Lake Phase, and perhaps all the way back to the finely worked points of the Paleoindian period, 8,000 years earlier (which would provide a striking example of *la longue durée*).

The care and detail invested on these points may be interpreted in the light of the symbolic role such objects played in a society with a long tradition of hunting large game (Duke 1991); these points were tied into notions of power and prestige associated with killing, a symbolic investment well documented elsewhere (Evans-Pritchard 1956: 236; Hodder 1979; Larick 1985). It is also worth considering that more rapid changes in point types characteristic of the Old Women's Phase might be tied into the same notions of power and prestige. Larick (1985), for instance, has suggested that amongst Maasai males, more rapid replacement of point types is tied into their perception of their own worldliness and status. Consequently, rapid style evolution takes place. Clearly this analogy will not suffice unmodified for a prehistoric situation taking place over a considerably longer time period, but it does demonstrate at least one process by which punctuated change can occur.

The adoption of the bow and arrow, associated with the Avonlea Phase, is also tied into this notion of hunting power and prestige. Not only is this "event" recognized archaeologically as a marker of transition, but it is also the product of structural change, intimately connected to individual negotiations of power within existing structures. An explanation of greater adaptive efficiency for point embellishment and the adoption of the bow and arrow has been rejected, since there is apparently no greater killing efficiency of Avonlea and later Old Women's Phase points compared to Besant points which lack such embellishment: all are found in the same area, all are of the same general time period, and all fulfilled essentially the same function in a communal kill situation where a long trajectory was not needed.

The same degree of symbolic importance does not seem to have been attached to Besant and Samantha points. While many are well made (although never equal to Avonlea points), most are much more asymmetrical than Avonlea and show much less control in body flaking. The heavier and slower atlatl continued in use. These differences perhaps result from the socio-structural character of the people of the Besant Phase. Were they an immigrant group from an area where there was less concentration on single animal species and, therefore, less of a tradition in hunting symbolism? Their movement into the Plains would have necessitated a rapid readjustment to bison-hunting practices and, through emulation, they would rapidly have become as efficient as indigenous groups. In such a scenario, the importance attached to hunting as a symbolic action was less quickly adopted, since it was a product of a historically specific long-term structure in indigenous cultures.

This structure of *mentalité* – hunting as symbolic action – may be traced through an approximately two thousand-year period, and probably originated well before that. Although it cross-cuts the temporal boundaries established by culture-historical studies, it is not consistently present in specific phases, as evidenced by its absence during the early part of the Old Women's Phase. The waxing and waning of the symbolic importance attached to hunting have implications for a greater understanding of the processes of cultural transmission during the period, and enhance notions based on traditional culture-history alone. The structure is transformed and amplified by the adoption of the bow and arrow, a product of individual action within an existing structural framework.

Processing

In contrast to the embellishment and more rapid stylistic change of Avonlea and Old Women's projectile points, artifacts concerned with processing seem more resistant to change. Certainly, there is no equivalent amongst processing tools of the Avonlea point, and it has proven extremely difficult to date sites by processing tools alone because of their more standardized shapes. This conservatism would have been encouraged actively by society and is reflective of different values attached to procurement and processing activities. Ethnoarchaeological studies in the material culture of females in Kenya's Baringo district, for example, show that conservatism is tied into notions of individualism within society; females are expected to conform to traditional notions of behavior, whereas men achieve status by being "worldly" and innovative (Hodder 1979; 1981).

There is evidence, however, for long-term change in the structural continuity of processing activity in one area: the adoption of pottery. A number of functional arguments can be given for the adoption of this technology, ranging from the appearance of new foodstuffs to the development of new cooking styles. Other complementary explanations, however, are also feasible for the adoption of an artifact not particularly well suited to this socio-technic environment (a friable and fragile object that had to be fired in an area devoid of surplus combustible material and then transported).

Avonlea groups may have adopted pottery within the context of its role in social negotiation, specifically between procurers and processors. An analogous situation has been explored by Braithwaite (1982) and Hodder (1982) in African agricultural societies, where pottery has a high utilitarian value, and where social power is negotiated through the decoration of pots, in such a way that the overall efficiency of the pot is not reduced. In southern Alberta, pots may have been used to achieve similar social goals, although in a slightly different way. Pottery was adopted precisely because it was not fundamentally necessary to processing and storage facilities. Brumley (1983: 185), for instance, noted that fire-broken rock, used to heat food or water in skin containers, is still found in ceramic-bearing sites in southern Alberta, the implication being that existing processing practices continued. Social discourse in material culture could then be carried out in a cultural sphere which would not interfere with existing practices. The long-term continuity of the processing structure is thus marked off and transformed by a recognizable event, the adoption of pottery. This event is best explained not by functional adaptation alone, but by its recursive relationship to other structures in society, within the context of individual action and social negotiation.

There is no reason to explain the adoption of ceramics by groups of the Besant Phase in the same way. Since the Besant Phase was intrusive, different contextual arguments are relevant. These relate, for instance, to Besant social organization prior to their movement into the Northern Plains, and to the economic and cultural ties of Besant Phase groups with groups located farther east. These topics deserve more detailed examination.

Historic period gender relations

The dialectical relationship between procurement and processing structures can be used as a means of assessing the specific dynamics of gender relationships of the area's aboriginal groups, specifically the Blackfoot, during the historic period. The traditional anthropological view of gender relations in historic Blackfoot society is that males were dominant, while females were essentially menial drudges: the mechanics of the fur trade made females into objects of capital needed by males to process furs and hide for profit (Klein 1983). Furthermore, different standards of morality applied to males and females (Ewers 1958). Some contradictory evidence, however, suggests that females may have had power in society. For example, females made, owned, and looked after the tipi (Wissler 1910; Lowie 1954), played significant roles in religious ceremonies (Weist 1980: 260), and in some Plains societies, including the Blackfoot, undertook men's roles in certain circumstances (Weist 1980). Alternative roles, of which the best known is the "manly-hearted women" (Lewis 1941), allowed some women access to the high levels of social status normally reserved for males (Medicine 1983).

The contradictory nature of this evidence has been reinterpreted by recent anthropologists as indicative of greater female equality, with the traditional interpretations of male dominance perceived as arising from the specific ideological positions of earlier observers, both specialist and non-specialist (Kehoe 1983; Weist 1983). At the risk of simplifying what was a very complex situation, it is suggested that the different interpretations are reflective not just of ambivalence on the part of anthropologists, but also of a real ambivalence in gender relations in the historic period: European contact rapidly altered gender relationships, and resulted in the confusing and sometimes contradictory appearances described above.

For example, European contact throughout the nineteenth century had a profound influence on the self-perception of the Indian male. From being an independent warrior, he became increasingly controlled by the European fur and hide trade. Territorial control was lost as settlers began to move west. Conversely, females became more important because of their ability to process hides and fur. One response was that males "over-reacted" in order to retain their sense of control and their position in society. Thus, males exerted greater dominance over females: there was a shift to polygyny as males became aware that more wives meant more wealth in trading (Lewis 1941). Male control of the mode of production was further stimulated by the particular form of European gender relations, itself a long-term structure of *mentalité*. European males imposed their own value system of gender inequality on the Indian, in trading only with Indian males; females in European society were generally prohibited from entering into such economic activity.

These gender relationships of the nineteenth-century Blackfoot did not spring up spontaneously. Rather, they are the direct product of individuals in aboriginal society altering and intensifying – through the event of European contact – the intertwined, long-term structures manifested archaeologically in procurement and processing. A clash of external and internal long-term structures thus contrived to produce the particular short-term situation described ethnographically.

Environment and economy

Long-term structural continuity in subsistence strategies and responses to the natural environment can be traced from the prehistoric into the historic periods. The environment exerted fundamental influences on aboriginal cultures of southern Alberta. The unpredictability of cultivated plant yields made the area unsuitable for any subsistence economy other than hunting and gathering. Seasonal variation in climate resulted in certain areas being used consistently through time. This is most noticeable in the Foothills belt where warming westerly winds called Chinooks create a more amenable winter habitation zone. The demands of living in this environment created similar adaptations throughout much of the Northern Plains.

Such conservatism is evidenced in the circular habitation structure, capable of being transported and withstanding the wind and temperatures of the Plains. On the evidence of stone circles or configurations, this type of structure has a long antiquity. There is some evidence for buried stone structures as early as the late Paleoindian period, for example, with more secure evidence dated to the ensuing Archaic period (T. Kehoe 1983: 338). Stone circles are numerous in southern Alberta, as in the Northern Plains generally; Wormington and Forbis (1965: 143) conservatively estimate a total of 600,000 for the former area alone.

Kill sites, whose location was determined by the presence of appropriate topographical features like a natural gathering basin and a cliff of a particular height, provided a means of dispatching the animals which took advantage of their instincts to stampede. These sites also show long-term continuity of use, as evidenced at Head-Smashed-In, Old Women's, and many others; evidence for communal bison hunting may be found as early as the Paleoindian period (Wilson and Davis 1978). These patterns of human–environmental relationships showed a remarkable resilience through time; incoming groups apparently adopted existing subsistence techniques, whether they were those of the Besant Phase, the One Gun Phase, or the strategies of the aboriginal immigrants into the Northern Plains in the historic period (Wissler 1914). The subsistence economy constitutes one example of the structure of *la longue durée*.

Although this bison-hunting pattern remained essentially unchanged, fluctuations in the environment may well have had some effect on human occupation of the area. Periods of higher precipitation not only increased the numbers of bison and other animals but also favored an increase in woodland animals like deer (Reher 1977; Duke 1981). Such a change is hypothesized for at least three climatic episodes: the Sub-Atlantic (500 BC – AD 400), the Neo-Atlantic (AD 900–1200), and the Neo-Boreal (AD 1500–1800).

There is evidence in at least two of these episodes, the Sub-Atlantic and Neo-Boreal, for population movement into southern Alberta. During the Sub-Atlantic, peoples represented by the Besant Phase entered the area and, although evidence is scant, their initial movement may have been caused by an increased demand in Hopewellian trading networks for Rocky Mountain obsidian, and possibly for bison meat and hides (Reeves 1983). Another indigenous population movement occurred during the Neo-Boreal with the appearance of the intrusive One Gun Phase, representing immigrants from the Middle Missouri. Thus, it may be concluded that during periods of higher precipitation population levels in southern Alberta rose because of immigration. There is no evidence for increases in indigenous populations during these periods, although this is extremely difficult to recognize.

In periods of lower precipitation, bison populations fell. It is also plausible that the decrease during the Scandic Episode (AD 400–900) was responsible for the decline after AD 450 in Alberta Besant sites of Knife River Flint imported from South Dakota (Reeves 1983). If Besant populations were part of a Northern Plains exchange network, their connections to the east would have become more tenuous as bison became scarcer, and as meat and hides became less available. Also, the loss of social ties with the east would have reduced the need (or ability) for Besant populations to remain as independent entities. Thus, they initiated the slow merger with indigenous populations, a process manifested archaeologically in the emergence of the Old Women's Phase.

In any comprehensive assessment of the impact of the environment on human behavior, it is necessary to view the environment not just as an external, determining phenomenon, but also as a cultural construct of the societies inhabiting it (Collingwood 1946: 200). This view introduces the notion of human action into the interpretation of economic behavior, and moves away from a strict determinism.

In this instance, hunting techniques must be placed within the context of procurement and processing and the dialectical relationship between the two. Viewing the process of change as *structure–event–structure* (Le Roy Ladurie 1979: 113–31) (the event being the adoption of the bow and arrow) may help to explain the evidence for a possible intensification in hunting practices during the last 2,000 years of Northern Plains prehistory (Kehoe 1973; Frison 1978; cf. Reeves 1978). In southern Alberta, there is evidence for larger numbers of animals being killed at one time and for shorter periods between kills (Duke 1981). This intensification continues into the historic period where the relationship between humans and bison may have approached what Higgs and Jarman (1972) defined as animal husbandry (Kehoe 1973).

The role of hunting as a symbolic activity is further affected by another event: its clash with European gender structures. A shift to individualism from communalism is manifested in the popularity of individual mounted hunting and in the heavy toll taken on bison herds, and this is tied into the changes in male self-perceptions during the nineteenth century (already discussed). Since hunting intensification seems to have been a continuous process throughout the last 2,000 years, spanning climatic episodes with different environmental carrying capacities, its explanation should not rely solely on ecological factors.

Concluding summary

The contributions which Braudel and *Annales* thinking generally can make to archaeological interpretation may be divided into two types: empirical and conceptual. This study has concentrated on empirical methods of analysis that allow explanations of specific data sets. Particular notions of time and structural continuity and change have been adduced to explain varying rates of artifactual and behavioral change in the later prehistory of southern Alberta. Different prehistoric phenomena, therefore, changed at differential rates that affected individuals in society in different ways. Structural change may be induced by a series of different events, ranging from structural clashes (as in the case of European worldviews and aboriginal structures) to the impact of internal human action on those structures, as evidenced by differential rates of change in procurement and processing artifacts. Inasmuch as these structures are transformed by events, new social conditions are created upon which human action operates in an endless *structure–event–structure* cycle.

The conceptual contribution of *Annales*, in terms of "Grand Theory" (Clark 1985), involves most importantly new notions about the flow and rhythms of history. These notions are particularly relevant for North American archaeology, which has been implicitly defined as a cultural anthropology of the past, with emphasis on short-term models of change. Braudel's concept particularly, with its sweep through time and space, offers to North American archaeologists a workable model which may transcend the restrictions of past analyses, and allow a reassessment of the traditional relationship between archaeology and ethnography; the outcome may allow archaeology to contribute independently to a better understanding of the human past. This has profound implications not just for archaeology but also for anthropology.

Acknowledgments
This chapter developed out of a wider research project on structure and event in the Northern Plains. I am most grateful to the following for their helpful comments and criticisms: Ian Hodder, Alice and Thomas Kehoe, Michael Wilson, Bernard Knapp, Tony Sinclair, Kathleen Fine, and Cynthia Duke.

References

Abrams, P. 1982 *Historical Sociology*. Shepton Mallet: Open Books.

Bailey, G. 1983 Concepts of time in Quaternary prehistory. *Annual Review of Anthropology* 12: 165–92.

Baerreis, D. and R. Bryson 1965 Climatic episodes and the dating of the Mississippian cultures. *Wisconsin Archaeologist* 46: 203–20.

Beales, D. 1981 *History and Biography*. Cambridge: Cambridge University Press.

Braithwaite, M. 1982 Decoration as ritual symbol: a theoretical proposal and an ethnographic study in southern Sudan, in I. Hodder, ed., *Symbolic and Structural Archaeology*, pp. 80–8. Cambridge: Cambridge University Press.

Braudel, F. 1972 *The Mediterranean and the Mediterranean World in the Age of Philip II*, vol. 1. London: Collins.

1973 *The Mediterranean and the Mediterranean World in the Age of Philip II*, vol. 2. London: Collins.

1980 *On History*. London: Weidenfeld and Nicolson.

Brink, J. 1986 *Dog Days in Southern Alberta*. Archaeological Survey of Alberta Occasional Paper 28. Edmonton.

Brumley, J. 1983 An interpretive model for stone circles and stone circle sites within southeastern Alberta, in L. Davis, ed., *From Microcosm to Macrocosm: Advances in Tipi Ring Investigation and Interpretation*, pp. 171–91. Plains Anthropologist Memoir 19. Lincoln: Augstums Printing Service.

Bryson, R. and W. Wendland 1967 Tentative climatic patterns for some late glacial and post-glacial episodes in Central North America, in W. J. Mayer-Oakes, ed., *Life, Land and Water*, pp. 271–98. Winnipeg: University of Manitoba Press.

Burnham, P. 1973 The explanatory value of the concept of adaptation in studies of culture change, in C. Renfrew, ed., *The Explanation of Culture Change: Models in Prehistory*, pp. 93–102. London: Duckworth.

Byrne, W. 1973 *The Archaeology and Prehistory of Southern Alberta as Reflected by Ceramics*. Archaeological Survey of Canada, Mercury Series 14. Ottawa.

Clark, S. 1985 The "Annales" historians, in Q. Skinner, ed., *The Return of Grand Theory in the Social Sciences*, pp. 177–98. Cambridge: Cambridge University Press.

Collingwood, R. 1946 *The Idea of Prehistory*. Oxford: Oxford University Press.

Dempsey, H. 1982 History and identification of Blood bands, in D. Ubelaker and H. Viola, eds., *Plains Indian Studies: A Collection of Essays in Honor of John C. Ewers and Waldo R. Wedel*, pp. 94–104. Washington: Smithsonian Institution.

Duke, P. 1981 Systems dynamics in prehistoric southern Alberta: 2000 B.P. to the historic period. Unpublished Ph.D. dissertation, University of Calgary, Calgary.

1991 *Points in Time: Structure and Event in a Late Period Northern Plains Hunting Society*. Boulder: University of Colorado Press.

Evans-Pritchard, E. 1956 *Nuer Religion*. Oxford: Oxford University Press.

Ewers, J. 1955 *The Horse in Blackfoot Indian Culture*. Bureau of American Ethnology, Bulletin 159. Washington: U.S. Government Printing Office.

1958 *The Blackfoot. Raiders of the Northwestern Plains*. Norman: University of Oklahoma Press.

Fabian, J. 1983 *Time and the Other: How Anthropology Makes its Object*. New York: Columbia University Press.

Forbis, R. 1962 The Old Women's buffalo jump, Alberta. *National Museums of Canada, Bulletin* 180: 56–123. Ottawa.

1977 *Cluny. An Ancient Fortified Village in Alberta*. Department of Archaeology, University of Calgary Occasional Paper 4. Calgary.

Frison, G. 1978 *Prehistoric Hunters of the High Plains*. New York: Academic Press.

Higgs, E. and M. Jarman 1972 The origins of plant and

animal husbandry, in E. Higgs, ed., *Papers in Economic Prehistory*, pp. 3–13. Cambridge: Cambridge University Press.

1975 Palaeoeconomy, in E. Higgs, ed., *Palaeoeconomy*, pp. 1–7. Cambridge: Cambridge University Press.

Hodder, I. 1979 Social and economic stress and material culture patterning. *American Antiquity* 44: 446–54.

1981 Reply to Davis. *American Antiquity* 46: 668–70.

1982 *Symbols in Action*. Cambridge: Cambridge University Press.

1985 Postprocessual archaeology. *Advances in Archaeological Method and Theory* 8: 1–26.

1987a The contextual analysis of symbolic meanings, in I. Hodder, ed., *The Archaeology of Contextual Meanings*, pp. 1–10. Cambridge: Cambridge University Press.

1987b The contribution of the long-term, in I. Hodder, ed., *Archaeology as Long-Term History*, pp. 1–8. Cambridge: Cambridge University Press.

Kehoe, A. 1983 The shackles of tradition, in P. Albers and B. Medicine, eds., *The Hidden Half*, pp. 53–73. Lanham: University Press of America.

Kehoe, T. 1958 The direct ethnological approach applied to an archaeological problem. *American Antiquity* 60: 861–74.

1973 *The Gull Lake Site: A Prehistoric Bison Drive Site in Southwest Saskatchewan* 1. Milwaukee Public Museums, Publications in Anthropology 1. Milwaukee.

1983 A retrospectus and commentary, in L. Davis, ed., *From Microcosm to Macrocosm: Advances in Tipi Ring Investigation and Interpretation*, pp. 327–42. Plains Anthropologist Memoir 19. Lincoln, NE: Augstums Printing Service.

Kehoe, T. F. and A. McCorquodale 1961 The Avonlea: horizon marker for the Northwestern Plains. *Plains Anthropologist* 6: 179–88.

Klein, A. 1983 The political economy of gender: a 19th century Plains Indian case study, in P. Albers and B. Medicine, eds., *The Hidden Half*, pp. 143–73. Lanham: University Press of America.

Kroeber, A. 1939 *Cultural and Natural Areas of North America*. University of California Publications in American Archaeology and Ethnology 8. Berkeley.

Larick, R. 1985 Spears, style and time among Maasai-speaking pastoralists. *Journal of Anthropological Archaeology* 4: 206–20.

Le Roy Ladurie, E. 1979 *The Territory of the Historian*. Chicago: University of Chicago Press.

Lewis, O. 1941 Manly-hearted women among the North Piegan. *American Anthropologist* 43: 173–87.

1942 *The Effects of White Contact upon Blackfoot Culture, with Special Reference to the Role of the Fur Trade*. American Ethnological Society Monograph 6. Seattle: University of Washington Press.

Lowie, R. 1954 *Indians of the Plains*. New York: McGraw-Hill.

McHugh, T. 1974 *Time of the Buffalo*. Lincoln, NE: University of Nebraska Press.

Medicine, B. 1983 "Warrior women" – sex role alternatives for Plains Indian women, in P. Albers and B. Medicine, eds., *The Hidden Half*, pp. 267–80. Lanham: University Press of America.

Morgan, R. 1980 Bison movement patterns on the Canadian Plains: an ecological analysis. *Plains Anthropologist* 25: 143–60.

Ray, A. 1974 *Indians of the Fur Trade*. Toronto: University of Toronto Press.

Reeves, B. 1978 Head-Smashed-In: 5000 years of bison jumping in the Alberta Plains, in L. Davis and M. Wilson, eds., *Bison Procurement and Utilization: a Symposium*, pp. 151–74. Plains Anthropologist, Memoir 14. Lincoln, NE: Augstums Printing Service.

1983 *Culture Change in the Northern Plains 1000 B.C. to A.D. 1000*. Archaeological Survey of Alberta Occasional Paper 20. Edmonton.

Reher, C. 1977 Adaptive processes on the shortgrass plains, in L. Binford, ed., *For Theory Building in Archaeology*, pp. 13–40. New York: Academic Press.

Sahlins, M. 1976 *Culture and Practical Reason*. Chicago: University of Chicago Press.

Sanderson, M. 1948 The climates of Canada according to the new Thornwaite classification. *Scientific Agriculture* 28: 501–17.

Shanks, M. and C. Tilley 1987 *Social Theory and Archaeology*. Cambridge: Polity Press.

Sinclair, A. 1988 Foraging for meaning; seeking structure in Palaeolithic society. Unpublished ms on file with author.

Stoianovich, T. 1976 *French Historical Method: The* Annales *Paradigm*. Ithaca, NY: Cornell University Press.

Weist, K. 1980 Plains Indian women: an assessment, in W. Wood and M. Liberty, eds., *Anthropology on the Great Plains*, pp. 255–71. Lincoln, NE: University of Nebraska Press.

1983 Beasts of burden and menial slaves: nineteenth century observations of Northern Plains Indian women, in P. Albers and B. Medicine, eds., *The Hidden Half*, pp. 29–52. Lanham: University Press of America.

Wilson, M. and L. Davis 1978 Epilogue: retrospect and prospect in the man–bison paradigm, in L. Davis and M. Wilson, eds., *Bison Procurement and Utilization: A Symposium*, pp. 312–35. Plains Anthropologist, Memoir 14. Lincoln, NE: Augstums Printing Service.

Wissler, C. 1910 Material culture of the Blackfoot Indians. *Anthropological Papers of the Museum of Natural History* 5: 1–78.

1911 The social life of the Blackfoot Indians. *Anthropological Papers of the Museum of Natural History* 7: 1–64.

1914 Material cultures of the North American Indians. *American Anthropologist* 16: 447–505.

Wormington, H. and R. Forbis 1965 *An Introduction to the Archaeology of Alberta, Canada.* Denver: Denver Museum of Natural History.

Young, T. C. Jr. 1988 Since Herodotus, has history been a valid concept? *American Antiquity* 53: 7–12.

8 Restoring the dialectic: settlement patterns and documents in medieval central Italy

JOHN F. MORELAND

In recent years archaeologists appear to have rediscovered history. For many the Annaliste history of Fernand Braudel has proved especially attractive. In this paper it is argued that an overemphasis on the determinism of long-term structures, and the lack of a dialectical relationship between the *longue durée* and the history of events fundamentally flaws Braudel's enterprise. Drawing upon the work of sociologists and anthropologists like Anthony Giddens and Pierre Bourdieu, an alternative theoretical perspective is provided and applied to further our understanding of the formation of hilltop towns in central Italy during the early Middle Ages. It is argued that this perspective, with its emphasis on the social contruction of reality and the recursiveness of the relationship between structure and agency, is similar to that of a later generation of *Annales* scholars like Georges Duby and Jacques Le Goff. Annalisme is not rejected: *le monde Braudellien* is.

Introduction

In the middle decades of this century a new form of historiography was developing in France. It was a form of history established in explicit reaction to the then dominant school of narrative political history. Founded by Lucien Febvre and Marc Bloch, *Annales* history flourished under Fernand Braudel; the banner of the *Annales* is now carried by such notable French historians as Georges Duby, Jacques Le Goff, and Paul Veyne. The output of these *Annales* historians has been stupendous, and it is dedicated by and large to the structures of everyday life, a subject of great relevance to archaeologists. Until relatively recently, however, archaeologists have singularly ignored the work and methodology of the *Annales*.

One reason why British archaeologists, at least, did not notice the development of a new historical movement across the Channel was that their attention was strongly focused on developments in archaeological thought across the Atlantic. The development of what was very self-consciously called the New Archaeology gripped the attention of those archaeologists who were interested in moving beyond the essentially descriptive and antiquarian approaches that had dominated British archaeology for so long.

Lewis Binford, who initiated this movement in 1958, describes in almost messianic tones how he conceived and ran "the first field season consciously conceived as the New Archaeology" in that year, and how he and Mark Papworth in the following decade carried the Good News to the traditionalists throughout the United States, while suffering the pillorying and disbelief which seems to be the common fate of all those who preach a new creed (Binford 1972: 133).

The New Archaeology sought to make archaeology a nomothetic science concerned with explaining the general *process* of societal change in the past, in opposition to an idiographic history which was presented as being concerned with the chronicling of unique and particularistic *events*. In this sense its foundation bears a strong resemblance to that of the *histoire annaliste* in reaction to a *histoire sorbonniste*, the latter obsessed with marriages, battles, and alliances. But this resemblance would have largely gone unnoticed by the proponents of the New Archaeology, who wilfully presented history as a Rankean monolithic entity, part of a justification for their program of renewal. They used an anachronistic conception of history as a straw man against which to pit their new science, and they can be situated alongside those whom Le Roy Ladurie chastises for their attacks on "Old Chronos":

> The social sciences [for this read New Archaeology], wishing to preserve a reputation for hardness and purity, began to operate a closed shop against history, which was accused of being a "soft" science. The attack was characterised by a great deal of ignorance and not a little gall on the part of the attackers, who had affected to forget that since Bloch, Braudel and Larousse, history too had undergone a scientific transformation. Clio had stolen the clothes of the social sciences [archaeology] and they had never noticed their nakedness . . . while the death of history was being widely proclaimed in certain quarters, it had simply gone through the looking glass in search not of its own reflection, but of a new world. (Le Roy Ladurie 1979: 26–7)

Archaeology and history

The relationship between archaeology and history has not been easy or satisfactory for either party, especially in recent years. Historians have pointed to the "dumbness" of the mute artifact, and have seen the archaeologist

> simply as an illustrator, to provide a few concrete relics to make vivid the written page – "Here is Queen Mary's coronation chair; this is a portrait of Alexander; this is the jaw bone of a neolithic sheep." (Renfrew 1979: 257)

In an otherwise interesting and illuminating article on Dark Age trade, Philip Grierson suggests that the reason the spade cannot lie is because it cannot even speak (Grierson 1959). This objectivization of the archaeologist's craft in the form of a spade, and the characterization of the latter as an *instrumentum mutum* has been a persistent theme of many historians who deal with archaeological data. A recent work on the Roman phases of the monastery at San Vincenzo al Volturno in Molise, Italy, contains the following comment:

> Evolution from villa to village to church or monastery is a frequent phenomenon of early medieval archaeology. Continuity is often surmised, but inevitably hard to demonstrate. At San Vincenzo, where continuity was broken, stages of change are hard to see, but *the spade's dumb mouth* gives us little help in understanding them. (Barnish 1992; emphasis added)

In a similar vein, Crawford (1987: 4) accepts without reservation Alcock's assertion that the "archaeologist who chooses to work in an historic period 'must recognise his dependence on historians'" (Alcock 1983: 57). Archaeology here truly is the handmaiden of history.

Historians have been further mystified by the activities of a new generation of prehistorians who have attempted to write the history of the greater part of the human past without what the former consider the indispensable aid of documents (Finley 1975: 88), and so have largely ignored the subject altogether.

For their part archaeologists have proclaimed themselves the saviors of the prehistoric "common man" who they see as being rendered mute by the social factors underlying textual production. Archaeologists point to the text as elite product, as "distorted" ideology, and as saying nothing about the base majority of the population. Only archaeology, they argue, can give history back to people.

Following on from the perception of text as distorted communication, some archaeologists have argued that we would do better to ignore this data set altogether and construct our histories from archaeological evidence alone. Thus in a recent book on the transition from Roman Britain to Saxon England, Arnold makes a virtue of the fact that his work deliberately ignores historical evidence; for him, archaeological and historical evidence are not even concerned with the same subject matter (1984: 163). Hodges' contention that "it is the archaeological record, not the fleeting gasps of contemporary observers, which provides a source of data on the pattern and process of the Anglo-Saxon conquest of southern and eastern Britain" (1986b: 70) should be read in much the same light. Essentially what Arnold and others advocate is that, given the uncertainties and vicissitudes of interpretation and dating connected with documents of this period, archaeology should stand by itself (Hope-Taylor 1977: 309; Arnold 1984: 165; see Hobsbawm 1979 for a critique of these "counterfactual" arguments).

Such feelings have been expressed in a manner which is both more forceful and more polemical by one of the great theorists of modern archaeology – David Clarke. Clarke was primarily concerned with the development of archaeology as an independent discipline "struggling to find its dimensions and assert its separate existence from bordering disciplines of greater maturity" (1978: 19), especially history. Clarke contends that archaeologists should set about the task of developing models and modes of data analysis which are specifically archaeological – that is, they are to be used for the classification, explication, and explanation of archaeological "facts."

> Archaeological data are not historical data and consequently archaeology is not history ... archaeology is archaeology is archaeology . . .[It] is a discipline in its own right, concerned with archaeological data which it clusters in archaeological entities displaying certain archaeological processes and studied in terms of archaeological aims, concepts and procedures. We fully appreciate that these entities and processes were once historical and social entities but the nature of the archaeological record is such that there is no simple way of equating our archaeological percepta with these lost events. (Clarke 1978: 11)

We may sympathize with Arnold's reservations about the inadequacies of the historical documentation for the fifth century in Britain, and with those of Grierson for the capacity of the spade to be anything more than an *instrumentum mutum*. Such cautions have been noted before (Sawyer 1978: 2–20; Myres 1986: 1–20), and certainly will be again, but should the information be so summarily dismissed just because we feel that it presents us with apparently insurmountable problems?

The immediate causes of what Renfrew has characterized as a "dialogue of the deaf" (Renfrew 1979) are differing conceptions of how to arrive at an objective "reality" of the past. On the one hand historians argue that archaeological material by its very nature is incapable of directly imparting information about the past: the mute stones do not speak. They have to be given voice through interpretation, and the introduction of this middleman between the past and its material remains in the present makes the desired goal of objectivity impossible. By contrast, the historical sources are held to speak directly to us. We speak their language. They can tell us what the past was really like.

On the other hand, archaeologists point to the restricted nature of effective literacy in most periods of the historical past and conclude that most textual data are subjective reflections of the aspirations and worldview of an elite. They refer to an ideal, not to any historic reality. Unlike textual data, the artifacts recovered by archaeologists are held not to have been consciously produced with communication across time and space in mind. As such they are presented as a resource from which an objective past "as it really was" can be reconstructed. Here the archaeological evidence is seen as passive. It is open to manipulation neither in the past nor in the present. In essence it is a given which offers us fairly direct access to aspects of the past. All that is necessary to gain that access is an interpretative technique, usually nothing more than common sense, though the more sophisticated might prefer the methodological rigor of new archaeology's middle-range theory (Binford 1983).

What we need to recognize is that the separation of archaeology and history in the study of periods with some form of documentary evidence has contributed greatly to the proliferation of histories of the great and the glorious on the one hand, and on the other the production of typologies of ring-headed pins and cremation urns or reports on the latest selection of carbonized seeds from a tenth-century deposit in a Tuscan hilltown. Both are vital to our attempts at "piecing together the past," but on their own, devoid of context or attempts to place them within a body of theory, they are certainly "dry bones, signifying nothing" (Collingwood 1946: 305).

A *rapprochement* between archaeological and historical data must take place; it is vital to our fuller understanding of those societies which have left material remains in both forms. But it can only take place if we "cease to refer to the (written) account as 'historical' as if the archaeological material lies outside history," and if we desist from separating the documentary and archaeological records on the basis of supposed conscious attempts to communicate, or otherwise (Barrett 1981: 216).

Archaeology and the *Annales*

In recent years some archaeologists have suggested that Annalisme and particularly Braudelian Annalisme offers the potential of producing this *rapprochement* between archaeology and history (e.g., Hodder 1987a). The essence of Braudelian thinking has been presented in the earlier chapters in this volume (see Smith, Knapp). Because of the perceived nature of their evidence, archaeologists have focused in particular on the Braudelian *longue durée*. Thus one of the foremost European early medieval archaeologists asserts that "Archaeology is an approach well suited to supporting the goals to which Braudel and the historians of the Annales school aspire. Its command of long time sequence is its real strength, as many prehistorians have realised. The timeless history – the *longue durée* – in which man is in constant rapport with his environment is the very essence of prehistory" (Hodges 1986a: 138). The belief that archaeological data are particularly appropriate to the study of the *longue durée* and the *conjoncture*, and historical data that of the event, leads to the suggestion that "The individual's observations of his/her time can be measured against a *reality* which we can observe. ... written documents are ... cultural expressions to be considered alongside the slower rhythms of time" (Hodges 1986a: 140, emphasis added). Archaeology, it is argued, allows us to "rewrite history, putting the tales of the virtuous relayed from the past to the present in their proper *scientific* place in the process of history" (Hodges 1986a: 140, emphasis added).

This archaeological fascination with Braudelian Annalisme probably stems from the fact that *le monde Braudellien* emphasizes the same structural variables which were regarded as important in many previous incarnations of archaeology, not least the new archaeology (see Fletcher, this volume). A Braudelian emphasis on the long-term structures of the environment, and the medium-term ones of the economy, can be paralleled in Higgsian economic archaeology (Higgs 1972) and the systemic, adaptive New Archaeology (Binford 1983). Archaeologists also take Braudel's emphasis upon the *longue durée* to support their case for a status independent of history since only they have access to the material records which are testament to the processes of long-term structures.

The reliance of archaeologists on Braudelian Annalisme does little to resolve the archaeological/documentary dilemma with which this volume is concerned. Although the Braudelian schema may be presented as a simple heuristic device, as a structure around and through which research can take place, as with orthodox Marxism, such constructs can become reified and shift from being enabling research tools to straitjackets of the historical process (discussed below).

The search for an objective past

The essential problem with the archaeological use of the *Annales* methodology, or to be more precise with that aspect of *Annales* thought outlined by Fernand Braudel, is that it largely ignores the constructed nature of the past, and the archaeologist's and historian's position as constructors in the present.

It is now somewhat of a commonplace in the philosophy of history to recognize that all history has the character of contemporary history due to its construction in the present, or that each generation writes history from the perspective of its own interests (Collingwood 1946). Braudelian history, however, seeks to re-create the past through the accumulation of as many *facts* about the past as possible (Hexter 1972). Similarly the new archaeology sought to use the methods of the natural sciences to generate facts, and ultimately laws, about the past which would allow its re-creation "as it really was" (Hodder 1986: 1–17; Shanks and Tilley 1987: 9–12).

The problem is that in both cases these "facts" were established within a framework which subordinated the role of individual thought and action. The individual agent in both the *monde Braudellien* and the new world of scientific rationalism created by the New Archaeologists simply *behaved* in response to the dictates of the environment's deep structures. Creativity, awareness, and purposeful action in both cases were removed from man and attributed to reified structural constructs. Such structural determinism creates a "people without history" just as effectively as do the Eurocentric and androcentric approaches to the past which have prevailed until recently, and which the decolonization process, the emergence of Third World histories, and the burgeoning of feminist approaches have done so much to dispel (Wolf 1982; Trigger 1984; Hodder 1984; 1986).

A recursive alternative

The numerous critiques of structuralism and systems approaches to archaeology and history should not encourage us to place undue emphasis on the role of the individual in the historical process (see Macfarlane 1979; Hodges 1989). In terms of material culture such considerations imply that each artifact or document is largely an autonomous expression of the thought process and mentality of the agent responsible for its execution (Shanks and Tilley 1987: 97). Given what we have just said about the construction of the past in the present, we must wonder to what extent this promotion of the cult of the individual is a product of the importance attached by the Thatcher government to the former era of imperial greatness, and to the notion that it was the motivation of a few entrepreneurs and explorers which made Britain "great," rather than the sweat and toil of millions.

In our post-modern world, deconstruction is fashionable. But in order to break down this myth of individualism we need only follow someone who had deconstructed the concept a century before it became the ideological cornerstone of the new Victorians. In the Introduction to the *Grundrisse*, Marx writes that

> The individual and isolated hunter and fisherman ... belongs to the unimaginative conceits of the eighteenth century Robinsades, which in no way express merely a reaction against oversophistication and a return to a misunderstood natural life, as cultural historians imagine ... It is rather the anticipation of "civil society" ... In this society of free competition, the individual appears detached from the natural bonds etc. which in earlier historical periods made him the accessory of a definite and limited human conglomerate ... [the] individual ... appears as an ideal whose existence they project into the past. Not as a historic result but as history's point of departure. (Marx 1973: 84)

The essential point here is that human beings live, produce, and reproduce within historically specific social structures. These social structures are the sedimented product of the intended and unintended consequences of human action in the past. They provide the field on which daily life is played out in the present, and they provide human agents with the practical knowledge of how to go on in life (Bourdieu 1977). They are a product of history, and of action in the past.

But they are also more than this, for a recursive relationship exists between human action, the products of that action, and social structures. Social structures – relations of production, kinship, etc. – are the medium as well as the outcome of social practice. Human action is articulated through social relationships, and is also the means by which those relationships are constructed, reproduced, and transformed. Human beings are not structure bound. They live within structures and reproduce and transform those structures through the intended or unintended consequences of their action (Giddens 1979; 1981).

Material culture is similarly the product of human action. It should not be seen as the result of the mentality of the artificer as the individualists would allow, nor as the consequence of motor responses to structural or environmental stimuli. It too is both the medium and the outcome of social practice. We have to see material culture as "socially determined individual production" (Marx 1973: 84), and to contextualize its production and circulation. Material culture cannot be seen as a simple reflection of past social systems. Nor is it a passive record which methodological advances will allow us to interpret in order to reach the past "as it really was." Rather, it is and was activated in the creation and protection of social relationships (see Hodder 1982; 1986).

If we are to see material culture as active in the reproduction and negotiation of social relationships, this must apply equally to documentary evidence, since it too represents "socially determined individual production" (Marx 1973: 84). Otherwise we ascribe a free will and consciousness to those who produce the written evidence – generally the elite – and imply that they somehow exist and operate outside the structures created for and by the rest of the population. This is to reproduce in exaggerated form the fallacies of the various forms of dominant ideology theses (see Abercrombie *et al.* 1980). If we can dismiss the claims that written accounts differ from other artifactual material in being individualistic, intentional, conscious productions, then the way is open to see both the textual and artifactual material in a similar light. Through a conception of all material culture as intrinsic to the constitution of the self and the reproduction and/or transformation of social relationships, we can start to consider the archaeological and historical data within the same interpretative framework. Whether we can reach the truth of the past is another matter and one best left in abeyance for the moment (but see Ricoeur 1984).

The capacity to integrate archaeological and historical data bases is denied those who adopt a strictly Braudelian approach because they work from a series of objective facts to reconstruct an objective past. The role of documents in the production and reproduction of social relationships in the past is never considered. The documents as artifacts are taken as a given, as reflective of social relations – not inherent in their constitution. In the same way the facts about the environment and economy created by the New Archaeologists rarely play a part in the constitution of the human agent and society in the historical past.

All this stems from the restoration of the dialectic which should connect the Braudelian *conjoncture* and the history of events (Hexter 1972: 533), here understood not as the history of individual men, but as the history of human action in the practice which constituted their daily lives. At the same time we accord people a say in controlling their own destiny.

But what of that other level, or rhythm of time? What of the geohistorical structures of the *longue durée*? How do these fit into an interpretative framework which stresses the knowledgeability and capabilities of the human actor in the past? For Braudel the *longue durée* is the time of almost imperceptible passing, theoretically the history of man in relationship with the environment (Braudel 1972: 20). In reality, Braudel's environmental determinism reduced this history of man to the history of the environment, and to the limits placed by the environment on human action. The environment is a hindrance "beyond which man and his experiences cannot go ... For centuries man has been a prisoner of climate, of the animal population, of a particular agriculture, of a whole slowly established balance from which he cannot escape without the risk of everything being upset" (Braudel 1980: 30). Braudel's environment is a structural rather than a dynamic factor (see Smith, this volume). As such it is presented as a given, as a stable monolithic entity. While this can be criticized from the perspective of geomorphology and earth sciences, it is perhaps more apposite to point out here that Braudel ignores the *dynamic* of man–environment relations. Not only are human beings excluded from the natural realm in the manner of classic succession theory in ecology, but there is little appreciation that man's perception of "this unchanging background" can radically alter with changing social and economic conditions: "One man's wilderness may be another's roadside picnic ground" (Nash 1967: 1, see also Moreland 1990).

Like the material world of cities and villas, the natural environment is to an extent socially constructed. Past people's perception of the landscape that surrounded them may have been radically different from our objective reality reconstructed through paleobotanical, paleozoological, and documentary evidence. As Chris Wickham has written in the context of a discussion on the nature of the constraints placed upon social development in mountainous regions of early medieval central Italy: "Geography, like grace, works through people, and people have their own ideas about geographical constraints, ideas that are not necessarily ours" (Wickham 1988: 6). He continues: "... even though geographical determinism does not lay down the laws of necessary, or even natural development, geography does none the less provide a major element in the logic of the situation, through which the social perception of the environment is transferred into action" (1988: 7). It is the social perception of the environment which is transferred into the action of which we have material cultural traces. This takes us to the second point to be considered. The fact that we know that the forests of Europe were cleared, or that the great fenlands of eastern England were drained with the development of the appropriate technologies, should not lead us to transplant the mentality of *Homo economicus* from the world of nineteenth- and twentieth-century Europe onto the minds and consciousness of the world's past populations.

To a large extent, therefore, environmental "constraints" are internal rather than external. The natural environment is internalized and is used in the production and reproduction of social structures. It is not in and of itself a constraint on human action, but is the place where human action occurs. As such it is not an objective, determining force, as in the geohistorical *longue durée*, but is an integral part of the *mentalité* of human populations. It does not stand at the top end of a hierarchical relationship with the structures of the *conjoncture* and the event, but rather exists in a dialectical relationship with them. It is not a "hindrance," nor does it travel "through vast tracts of time without changing" (Braudel 1980: 75). It changes as man's perception of it changes, and the latter changes as a product of the recursive relationship between structure and human action (see also Cronon 1987).

The notion of the dialectical or recursive relationship between structure and event, and the realization that the environment is internalized allows us to restore a nondeterministic unity to the Braudelian conception of structural ordering. To what extent this conception remains Braudelian, or even Annaliste, can be debated, although it clearly accords better with the work of the

Figure 8.1 Hilltop town in Molise

more recent generation of *Annales* scholars. Whatever the case may be, such a conception of the relationship between environment, structure, and event restores people as motor forces in historical change. It is not to argue for the primacy of the individual and individualism (*contra* Rahtz 1988), but simply to assert that humans create social structures, that they work in and through those structures, and that they have the capacity to reproduce and/or transform them. Here we can do no better than repeat the much-quoted words of Marx: "Men make their own history, but they do not make it just as they please; they do not make it under circumstances chosen by themselves, but under circumstances directly encountered, given and transmitted from the past. The tradition of all the dead generations weighs like a nightmare on the brain of the living" (Marx 1963: 15).

The remainder of this chapter attempts to demonstrate the usefulness of this proposition, and that of recursivity as outlined above, paying particular attention to the importance of considering both texts and artifacts as "socially determined individual production," and to the role of the past in the present.

Texts and settlements in early medieval central Italy

> . . . the situation of the place [*Capranica* near Sutri] and its obvious fertility were, as they became known, responsible for attracting, little by little a fair number of inhabitants, who created a citadel for themselves on a mound of sufficient eminence. (Petrarch 1337, quoted in Luttrell 1975:270–1).

Such was a fourteenth-century explanation for a process – called *incastellamento* by Italian historians – which led to the creation of the nucleated hilltop villages which so typify the central Italian countryside (Figure 8.1). In the modern Sabina, the landscape is dominated by a series of small towns that sit perched on rocky crags and promontories, surrounded by lowlands which, until after the end of the First World War, appear to have been almost totally devoid of settlement. Even until 1934 only 16.5 percent of the population in this area lived outside these locales (Toubert 1973: 200). These settlements totally dominate the lives and consciousness of people in this area.

Such is the apparent timelessness and solidity of these places, appearing as they do to grow immediately out of the rock on which they sit, that one might suppose they had always been there, that they represent continuity from a most ancient form of settlement. However, we know that this was not the case. They are a phenomenon of relatively recent date, but the precise date is a matter of some considerable discussion. Documentary sources suggest a tenth- to eleventh-century date for the formation of these hilltop towns (Toubert 1973; Settia 1984;

Figure 8.2 Map of Italy showing the principal sites mentioned in the text

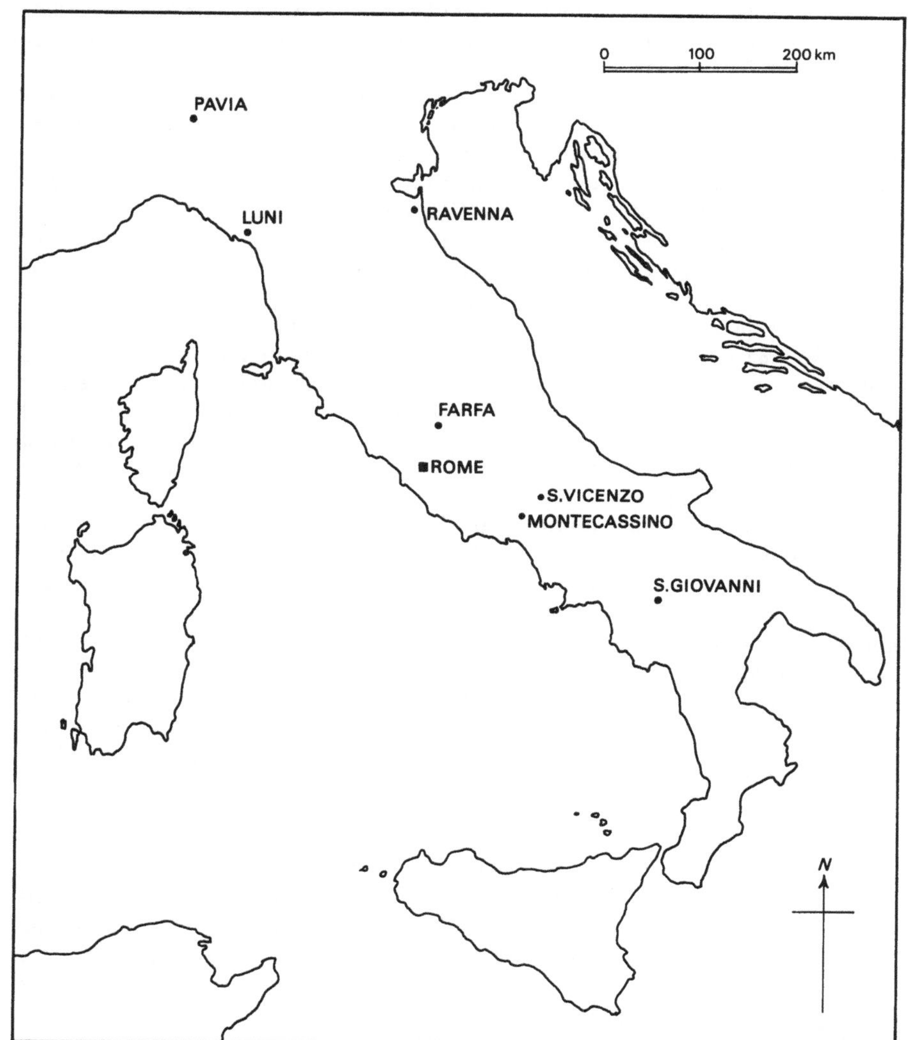

Wickham 1985a); archaeological surveys throughout Italy, and more recently around two of the great medieval monasteries of the Peninsula – Farfa in Sabina in Lazio (Moreland 1986; 1987), and San Vincenzo al Volturno in Molise (Hayes 1985; Hayes *et al.* 1990) (Figure 8.2) – have shown that in the Roman period the land was worked from a large number of villas fairly evenly dispersed across the landscape. The archaeological evidence, furthermore, shows a marked decrease in the numbers of these villas from the second century onwards; in both South Etruria and the Sabina (Figure 8.3) there had been a fall of some 86 percent in the number of villa sites recorded between the end of the first and the mid-fifth centuries AD (Hodges and Whitehouse 1983: 40; Moreland 1988). After this date, analysis of settlement patterns and numbers becomes increasingly difficult because of the disappearance of the archaeologist's prime dating tool for late antiquity – African Red Slip (hereafter ARS) (Hayes 1972), and the controversy over the dating of another late antique/early medieval type fossil – Forum Ware (Whitehouse 1965; 1980; Whitehouse and Potter 1981; Whitehouse *et al.* 1985).

Figure 8.3 Areas of the main field surveys carried out north of Rome by the British School at Rome

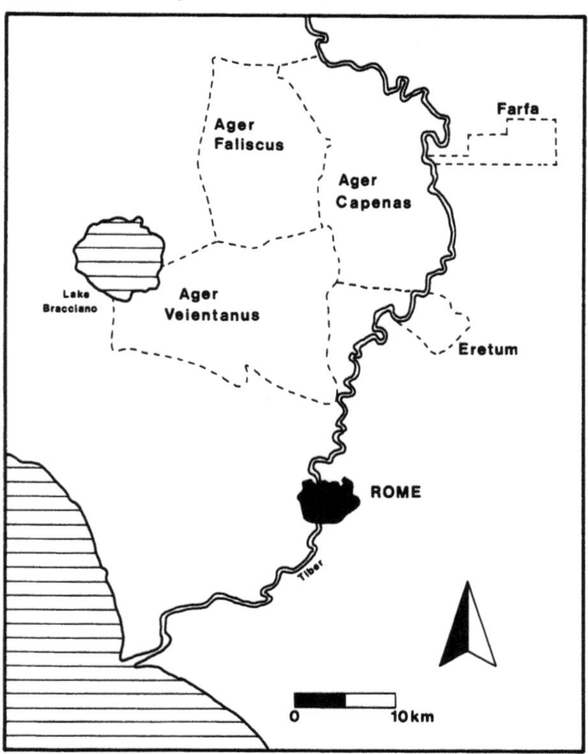

The scale of the productive, transportational, and distributive networks of the early and mid-imperial periods (first to third centuries AD) made available the early forms of ARS to practically all levels of society. The collapse of the infrastructural supports of the Roman edifice in the later imperial period (fourth to sixth centuries AD) of necessity reduced the amount of ARS produced and therefore altered its availability and range of consumers (Fentress and Perkins 1988). This unique pottery became an elite product and perhaps a symbol of some continuing relationship with the notional greatness of a decaying core. Those sites in central Italy on which the latest forms of ARS are found do not therefore represent the sum total of occupation, nor do they provide a reliable key to relative population decline in the later imperial period as some have argued (Hodges and Whitehouse 1983). Rather they are the loci at which "power over" was concentrated (Giddens 1979; 1981).

Excavated examples like those of the fifth and sixth centuries at San Vincenzo al Volturno (Hodges and Mitchell 1985) and San Giovanni di Ruoti (Small 1983) were the centers from which power of an increasingly private nature (as opposed to the public authority conferred by the state) was exercised (Wickham 1984). An architecture of basilican construction and strongly fortified towers on both sites are eloquent testimony to the growth of strong personal ties of dependency in a milieu where the state, though terminally weakened, still persisted at least on the level of a conceptual core.

With the collapse of the state in the seventh century such villa sites may not have lost their efficacy as points around which social life was structured. They probably formed the centers of *curtes* (manorial estates) recorded in the eighth-century documentation preserved in the great monastic archives (Andreolli and Montanari 1985). The archaeological evidence for this continuity is still tenuous but nonetheless persuasive. Preliminary indications from the Farfa survey suggest that some villa sites in the monastic *terra* (estate) may have remained in occupation throughout the Italian "Dark Ages" (Moreland 1988). Combined with the results of recent excavations at Monte Gelato in South Etruria (Potter and King 1988), where a villa was replaced by an early medieval church, and with earlier excavations in central Italy which demonstrate the same sequence, the argument that villas remained essential structuring elements in the landscape of seventh- and eighth-century Italy seems justified (see also Cambi and De Tommaso 1988: 472–6). The continuity of settlement may have been encouraged by a desire on the part of the elite to legitimate their local power through ties with an age-old

Figure 8.4 The present-day monastery of Farfa in Sabina

system. The sites themselves, as material culture, may thus have been important in reproducing relations of power in central Italian society.

What, then, of the ninth century? Did a dispersed pattern of settlement persist right up to the documented date of *incastellamento*? The answer must be a qualified yes. Many of the *curtes* centers may have remained but some changes were taking place, changes which were both a product of the tightening of social relations, and the means through which such increased control was mediated. In the *Ager Faliscus* in South Etruria (see Figure 8.3), ninth-century occupation has been demonstrated for some hilltop sites (see Potter 1979: 1987; Cameron *et al.* 1984). The Farfa survey also produced evidence for the early medieval occupation on the tops of small prominent hills (Moreland 1986; 1987), while at San Vincenzo the site of Vacchereccia also contained sherds of ninth-century (?) Forum Ware (Hodges *et al.* 1984). Is this, then, evidence of *incastellamento*? Does this ninth-century date not contradict that given by the documentary sources? The answer in this case is an unequivocal no. These hilltop sites should be seen in the context of agrarian reorganization and the tightening of social relations. They were essentially additional to, and did not replace, a dispersed pattern of settlement. As such they are not part of the *incastellamento* process, which involved the wholesale reorganization of settlement patterns, the patterns of landholding, and the religious topography (Toubert 1973). To see the significance and role of these ninth-century sites we must look at those areas where the contextual evidence is best. In central Italy this necessarily means the *terrae* (estates) of large monasteries like San Vincenzo al Volturno and Farfa in Sabina (Figure 8.2), where extensive archaeological research has taken place and where the documentary evidence is both full and extensively studied (Toubert 1973; Whitehouse *et al.* 1979; 1981; Hodges and Mitchell 1985; Wickham 1985a; Moreland 1986; 1987).

Farfa and San Vincenzo

From small religious centers in the eighth century, San Vincenzo and Farfa grew to become the largest landowners in their regions (Figure 8.4), reaching their zenith in the ninth century. Extensive building campaigns in the second decade of that century under Abbot Epiphanius at San Vincenzo (Hodges and Mitchell 1985), and at Farfa in the third decade under Abbot Sicardus, produced veritable monastic cities – centers of power and opulence (McClendon 1986). The material trappings of the Carolingian renaissance were incorporated within the built fabric of the monasteries, and expressed the ideology of the Church ascendant in areas far from the heartlands of the empire. Carolingian patronage made both monasteries imperial establishments, and there seems no doubt that the "Carolingian connection" was significant in the physical expansion of the monastic

Figure 8.5 Farfa's principal *castelli* in the area covered by the Farfa field survey

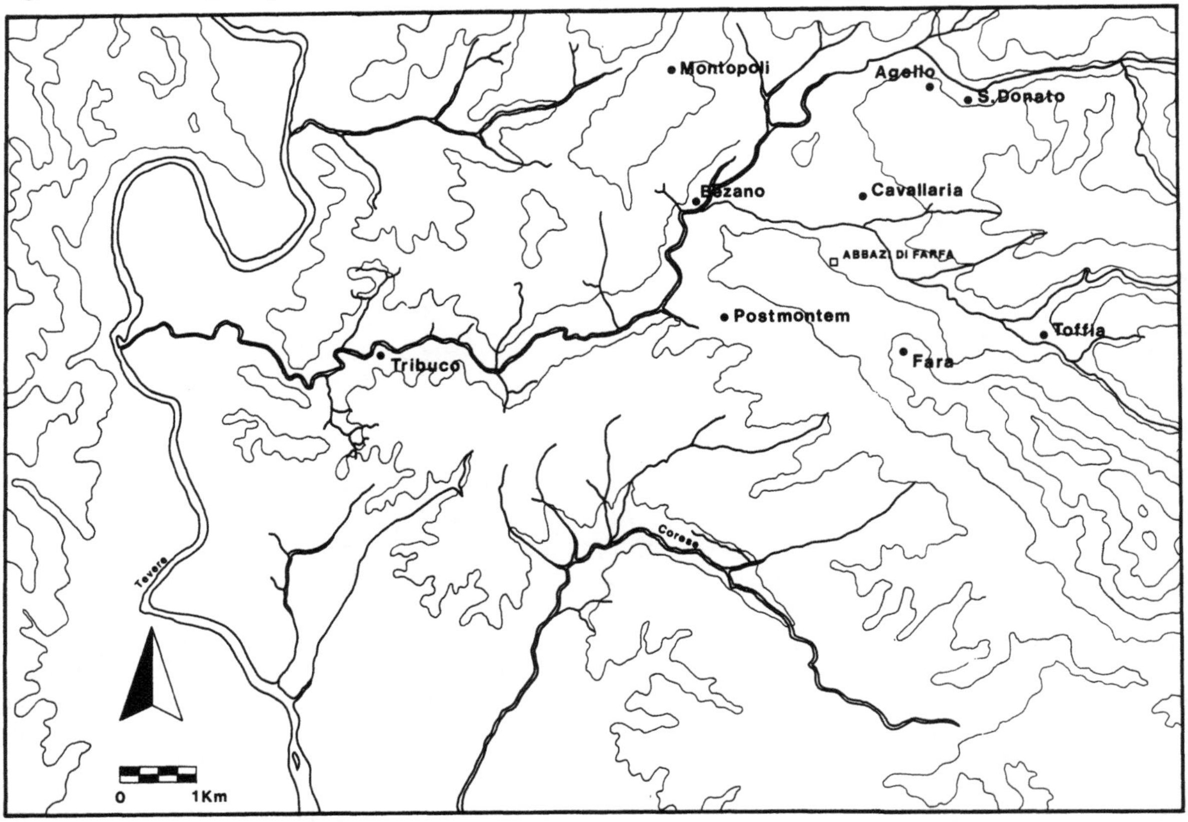

complexes and in the growth of their landed wealth (Hodges *et al.* 1985).

But this cannot be the full story. In an age when transportation of people and products must still have been a dangerous and risky exercise, exploitation of regional production and labor would have figured largely in monastic strategies. At first glance, however, there is little evidence for an intensification of regional production in the areas around San Vincenzo and Farfa (Hodges *et al.* 1985). Hardly any archaeological evidence exists for a change in settlement patterns in terms of either numbers or location, while historical sources speak of continuity in the *sistema curtense* (the system of resource management based on the *curtes*, or manorial centers) around Farfa. At San Vincenzo an even more basic agrarian unit exploited the newly acquired monastic lands – small bands of three to five people of servile or semi-servile status (Wickham 1985a).

Agrarian productivity, however, can also be enhanced by increasing the effectiveness and efficiency of existing social relationships. Greater control over peasant labor and production can be achieved by closer supervision of the productive process, and by the use of devices to increase the amount of information processed. This points to the real significance of both the ninth-century hilltop sites located at Farfa and San Vincenzo, and the increase in the number of documents in the monastic archives for this period. Because the documents record the donation of lands and provide details of the boundaries of such properties it is possible to assign functions and names to some of the sites located through field survey. The significance of this stems from the fact that hilltop sites in the Farfa region seem to have been involved in the close administration of the monastic patrimony.

One site, immediately opposite the monastery, is called *Cavallaria* in the tenth-century texts (see Figure 8.5), while an account from the monastic chronicle – the *Chronicon Farfense* – recording the ninth-century grandeur of the monastery describes this location as the palace for the administration of justice (Zucchetti 1927:

2). The other site lies about 2 km west of the monastery and can be identified with the settlement called *Bezanum* (Figure 8.5). *Bezanum* is mentioned in a document of AD 750 as a ducal *curticella* (a form of *curtes* settlement) (*Regesto di Farfa* [*R.F.*] II, 28), while a document of 776 suggests that the site contained an oratory dedicated to San Vito, and that the "duke" was responsible for the administration of the stock in that area (*R.F.* II, 93). Again the administration of a sector of Farfa's patrimony was a prime function of this site. *Bezanum* effectively overlooks the entrance to the valley in which the monastery sits, and controls the routes along which animals and herders would have passed on their way to and from the winter grazing of the Tiber lowlands and the summer pastures in the interior of the Sabina (Wickham 1985b). The road from Rome to the monastery also passed close by, and thus we might imagine that the ducal site not only controlled access to the monastery but also collected tolls and taxes.

The site of *Vaccherecccia* lies close to the monastery of San Vincenzo in a commanding position over the flat Rochetta plain (Hodges *et al.* 1984). It thus oversees the productive heart of San Vincenzo's *terra* (estate) and the main access routes to the monastery from the south. The site has no ninth-century documentation, but finds of Forum Ware suggest such a date, while the similarity in its location and material culture to that of *Bezanum* and *Cavallaria* makes a similar administrative function possible.

The same is probably true of another site in the middle reaches of the Biferno valley called *Santa Maria in Civita* or D85 (Hodges *et al.* 1980). Here excavations revealed a rich material cultural assemblage including glass vessels from the Veneto, soapstone from the Alps, and sherds of Forum Ware type. This site overlooks the lowest crossing point of the Biferno River and the main road up the valley, so it too is ideally located for the purposes of administration, as well as toll and tax collection, although this time probably for local secular rather than ecclesiastical powers.

It can be argued therefore that all these sites should be seen as focal points for the increased control of local populations. Their rich material culture suggests a prominent place in the settlement hierarchy, while their hilltop locations and dominance of local communications point to their role in what Foucault might have called surveillance (Foucault 1979) – the collection, collation, and recording of information.

This takes us back to the documents which record these settlements. Archaeologists and historians have traditionally looked at these documents in a normative fashion. They concentrated on the *content* of the document and extracted names, dates, and aspects of agrarian organization. But as material culture produced within a particular social, political, and cultural milieu, the *form* of the document – its very existence – tells us something about attempts to reinforce relations of power in ninth-century central Italy.

Because this is not the place to draw out the implications of literacy and written forms of discourse (see Goody 1977; Stock 1983), suffice it to say that the development of written forms of recording are of fundamental importance: they increase the capacity to store and control information and knowledge relevant to the administration of both people and resources in past social systems (Giddens 1981: 94–5). Great Italian monasteries like San Vincenzo and Farfa recorded the donations given to them by pious donors as a way of formalizing the donations and securing them against the claims of later generations. Effective administration of the estates they built up, however, required that more and more information be recorded, stored, and processed. The documents should therefore be seen as more than an indication of increased control over social relations; along with the hilltop sites, they were the means by which that control was exercised. Both were fundamental to the perpetuation of the monasteries' temporal power, so eloquently expressed in the magnificence of their built fabric.

With the collapse of the Carolingian empire in the middle decades of the ninth century and the loss of support and input from the core, the importance of such control strategies must have increased significantly. The reproduction of social relations increasingly relied upon strategies devised and implemented at the local level. The late ninth century saw the effective disintegration of the Carolingian state apparatus in Italy, and the emergence of what Wickham has called "a pullulation of little powers" (Wickham 1981: 168). The reality of feudal social relations was revealed with the removal of the ideal veneer of the Carolingian state. The political turmoil of the period posed a serious threat to the monastic patrimonies, as did the incursions of raiding bands of Saracens and Hungarians.

When the event was the focus of historiographic and archaeological thought, it was argued that the danger and feeling of insecurity caused by the Saracenic and Hungarian incursions caused *incastellamento*: people literally fled to the hills to avoid the depredations of the infidel. Such reliance on external threats, on events, fits well with a view of society as essentially unchanging and with a consensualist picture of social relations. It negates, however, the importance of contradictions within society as a source of transformations, and underplays the significance of changing relations of power and domination. It is a politically charged notion and falls in the face of the evidence. The Arab raids were largely eliminated by the end of the ninth century, and the rapid movements of small bands of Hungarians over the Italian countryside in 899, 937, and 942 (Settia 1984; Leggio 1986) can hardly have been instrumental in such a major tranformation as *incastellamento*. In fact the Saracenic raids were a product rather than a cause of the political turmoil of late ninth-century Italy. They were simply another manifestation of the disintegration of the state and the growing importance of local power and control (Toubert 1973: 312–13). They resulted from and contributed to the reinforcement of local power at the expense of centralized authority. A dialectical or recursive relationship existed between structural change and events.

The Saracenic attacks, however, did have a tangible effect on the fortunes of both San Vincenzo and Farfa. The *Chronicon Vulturnense*, San Vincenzo's chronicle, records in explicit detail the destruction of the monastery by a band of Saracens on the morning of Tuesday, 10 October 881. We believe that we have found archaeological evidence of this particular event in the form of extensive destruction layers containing Saracenic arrowheads (Moreland 1985). The Saracens never stormed Farfa: the monks managed to resist them for seven years and eventually left in three groups carrying the treasure of the monastery with them (McClendon 1986: 9; *Chronicon Farfense* I, 31). Their flight echoes that of the monks of San Vincenzo to Capua after the terrible events of 881. This was the ninth-century nadir for both monasteries, and their smoking ruins must have stood in sharp contrast to the zenith they had reached in the earlier part of that century.

These ruins also reflect the fortunes of the monastic patrimonies, since many of these had fallen into the hands of local secular powers (Wickham 1992), and the rest may have suffered from the lack of direct monastic management. The monks returned from exile to both San Vincenzo and Farfa in the second decade of the tenth century, and proceeded to implement a series of strategies to rebuild their estates and to reassert their control. To achieve these aims they drew upon strategies for increased administration and control developed in the ninth century. Thus the use of written documents to record the administrative process became more significant and is reflected in the vastly increased number of documents we have from the tenth century. Similarly the ninth-century hilltop towns may have been used as conceptual models for the location of the tenth-century population.

It must be remembered that the past is and was a resource to be drawn upon constantly and interpreted in the constitution and negotiation of social relationships. The grounding of the tenth-century present in the ninth-century past, in the period of Epiphanius and Sicardus, may have conferred a degree of legitimacy and "naturalness" on a process (*incastellamento*) which it would have otherwise lacked. *Incastellamento* is a perfect example of how changes in the settlement pattern, and in other societal structures, are not the product of collective behavioral response to environmental change or other external stimuli. Instead *incastellamento* was the product of the dialectic between purposeful human action and past structure.

Although the demographic catastrophe theory for late antiquity and the early middle ages has been overstated, there probably was a significant drop in the population levels such that by the eighth century it may be suggested that people were a relatively scarce resource. The relativity in this equation stems from the fact that such resources are adjudged plentiful or otherwise according to the demands made of them and the "need" for them. With the dominance of feudal social relations, the ability to control people became the principal factor in the establishment and maintenance of power relations through the access this provided to what Anthony Giddens has called "allocative resources" – natural material products (Giddens 1979; 1981). People were not only a productive resource but also essential elements in the constitution of the "little powers" which now comprised central Italy. At one and the same time they formed the productive force of a society based on feudal social relations, as well as a symbol of the power and authority of elites. In the face of competing local powers for control of the "authoritative resources" (people – and here we should remember that in many parts of central Italy secular elites were the initiators of the *incastellamento* process), the location of people in concentrated settlement on hilltops served to establish a series of horizontal bonds that went beyond the elementary structure of kinship. The identification of the people with a particular locale, seen both in the new settlement pattern and in the naming of people in the documents, would, one might say, have created a sense of community that reinforced both territorial and political control. At the level of the peasant producer, the relocation in the hilltop settlement was a physical manifestation of the relations of power exercised by the elite. The constitution of the group – through daily practice, through living, praying, and working together – was a potent force in fending off rival claims to land and people.

The settlement patterns and the *incastellamento* leases were thus both the medium and outcome of attempts to reinforce relations of power and domination. The profound significance of the creation of hilltop settlements and the increasing pervasiveness of the written word cannot be minimized. Settlements are not neutral, objective spaces. The ordering of daily life in and through settlements creates what Pierre Bourdieu has called *habitus*, the means by which people order their lives and view the world (Bourdieu 1977). The spatial distribution of people within the hilltop settlements was a direct manifestation of relations of power and the ideal ordering of feudal society. Here Georges Duby's "three order construct" became a part of lived experience (Duby 1983). The dominance of the *oratores* (those who pray) and the *bellatores* (those who fight) was reflected and reproduced in the central location of the church and castle, while the houses of the *laboratores* (those who work) ringed the settlement with their backs frequently forming the enclosing circuit of the site.

It is, however, somewhat ironic that by the time the three order construct had found its material form, forces were at work which negated its impact. The world was becoming more complex at the very moment when central Italy's orders took their places beside each other in the *castelli*. Social divisions within the *castelli* created a "middle class" of *boni homines* (Toubert 1973: 151; 1976: 699–700); the Cluniac reform program introduced at Farfa in the late tenth and early eleventh century linked the monastery to a pan-European movement and involved it in concerns beyond the region (McClendon 1986: 100), while the distribution of fine ceramic wares like Sparse Glaze to non-elite sites points to the expansion of extra-regional production and distribution networks (Moreland 1988).

The discovery of these areas outside the *castelli* has important implications for our conception of the nature of power relations in early medieval central Italy. Power is not seen as concentrated at the top of social hierarchies; it is possessed by everyone. Just as dominant ideologies and high culture should not be seen as assimilated by a dumb, passive, and wholly receptive lower class, so the desire of the elites to strengthen their control over people did not remove from everyone the power and capacity to take purposeful action at variance with those desires.

In the Sabina, some of the texts are explicit about the relationship between the creation of a *castello* and the control of people. They make it clear that the purpose of the foundation was the *congregatio populi*, the *amasamentum hominum*, and the *consolidatio fundorum* (the consolidation of lands and the aggregation of people) (Toubert 1973: 337). But this did not always work. Although the *castellum* of *Postmontem* (see Figure 8.5) was founded by Farfa before 970 (Toubert 1973: 444), documentary references to forms of dispersed settlement in the area right into the eleventh century show that it was never fully "incastellated" (Wickham 1985a: 64–5). Even here, so close to the monastery of Farfa, the domination of the *castellani* was not complete, and the power of the peasantry to make choices, resist, and refuse was not totally eroded.

The creation of *castelli* and the recording of rights and duties were double-edged weapons: the rights of the lessees were materialized and fixed in the texts, and infringements could be (and were) challenged in court (Wickham 1986). *Castelli* could also become foci of resistance to the *castellani*, as Montecassino found to its cost when Norman help had to be requested in order to crush rebellions against its authority, rebellions that were focused on some of its own *castelli* (Wickham 1985a: 43–4).

Conclusion

This example provides a clear demonstration of the complex relationship between structure and agency so absent in the Braudelian scheme; it shows that although people worked within and through structures, they were not structure-bound. They could and did take action, and even used facilities (like the *castelli*) that constituted elements of structure to further their own ends. This is also seen clearly in the cases where peasants themselves founded *castelli*, as with those constructed in *Tuscia Romana* (Wickham 1985a: 72–3). These peasant *castelli* have been seen as symbols of resistance by small owners to attempts by local lords (including Farfa) to exercise control in this area. The interaction of structure and agency is seen from the fact that, although the peasants took action which resulted in the construction of *castelli*, they chose as a symbol of their resistance the very elements of the *incastellamento* structure which were the basis of seigneurial power.

I have attempted in this study to outline an approach that might lead to a resolution of the archaeological/documentary dilemma. Such a resolution can only be achieved if we move beyond approaches where any data set is dismissed as biased, "dumb," or otherwise inappropriate to our arriving at the past "as it really was." If we realize that, just as we construct the past, so people in the past constructed themselves and their social relationships in and through material culture, the importance of studying all material culture as "socially determined individual production" and as the bearer of meaning and signification becomes apparent.

Advocacy of such an approach should not be taken to suggest that I dismiss out of hand the usefulness of an *Annales* approach as a means for achieving our ends, for as I stated at the outset, a single *Annales* approach does not exist. I have questioned the value of a strictly Braudelian approach simply because it is the one most commonly adopted by archaeologists as representative of the *Annales*. But the works of Georges Duby and especially Jacques Le Goff, with their emphasis on the social construction of reality and on the recursive relationship between structure and agency, are also written under the sign of the *Annales* and present, I believe, an Annalisme which historians and archaeologists should pursue to their mutual advantage.

As I have attempted to demonstrate, what must be added to the theoretical perspective of the new history is a theory of material culture. Although the Annalistes can see that the documents are texts to be read, documents (where they exist) are still seen as the primary source for the construction of the past. Although Braudel in both his great works lays great stress on the city as a dynamic force in European history, it is the city of objective charter, testimony, and deed. It is rarely the city constructed and endowed with meaning which fascinated Rykwert (1976) on one level, and Calvino (1979) on another. What must be done to allow a *rapprochement* between history and archaeology to take place is to construct a theory of material culture, to transform the spade into an *instrumentum vocale*, and to give artifact and document equal voice. A real dialogue – not that of the deaf – can then begin.

Acknowledgments

This chapter is largely based on research carried out for my doctoral thesis (University of Sheffield, September 1988). I thank my thesis supervisor Dr. Richard Hodges, and all those who were involved in any way in the fieldwork that provided the substantive data incorporated within that thesis, in particular Helen Patterson, co-director of the Farfa Project. The British School at Rome funded the project, and Dr. Graeme Barker (then director of the School) provided endless encouragement and ideas. The monks at the monastery of Farfa in Sabina were kind and hospitable hosts during the three seasons of fieldwork. Conversations with Drs. Tom Brown, Neil Christie, David Whitehouse, and Chris Wickham helped to make some sense of the results of the fieldwork; with regard to the theoretical framework developed in my thesis and elaborated here I owe an especial debt to Mark Edmonds, Matthew Johnson, and Julian Thomas. My special thanks, however, go to Sig. Tersilio Leggio (Soprintendente Honorario per il Lazio) for his inestimable local knowledge and his time, and to Prue.

The chapter was written mainly during my stay as a visiting professor in the Department of Classics at Wesleyan University; I thank Wesleyan University also for funding my trip to Baltimore to make the oral presentation. The final version benefited from conversations with my colleagues there, especially Profs. Carla Antonaccio, Doug Charles, and Clark Maines. As ever, the errors remain my own.

References

Abercrombie, N., S. Hall and B. Turner 1980. *The Dominant Ideology Thesis*. London: Allen and Unwin.

Alcock, L. 1983 The archaeology of Celtic Britain, fifth to twelfth centuries AD, in D. Hinton, ed. *Twenty Five Years of Medieval Archaeology*, pp. 48–66. Sheffield: Department of Prehistory and Archaeology.

Andreolli, B. and M. Montanari 1985 *L'azienda curtense in Italia*. Bologna: Clueb.

Arnold, C. 1984 *Roman Britain to Saxon England*. London: Croom Helm.

Barnish, S. 1992 Christians and countrymen, in R. Hodges, ed., *Excavations and Survey at San Vincenzo al Volturno 1980–1986*. London: British School at Rome.

Barrett, J. 1981 Aspects of the Iron Age in Scotland: a case study in the problems of archaeological interpretation. *Proceedings of the Society of Antiquaries of Scotland* 111: 205–19.

Binford, L. 1972 *An Archaeological Perspective*. New York: Academic Press.

1983 *In Pursuit of the Past*. London: Thames and Hudson.

Bourdieu, P. 1977. *Outline of a Theory of Practice*. Cambridge: Cambridge University Press.

Braudel, F. 1972 *The Mediterranean and the Mediterranean World in the Age of Philip II*. London: Collins.

1980 *On History*. Chicago: University of Chicago Press.

Calvino, I. 1979 *Invisible Cities*. London: Picador.

Cambi, F. and M. De Tommaso 1988 Ricognizione archeologica nel comprensione di Abbadia S. Salvatore. Rapporto preliminare 1987–1988. *Archeologia Medievale* 15: 471–80.

Cameron, F., G. Clarke, R. Jackson, C. Johnson, S. Philpot, T. Potter, J. Shepherd, M. Stone and D. Whitehouse 1984 Il castello di Ponte Nepesino e il confine settentrionale del ducato di Roma. *Archeologia Medievale* 11: 63–148.

Clarke, D. 1978 *Analytical Archaeology*. London: Methuen.

Collingwood, R. 1946 *The Idea of History*. Oxford: Oxford University Press.

Crawford, B. 1987 *Scandinavian Scotland*. Leicester: Leicester University Press.

Cronon, W. 1987 *Changes in the Land: Indians, Colonists and the Ecology of New England*. New York: Hill and Wang.

Davies, W. and P. Fouracre (eds.) 1986 *The Settlement of Disputes in Early Medieval Europe*. Cambridge: Cambridge University Press.

Duby, G. 1983 *The Three Orders: Feudal Society Imagined*. Chicago: University of Chicago Press.

Fentress, E. and P. Perkins 1988 Counting African Red Slip ware. *L'Africa Romana* 5: 205–14.

Finley, M. 1975 *The Use and Abuse of History*. London: Chatto and Windus.

Foucault, M. 1979 *Discipline and Punish*. London: Peregrine.

Giddens, A. 1979 *Central Problems in Social Theory*. London: Macmillan.

1981 *A Contemporary Critique of Historical Materialism*. London: Macmillan.

Goody, J. 1977 *The Domestication of the Savage Mind*. Cambridge: Cambridge University Press.

Grierson, P. 1959 Trade in the Dark Ages: a critique of the evidence. *Transactions of the Royal Historical Society* (5th series) 9: 123–40.

Hayes, J. *Late Roman Pottery*. London: British School at Rome.

Hayes, P. 1985 The San Vincenzo survey, Molise, in S. Macready and F. Thomson, eds., *Archaeological Field Survey in Britain and Abroad*, pp. 129–35. London: Society of Antiquaries, Occasional Paper 6.

Hayes, P., J. Patterson, R. Hodges, P. Roberts and C. M. Coutts 1992 The San Vincenzo survey, in R. Hodges, ed., *Excavations and Survey at San Vincenzo al Volturno 1980–1986*. London: British School at Rome.

Hexter, J. 1972 Fernand Braudel and the Monde Braudellien. *Journal of Modern History* 44: 480–539.

Higgs, E. (ed.) 1972 *Papers in Economic Prehistory*. Cambridge: Cambridge University Press.

Hobsbawm, E. 1979 An historian's comments, in B. Burnham and J. Kingsbury, eds., *Space, Hierarchy and Society*, pp. 247–52. British Archaeological Reports, International Series 59. Oxford: BAR.

Hodder, I. 1982 *Symbols in Action*. Cambridge: Cambridge University Press.

1984 Archaeology in 1984. *Antiquity* 58: 25–32.

1986 *Reading the Past*. Cambridge: Cambridge University Press.

1987a The contribution of the long term, in I. Hodder, ed., *Archaeology as Long Term History*, pp. 1–8. Cambridge: Cambridge University Press.

(ed.) 1987b *Archaeology as Long Term History*. Cambridge: Cambridge University Press.

Hodges, R. 1986a Rewriting history: archaeology and the *Annales* paradigm, in H. Kuhnel, ed., *Alltag und Fortschritt im Mittelalter*, pp. 137–49. Krems: Krems Institute for Medieval Studies.

1986b Peer polity interaction and socio-political change in Anglo-Saxon England, in C. Renfrew and J. Cherry, eds., *Peer Polity Interaction and Socio-Political Change*, pp. 69–78. Cambridge: Cambridge University Press.

1989 *The Anglo-Saxon Achievement*. London: Duckworth.

(ed.) 1992 *Excavations and Survey at San Vincenzo al Volturno 1980–1986*. London: British School at Rome.

Hodges, R., G. Barker and K. Wade 1980 Excavations at D85 (Santa Maria in Civita): an early medieval hilltop settlement in Molise. *Papers of the British School at Rome* 48: 70–124.

Hodges R. and J. Mitchell (eds.) 1985 *San Vincenzo al Volturno: The Archaeology, Art, and Territory of an Early Medieval Monastery*. British Archaeological Reports, International Series 252. Oxford: BAR.

Hodges, R., J. Moreland and H. Patterson 1985 San Vincenzo al Volturno, the kingdom of Benevento and the Carolingians, in C. Malone and S. Stoddart, eds., *Papers in Italian Archaeology 4*, pp. 261–85. British Archaeological Reports, International Series 246. Oxford: BAR.

Hodges, R. and D. Whitehouse 1983 *Mohammed, Charlemagne and the Origins of Europe*. London: Duckworth.

Hodges, R., C. Wickham, J. Nowakowski, P. Grierson, H. Patterson, V. Higgins and P. Herring 1984 Excavations at Vacchereccia (Rocchetta Nuova): a late Roman and early medieval settlement in the Volturno valley, Molise. *Papers of the British School at Rome* 52: 148–94.

Hope-Taylor, B. 1977 *Yeavering: An Anglo-British Centre of Early Northumbria*. London: HMSO.

Le Roy Ladurie, E. 1979 *The Territory of the Historian*. Hassocks: Harvester.

Leggio, T. 1986 Le principali vie di communcazione nella Sabina Tiberina tra X e XII secolo. *Il Territorio* 2: 3–19.

Luttrell, T. 1975 Review of P. Toubert's *Les Structures du Latium médiéval*. *Medieval Archaeology* 19: 269–74.

McClendon, C. 1986 *The Imperial Abbey of Farfa*. New Haven: Yale University Press.

Macfarlane, A. 1979 *The Origins of English Individualism*. Oxford: Blackwell.

Marx, K. 1963 *The Eighteenth Brumaire of Louis Bonaparte*. New York: International Publishers.

1973 *Grundrisse*. Harmondsworth: Penguin.

Moreland, J. 1985 A monastic workshop and glass production at San Vincenzo al Volturno, Molise, Italy, in R. Hodges and J. Mitchell, eds., *San Vincenzo al Volturno: The Archaeology, Art and Territory of an Early Medieval Monastery*, pp. 37–60. British Archaeological Reports, International Series 252. Oxford: BAR.

1986 Ricognizione nei dintorni di Farfa, 1985. Resoconto preliminare. *Archeologia Medievale* 13: 333–44.

1987 The Farfa survey: a second interim report. *Archeologia Medievale* 14: 409–18.

1988 Archaeology, history, and theory: settlement and social relations in central Italy AD 700–1000. Unpublished Ph.D. thesis, University of Sheffield.

1990 From the primeval to the paved: environment, perception, and structural history. *Scottish Archaeological Review* 7: 14–23.

Myres, J. N. L. 1986 *The English Settlements*. Oxford: Oxford University Press.

Nash, R. 1967 *Wilderness and the American Mind*. New Haven: Yale University Press.

Potter, T. 1979 *The Changing Landscape of South Etruria*. London: Elek.

1987 *Roman Italy*. London: British Museum Publications.

Potter, T. and A. King 1988 Scavi a Monte Gelato presso Mazzano Romano, Etruria meridionale. Primo rapporto preliminare. *Archeologia Medievale* 15: 253–312.

Rahtz, P. 1988 Decision making in the past. *Archaeological Review from Cambridge* 7: 210–18.

Renfrew, C. 1979 Dialogues of the deaf, in B. Burnham and J. Kingsbury, eds., *Space, Hierarchy and Society*, pp. 253–9. British Archaeological Reports, International Series 59. Oxford: BAR.

Ricoeur, P. 1984 *The Reality of the Historical Past*. Milwaukee: Marquette University Press.

Rykwert, J. 1976 *The Idea of a Town*. London: Faber and Faber.

Sawyer, P. 1978 *From Roman Britain to Norman England*. London: Methuen.

Settia, A. 1984 *Castelli e villaggi nell'Italia Padana*. Naples: Liguori Editore.

Shanks, M. and C. Tilley 1987 *Social Theory and Archaeology*. Cambridge: Polity Press.

Small, A. 1983 Gli edifici tardo-antico a San Giovanni, in M. Gualtieri, M. Salvatore, and A. Small, eds., *Lo scavo di San Giovanni di Ruoti e il periodo tardoantico in Basilicata*, pp. 24–46. Bari: Centro Accademico Canadese.

Stock, B. 1983 *The Implications of Literacy: Written Language and Modes of Interpretation in the Eleventh and Twelfth Centuries*. Princeton: Princeton University Press.

Toubert, P. 1973 *Les Structures du Latium médiéval*. Rome: Ecole Française.

1976 *Studies sur l'Italie médiévale*. London: Variorum.

Trigger, B. 1984 Archaeology at the crossroads: what's new? *Annual Review of Anthropology* 13: 275–300.

Whitehouse, D. 1965 Forum Ware: a distinctive type of early medieval glazed pottery from the Roman Campagna. *Medieval Archaeology* 9: 55–63.

1980 Forum Ware again. *Medieval Ceramics* 4: 13–16.

Whitehouse, D., L. Constantini, F. Guirobaldi, S. Passi, P. Pensabene, S. Pratt, R. Reece and D. Reece 1985 The Schola Praeconum II. *Papers of the British School at Rome* 40: 163–210.

Whitehouse, D., C. McClendon and P. Donaldson 1979 Farfa: nota preliminare. *Archeologia Medievale* 6: 270–3.

1981 Farfa. Seconda nota preliminare. *Archeologia Medievale* 8: 566–8.

Whitehouse, D. and T. Potter 1981 The Byzantine frontier in South Etruria. *Antiquity* 55: 206–10.

Wickham, C. 1981 *Early Medieval Italy: Central Power and Local Society 400–1000*. London: Macmillan.

1984 The other transition: from late Antiquity to feudalism. *Past and Present* 103: 1–25.

1985a *Il problema dell'incastellamento nell'Italia centrale: l'esempio di San Vincenzo al Volturno*. Florence: Al Giglio.

1985b Pastoralism and underdevelopment in the early middle ages. *Settimane di Studio* 31: 401–55.

1986 Land disputes and their social framework in Lombard-Carolingian Italy, in W. Davies and P. Fouracre, eds., *The Settlement of Disputes in Early Medieval Europe*, pp. 105–25. Cambridge: Cambridge University Press.

1988 *The Mountains and the City*. Oxford: Oxford University Press.

1990 Monastic lands and monastic patrons, in R. Hodges, ed., *Excavations and Survey at San Vincenzo al Volturno 1980–1986*. London: British School at Rome.

Wolf, E. 1982 *Europe and the People Without History*. Berkeley: University of California Press.

Zucchetti, G. 1927 Il 'Liber Largitorius' del notaris monasterii Pharphensis. *Bullettio dell'Instituto Storico Italiano* 44: 1–258.

PART III
OVERVIEW AND PROSPECTS

9 *Annales* and archaeology

RICHARD W. BULLIET

The potential significance of the *Annales* school of history for archaeologists depends upon what is understood by "the *Annales* school of history." As the relentless accumulation of human knowledge and the passage of time have conspired to break the totality of human understanding into discrete disciplines, subdisciplines, and specializations, so-called "interdisciplinary" adventures have become challenging, and sometimes seem heroic. The risk for appropriators of ideas and approaches originating in disciplines other than their own is that they will not properly understand them, or may wilfully misunderstand them, and thus will misapply them in a way that exposes the appropriators to criticism or ridicule. Social Darwinism is an apt example of such misapplied interdisciplinary appropriation. Yet how deeply must a scholar be steeped in the donor discipline to minimize the risk of such criticism? And, more to the point, if the conceptual borrowing proves of value for the receiving discipline, does this value outweigh the possible defect of the idea not being accurately and fully understood?

In consideration of these possible concerns, several propositions can be put forward regarding the papers contained in this book and their implications for archaeology:

First, the authors of the papers do not all understand the *Annales* school in the same way. Consequently, they apply significantly different insights deriving from their differing understandings.

Second, the *Annales* school itself does not have sufficient coherence and self-understanding to make appropriating ideas from it an easy or straightforward task.

Third, there is ultimately nothing in the *Annales*

school that can take archaeologists much farther intellectually than they have already gone.

And finally, like the fabled bumblebee that defied the predictions of the aeronautical engineer that its wing area would be insufficient to bear it aloft, this effort at interdisciplinary cross-fertilization flies, and buzzes, and makes honey.

The first of these propositions will be self-evident to anyone reading the individual contributions in this book. For Roland Fletcher and Michael E. Smith the *Annales* school is epitomized by the work of Fernand Braudel, and in particular by Braudel's elaboration of a scheme of temporal hierarchies. But other authors – e.g., Knapp, Moreland, and Bulliet – pay little or no attention to Braudel or to temporal hierarchies. Moreover, several of the most prominent exemplars of the *Annales* school, such as Marc Bloch, Lucien Febvre, and Georges Duby, are referred to only infrequently.

This lack of convergence in understanding the *Annales* school is, of course, exactly what one should expect in interdisciplinary foraging. Scholars looking to the discipline of physics for intellectual insight, for example, might well find something stimulating in the notion of critical mass, or in Heisenberg's uncertainty principle, or in the phenomenon of phase changes in elements going from gases to liquids to solids without feeling an obligation to reconstruct, or even to understand, the history of molecular and atomic theory. If one scholar adapts one of these ideas to one purpose in his own discipline, and another adapts another to a different purpose, neither is normally expected to set their adaptation within the context of the other's appropriation from the field of physics. Yet if someone were to undertake an analysis of the totality of such borrowings, he or she might well find lapses and discontinuities in the understanding of what the particular borrowed ideas meant, and how they evolved, within the context of physics.

If the disciplines are sufficiently remote from one another, as are history and physics, for example, one can ward off the charge of inadequate understanding and irresponsible appropriation by making it clear that the physical theory or phenomenon is being used only analogically or metaphorically. When the disciplines are close, however, as history is to archaeology, this is more difficult to sustain. When archaeologists reflect upon Braudel's scheme of temporal hierarchies consisting of events, *conjonctures*, and the *longue durée*, it is difficult to look upon it as a stimulating analogy to some rather different scheme in archaeology. It seems more appropriate to examine Braudel's ideas in detail because they actually can address archaeological data; yet, at the same time, they offer no insight for understanding change over time spans longer than a few centuries, which are precisely the time spans many archaeologists have to consider. Thus, an archaeologist concerned with understanding an array of artifacts from a single stratum of a site, or from several strata spread over a few centuries, might find Braudel's view instructive; while another archaeologist concerned with several thousand years of primate evolution might find them useless.

Would it be better, therefore, for archaeologists to study carefully the development and complexity of the *Annales* school and then determine whether, in its total approach, it can be *used*, and not just borrowed from in an occasional manner? This might be so if the *Annales* school presented a coherent, unified, and theoretically conceptualized body of thought about human society over time. But our second proposition maintains that the *Annales* school does not, in fact, have these properties.

Annales: Economies, Sociétés, Civilisations is a French historical journal. As such, its typical offering over the past seven decades has been the article. More than a thousand articles have appeared embodying a myriad of ideas, techniques, and speculations. While there has been an overall concern with social and economic history and a general eschewal of political and biographical narrative, perhaps the main characteristic of the contributors to *Annales* has been their quest for alternatives to what they have seen as traditional ways of writing history. Thus one author will concern himself with the possible historical implications of the geographical distribution of blood types in the Pyrenees, while another investigates the diet of eighteenth-century French boarding schools, and a third studies birth control in the early Byzantine empire. What draws the authors together is less a shared method or the exploration of a common theory than the desire to pose new historiographical problems and attack them in new and different ways.

To be sure, many *Annales* historians have also written books in which they have developed and systematized insights and techniques they first explored in article form. But the journal has continued to be the home of articles, and efforts to introduce the *Annales* approach to historians outside France have several times taken the form of publishing collections of articles intended to typify its contents.

The first volume of a series of selections from *Annales* in English edited by Robert Forster and Orest Ranum opens by characterizing the *Annales* approach for the benefit of American readers who in 1975 were still generally unfamiliar with the journal:

> The intellectual aims of the *Annales* from their beginning about fifty years ago have been threefold: (1) a comparative and interdisciplinary approach to history that attempts to "mine" the social sciences in order to fashion a "social history" in the widest sense of the term, (2) an effort to embrace the whole of human activity in a given society (*histoire totale*), and (3) a conscious rejection of narrative history and classical biography in favor of problem-oriented history. The editors of the *Annales* never tire of such phrases as "social structure" – a static slice of society from top to bottom – and the "*longue durée*" – the long-run development of one hundred to two hundred years. The "event" is held in disrepute. (Forster and Ranum 1975: vii)

This statement can be compared with one by noted Annaliste Emmanuel Le Roy Ladurie in his essay "History that stands still": "For half a century, from Marc Bloch to Pierre Goubert, the best of French historians, systematically systematizing away, have in fact been structuralists. Sometimes they realized it themselves; sometimes they did not; all too often nobody else realized it at all" (Le Roy Ladurie 1981: 5).

"Structure" is obviously the key to harmonizing these two summary views. The *Annales* approach does indeed involve historians relating data to social and temporal structures rather than to narratives. The more tell-tale parts of these quotations, however, are Ladurie's observation that the *Annales* historians were only occasionally self-aware in adopting this approach, and Forster and Ranum's observation that the *Annales* historians "mined" the other social science disciplines for ideas.

Lack of self-awareness is important because many historians wrote what they considered to be good history and found a home for their work in the pages of *Annales* without ever feeling that they were participating in the creation of a school or following the dictates of a school. To give a personal example, I once wrote an article on the reasons for the disappearance of wheeled vehicles in the late ancient Middle East (Bulliet 1969). A friend suggested that *Annales*, a journal I had at that time never heard of, might be interested in publishing that sort of thing. They did publish it, and eventually the editors of *Annales* selected it for inclusion in a book entitled *Social Historians in Contemporary France: Essays from* Annales (1972). This book was meant to familiarize American historians with what the *Annales* approach signified. Therefore the articles it contained should certainly be considered exemplary of that approach.

The import of this story is that the desire to move away from narrative history, to do something different, to utilize data in different ways, and to call upon interesting ideas from other disciplines has struck many historians in many different countries during recent decades. For some, *Annales* has afforded a publishing opportunity, for others, perhaps, it has suggested possibilities. But for many historians it has seemed less to provide a specific formula to follow than an opportunity to gain a hearing for new and adventurous ideas.

As Forster and Ranum point out, dozens of ideas from other social sciences have found their way into the articles included in *Annales*, and the interdisciplinary borrowing is not limited to the social sciences. Contributors have typically posed problems for themselves, often problems of making use of awkward data, and attempted to solve them by whatever techniques they could borrow or invent. Among these borrowings, of course, have been archaeological data and ideas of all sorts.

In trying to understand the *Annales* school, therefore, the key ingredients are not so much specific ideas or structures as innovative techniques, orientation toward solving problems, experimentation with intractable and non-traditional historical data, and great diversity in seeing that the human past may be reconstructed in myriad ways. Unlike the term "narrative history," non-narrative history cannot be easily defined. Within it there may be other definable approaches, such as psycho-history or quantitative history, but Annaliste history is not one. The word "structuralist" can be applied, but all it really means is that *Annales* historians imaginatively put data together to see whether the way they fit tells them something interesting about the past. What the data are and how to fit them together and analyze them are questions that scores of historians have answered differently in the pages of *Annales*.

This, then, brings us to our third proposition, namely, that the *Annales* approach is not likely to take the field of archaeology much farther than it has already gone. This is the viewpoint of a historian, of course, but a historian who has read a good many archaeological works and learned much from them. For me and for other historians who have published in *Annales*, archaeology has been a source of ideas and methods. Just as an archaeologist, or other social scientist, might look at the *Annales* approach to history and see in it stimulating concepts, historians can see the same thing in archaeology. The disputes among archaeologists over where their profession is going are of no more import to the historian looking for something stimulating than are the quarrels of historians over the proper evaluation of the "event."

History is a very old profession, archaeology a young one. However, both have undergone similar tests during the past two centuries: the test of scientific method, the test of relativism, the test of racism, the test of elitism, the test of subdisciplinary fragmentation. Each discipline has progressed through these challenges in its own way, sloughing off benighted ideas and approaches and fighting over the proper value and interconnection of newer and more sophisticated ones. Archaeologists' responses to a Binford or a Renfrew differ from historians' responses to a Pirenne or a Braudel because the evolution of cognate debates in the two disciplines is inherently different.

Wherever archaeology is, it got there without help from the historical profession; and wherever it may be going, it will get there without the *Annales* school. Interdisciplinary borrowing is like a blood transfusion. It may give vital sustenance temporarily, but the receiver cannot depend on the donor in the long run. It must manufacture from its own substance its own source of vitality. Though it may initially utilize the donated material in doing this, survival depends entirely upon the inherent capacity of the receiver to grow and prosper.

These sentiments may be self-evident, but they are germane to any proper appreciation of a book of this sort. They also lead to our final proposition, namely, and without the apian metaphor, that this has been an intellectually profitable undertaking. No attempt is made in these papers to force a harmony of ideas or adopt an evangelical attitude. Some papers concentrate on specific cases which the authors feel exemplify how some aspect of the *Annales* approach can help make sense of archaeological data. Other authors put the emphasis more on structure than on content but specify the particular structure that interests them without trying to reduce the *Annales* approach to that single set of ideas.

It is also noteworthy that this book has taken the form of a collection of articles containing examples of applications rather than a discourse by a single author on a putatively convergent development of archaeology and the *Annales* school. Practically trying out new ideas in articles has been the hallmark of *Annales: Economies, Sociétés, Civilisations* during decades when many historians have grown more accustomed to talking about the writing of history than actually doing it.

Above all, however, the value of this collection is its demonstration of the willingness of archaeologists to look outside their discipline. The *Annales* school has persistently courted such interdisciplinary connections without becoming wedded to any one of them in particular. The results have unquestionably enlivened the historical profession even when the liveliness has taken the form of defensive polemic. However much Historian A may quarrel with Historian B over the propriety of some gleaning from another discipline, the ultimate benefit for the profession lies in other historians reading A's and B's works and gaining a sense that there is energy and excitement there, and interesting work to be done, in a way that might have escaped them if there had been no debate to sharpen the issues.

As a historian, I certainly cannot predict what impact the *Annales* school may have on archaeology. Nor can I read the articles in this collection in the way another archaeologist might read them. But they represent several different and challenging visions of interdisciplinary experimentation, and that can only be viewed as a sign of vigor in the archaeological profession and a harbinger of future debate and growth.

References

Annales (editors of) 1972 *Social Historians in Contemporary France: Essays from* Annales. New York: Harper and Row.

Bulliet, R. W. 1969 Le chameau et la roue au Moyen-Orient. *Annales: Economies, Sociétés, Civilisations* 24: 1092–1103.

Forster, R. and O. Ranum 1975 *Biology of Man in History: Selections from the* Annales: Economies, Sociétés, Civilisations. Baltimore: John Hopkins University Press.

Le Roy Ladurie, E. 1981 *The Mind and Method of the Historian* (translated by Siân and Ben Reynolds). Chicago: University of Chicago Press.

10 What can archaeologists learn from Annalistes?

ANDREW SHERRATT

Since archaeologists and historians have a common interest in the human past, their continuing capacity to ignore each other's existence is rather surprising. To some extent this is because each lives up to the other's caricature: one apparently obsessed with the trivial detail of pottery classification, the other with the equally trivial (but more readable) details of personal lives. To the extent that this is true, New Archaeology was the great breakout from the first stereotype; Braudelian history from the second. Archaeologists, typically, took fifteen years longer.

Of course there had been many earlier works both of history and archaeology which far transcended these stereotypes; but from the point of view of the sociology of knowledge there is a striking similarity in the common rhythm which underlay the post-war development of innovative work in both disciplines. What both Binfordians and Braudelians had in common was a powerful, self-conscious determination to be seen as the dominant school of interpretation within their own disciplines, which ultimately led to their successful capture of a secure academic territory with its publications, pupils, and imitators. Both saw themselves as leading a major theoretical reorientation with more relevance to post-war society, replacing a redundant generation of scholars concerned simply with the collection of disconnected facts. Both expressed an impatience with narrative, and espoused a broadly ecological and demographic standpoint, subsuming individuals within broader social forces, and trying to quantify whatever was capable of being measured (while tending to ignore what could not). Both reacted from "kings and battles" or "tombs and temples" towards the study of the common man and his means of subsistence and livelihood – *les structures du quotidien.*

These resemblances are striking, but there they end. Although dealing with similar subject matter, their styles were entirely different. Had the two movements resembled each other more closely, they would surely have discovered each other in less than the four decades which have now elapsed since Braudel's programmatic inaugural address to the Collège de France in 1950 (English version in Braudel 1980). The difference lay less in their choice of themes than in their treatment of them. Eric Higgs' students did indeed discover Le Roy Ladurie, and his descriptions both of climatic influences on agriculture, transhumant pastoralism, and long-term cycles of demographic change; but generally there was too high a ratio of facts to theory for New Archaeologists[1] to cope with. For whereas archaeologists sought ever more abstract models, by analogy with (their perception of) their scientific peer group, Annaliste historians reveled in facts: more facts than had ever been treated as history before. Such new historiography reached its apogee with the 6 cm (paperback) of shelf-space taken up by Braudel's *Mediterranean*, or the 12 cm (paperback again) taken up by his *Civilization and Capitalism*, dazzlingly synthesizing a vast panorama of evidence. This was scholarship, with a professional breadth and depth that made most archaeologists seem like amateurs, or at least like specialist craftsmen skilled only in a single medium. Archaeologists by and large preferred the abstract to the concrete, and reserved their detailed efforts for statistical manipulation of their more recalcitrant numerical data, whose interpretation was more problematic than that provided by the written word or the pictorial image. When, eventually, archaeologists looked to Paris, it was to the abstractions of structuralist anthropology rather than to the thick description of Annaliste historians.

The history of a difference

These different attitudes to rather similar sorts of new information reflect the differing origins and trajectories of archaeological and historical studies (see also Knapp, Introduction, this volume). History has an established position in academia: children learn it at school, and (along with theology and law) it has a respectable ancestry in the universities. There it typically has an established place in the academic pecking-order, and it has traditionally been a training ground for politicians and administrators. While this has inevitably directed its researches to subjects concerned with the legitimacy of the state and established interest groups, its very size has allowed it to explore other themes, however marginally. Archaeology, by contrast, has had a less secure place: it has grown by the diversification of history or classics; or, somewhat later, from geography and anthropology. Often it has had a base in museum collections before being recognized as a university subject. Few undergraduates in the pre-war world studied archaeology as a major component of a first degree, and the mass production of archaeology students has been a post-war phenomenon (i.e., post-1945). Archaeology, especially in the United States, carved out its territory from anthropology. Its assertiveness was a feature of its relatively small size and rapid growth. Imaginative historians, by contrast, had both a larger field within which to grow and an already established tradition within which to work.

When archaeologists talk of an Annaliste paradigm, it is usually Braudel and his pupils whom they have in mind. Yet this was already the second phase of the *Annales* tradition, following the "dazzling early period" (Braudel's phrase) of Bloch and Febvre which established the base that was built on by Braudel. Febvre brought an interest in landscape history, Bloch a concern for agrarian economic and social structures. The post-war phase of the Annaliste tradition thus grew more organically from its predecessors than did the similarly ecologically minded New Archaeology, which had the more self-conscious character of a revelation. French history was thus "pre-adapted" to the intellectual temper of post-war concerns, having a holistic tradition of anthropogeography (itself partly the result of a disappearing French rural lifestyle) which had no direct counterpart in history, even in Britain (Lewthwaite 1988).

While there were some comparable echoes of Febvre's interests in Britain,[2] they were dispersed among several disciplines: geography itself, historical geography (which was a fairly marginal activity), and classical studies (notably J. L. Myres). It was perhaps the strength of British social anthropology, with its "colonial" subject matter (especially in Africa and Melanesia) which robbed a geographical and ethnographic approach to European rural societies of much of its vitality. The main interest in Bloch came from economic historians (like M. M. Postan) or from Marxists. In both cases the complementary dimension of Febvre had less appeal: they were concerned principally with agrarian productivity and the social structures within which it was exploited. Braudel, therefore, had a uniquely powerful and sympathetic audience among French historians to which to address his program; he could stress continuity with an already established (if minority) tradition, rather than adopting the New Archaeologists' stance of rupture with an uncomprehending orthodoxy.

Confronting traditions

This to some extent explains the different styles and approaches of otherwise similar post-war developments in archaeology and history (cf. Ricoeur 1980). Both movements looked to new, and rather similar, areas of subject matter, but in quite different ways. One looked to science for an appropriate methodology, the other continued its emphasis on description and humanistic insight. One went self-consciously for "theory," the other for experience. This explains some of the ambivalence felt by archaeologists about Annalistes.

Anglo-Saxon archaeologists are puzzled by a school with a paradigm but no explicit models, since this is the form in which they typically incorporate other disciplines: they expect to be able to load their own data and run an imported program on them; but in this case there is no such program. Annalistes generally do not talk of models – and when they do, they mean something different from archaeologists. Thus Braudel's "model of the Mediterranean economy" (1972: 418–60) was an exercise in accountancy rather than writing equations or identifying feedback loops. In so far as the Braudelian version of Annalisme has a theory, it is a theory written for it from North America: from the Braudel Institute at the State University of New York at Binghamton, Immanuel Wallerstein's multi-volume work *The Modern World-System* in effect systematizes Braudel's larger insights on the global economy. The rapid archaeological reaction to Wallerstein, in contrast to the slow recognition of Braudel, is symptomatic: archaeologists, recognizing it as the kind of model they are used to, have seized upon it eagerly and applied it to situations around the world; but Braudel himself, while commending it and using its terminology, nevertheless had his reservations – precisely because it is expressed as a model ("a *little too systematic*, perhaps, but ... extremely stimulating": Braudel 1984: 70, emphasis added).

Even the famous structure/conjuncture/event distinction is hardly a consciously constructed model, for it is in essence no more than the autobiography of Braudel's doctoral thesis (begun in 1923 and defended in 1947 at the Sorbonne), as it grew from a conventional study of the diplomacy of Philip II to encompass successively both social history and human and even physical geography. The three levels of analysis are the strata of this accretion, and represent the three divisions of the thesis – canonized in its publication in 1949 as the paradigmatic work of the school. Its very name, *The Mediterranean in the Age of Philip II*, suggests a somewhat incongruous juxtaposition of incommensurate entities, resulting from its author's shift of emphasis and perspective. Certainly there is no closely argued etiological analysis: just a convenient division for the purposes of exposition, much as J. L. Myres twenty years earlier had written successive chapters of *The Cambridge Ancient History* (1923) on geology, prehistory, and Greek civilization.

In consequence of this lack of explicit theorizing, there has been no agonized reappraisal of the relationship between structure and agency, which has characterized the change from new (processual) to post-processual archaeology. Individual members of the school (best exemplified by Le Roy Ladurie) have moved painlessly[3] from writing about demographic cycles to doing fine-grained ethnography from historical sources – and each genre has produced its best-seller (Le Roy Ladurie 1974; 1980). Thus the same historian who appealed to the Higgsians can now appeal to the Hodderites. Instead of writing prescriptions of how to do it, Annalistes just get on with it – osmotically absorbing the influences of their immediate Parisian environment (which incidentally has included, in alphabetical order, Althusser, Baudrillard, Bourdieu, Foucault, Godelier, Gourou, Lacan, Lévi-Strauss, Meillassoux ...). While their English counterparts have been closely identified with Marxism (Hobsbawm, Hilton, Hill: see Himmelfarb 1987), these French historians have tended to leave such ideological disputes to the anthropologists. *Bella gerant alii*: let others wage wars; Annaliste historians simply metamorphose.

Critique

This stance has its drawbacks. Neither archaeologists nor historians can find the Annaliste approach (and Braudel's in particular) entirely satisfactory. Historians typically admire the breadth of scholarship, and the widened horizons that it brought, but find something lacking (e.g., Hufton 1986). Human agency has simply been lost sight of, both in the geological perspective of Braudel[4] and even in the miniature studies of peasant communities of Le Roy Ladurie – situated as they were within larger political entities and centers of power. The human beings are there, but the most powerful actors – the politicians – are largely missing. The picture has been filled out, but the central problems remain. This is even more acute for the prehistorian, since it is the emergence of these very centers of political power which demand his or her attention – and there is no "traditional" framework to fall back on to supply a conventional structure which can be taken for granted in looking at patterns of everyday life.

While I have already suggested that the most quoted Braudelian concept – the three-tiered "wedding-cake mode of analysis" (Stone 1985) – is symptomatic of the *Annales mentalité* rather than acting as a prescriptive methodology, its simple equations and lack of articulation are nevertheless expressive of its attitude, and may be criticized as both constricting and outdated. It smacks too much of environmental determinism and vulgar materialism to stand up to prolonged critical scrutiny. Archaeologists do not need to be encouraged to believe that ideology, religion, and politics are superstructural and idiosyncratic, or that the way forward lies in a positivist belief in quantification. We have painfully outgrown such attitudes, and have no need to import them afresh.

Nor is the content of the famous Braudelian tripartite division conveniently ready for archaeological use: the celebrated *longue durée* turns out in practice to be only 300 years long, and the fifteenth-century starting point of Braudel's world picture is never treated as the culmination of a human story, which from an archaeological point of view really begins about 4000 BC, or even with the beginnings of the Neolithic. Equally important (and part of the same set of attitudes) is the firmly Eurocentric focus of French historiography, even when writ large by Braudel: the Ancient World and the Orient are alike consigned to the realm of unchanging, cyclical activity beyond the rhythms of world time: "There are always some areas world history does not reach, zones of silence and undisturbed ignorance" (Braudel 1984: 18). This (mis)reading of the world pattern (cf. Wolf 1982) has been absorbed and built into Wallerstein's *Modern World System*, as Jane Schneider (1977) elegantly pointed out – which is why such a pattern seems at many points to contradict the archaeologist's view of a dynamic past long before the fifteenth century.

Interestingly, the one Annaliste historian whose perceptions came closest to this archaeological view is the one who is never referred to in these discussions: the orientalist, Maurice Lombard, who was a close contemporary of Braudel. His three volumes entitled *Etudes d'économie médiévale*, concerned successively with coinage, the trade in metals and metalwork, and textiles in the Arab world, deal with a vast area of Eurasia in the fifth to twelfth centuries AD, with some comparative analysis of earlier periods in the first volume (Lombard 1971; 1974; 1978). Although never translated into English, they are among the most stimulating volumes I have ever encountered.[5] All are distinguished by their vast scholarship (much of it from Arabic sources), a due attention to archaeological data, and especially by a breathtaking (I use the word advisedly) use of maps. The foldouts at the end of his volume on metalwork (1974) show the kind of reconstructed trade routes that archaeologists dream of; and the area encompassed reaches from the Atlantic to the Pacific. Lombard thus breaches the two major constraints, in time (before 1500) and space (the Arab world, as well as Europe), which have restricted the classic Annaliste area of analysis.[6] By focusing on Islamic trade, Lombard broke the Eurocentric stereotype which regarded the "rise of the West" as synonymous with the course of European history, to which the Arabs were an irrelevant interruption; and in so doing, he turned the Pirenne thesis on its head (Le Goff 1988: 54–5).

Yet Lombard is largely ignored, not only by archaeologists for whom his work ought to be crucial (Hodges 1982; Hodges and Whitehouse 1983) but also by historical critics and commentators on the Annaliste tradition. This can only be because of the dominance of European and agrarian interests in the *Annales* school and in French and European history more generally. One factor which has reinforced this commitment is the role of history in creating a sense of identity among French intellectuals, many of whom were of Jewish origin, in the long aftermath of the *affaire Dreyfus* (Bernal 1987: 367). It is noteworthy how many of the leading figures in the French social sciences (notably, of course, in the development of Marxist thought) come from this background,[7] from Durkheim onwards. Anthropology has been a notable beneficiary: both Mauss and Lévi-Strauss came of rabbinical parentage (Wolf 1987: 115). In history, this phenomenon is best exemplified in the work of Marc Bloch himself (Fink 1989). Was it, perhaps, his desire to demonstrate "patriotism without nationalism"[8] that provided the motivation for works such as *Les Caractères originaux de l'histoire rurale française* (1931: English translation 1966)? Braudel's last work, too, was *L'Identité de la France* (1986: English translation 1988). The *Annales* school has a strand of Romantic attachment which is alien to the Enlightenment sympathies of cultural materialism and the New Archaeology.

Finally, and of particular relevance here, is the question of why *French* archaeology and Annalisme have largely ignored each other's existence. It is quite remarkable how few illustrations Braudel takes from archaeology. His books are adorned with plentiful representations (paintings, prints, carvings) but no actual examples of the tools or field systems he discusses, and only one photograph (1981: 277) of a rather bare excavation of a medieval house. The fault lies partly with archaeology: medieval archaeology – by contrast with the study of the Paleolithic – was slow to develop in the pre-war period, and often did so in the hands of amateurs (Flon 1985: 116); the main advances were made in north-west Europe (north Germany, the Netherlands, Scandinavia, Britain). French archaeologists have generally found more excitement and inspiration in the abstractions of structuralism (e.g., Leroi-Gourhan 1964–5) than in the documentary wealth of conventional (even Annaliste) history. Many, too, had no interest beyond trenches and pots (Courbin 1988). Yet if *Civilization and Capitalism* were to be written today, it would have to incorporate a huge amount of archaeological data, of the kind that accumulates each year in the pages of *Archéologie médiévale* and a whole row of other lively European journals which exemplify and test the ideas of Braudel, Duby, and others. Exemplify, test, and indeed transform: for the physical structures recovered by archaeology are not merely a reflection of the historical process but a significant component of it (see Moreland, this volume). Culture is not just the idiosyncratic residue left behind in the analysis of social structure, but a powerful motivation and constraint of human action (Appadurai 1986).

The lessons for archaeology

So what *can* archaeologists learn from the Annalistes? Certainly, their phraseology is catching: their intuitive grasp of what is going on is reflected in the way in which I have already had occasion to refer to their collective *mentalité*, and to describe their recent history in terms of the post-war cycle of economic and academic growth. Is there, then, some systematic way in which their insights can be taken into archaeology?

In the first place, we can widen our expectations: not all serious students of the past, dealing with phenomena very similar to our own daily concerns, go about it in the same way. A constant *Methodenstreit* is not necessarily the normal condition of a human science. The free competition of major studies exemplifying current ideas may be a better way of organizing the growth of knowledge than centrally planned research designs based on elaborate theoretical prescriptions. Despite the deficiencies which can be attributed to the Annalistes, they have continuously produced major works of scholarship which are both important and readable. Indeed, they have consistently produced books which have been best-sellers in an educated popular market. This is not an incidental characteristic, for it reflects the way in which the facts they have collected are interesting in themselves, rather than being passive data to be manipulated by a clinical investigator. Fact and theory do not appear as antitheses, to be constantly confronted in controlled situations; there is an organic relationship between them, which makes the difference hard to specify.

This is why archaeologists have such difficulty in finding easy formulae to adapt to their own ends. It is a different mode of apprehension, not dependent on constantly fulfilling a predetermined methodological plan: it is the work of poets, not grammarians, and that is why it reads so well. This quality can only be described as historical imagination, which succeeds because it is grounded in a broadly based understanding of the conditions of the time, and has a factual as much as a theoretical coherence. Added to such an achievement, theoretical criticism has a purpose; without it, the enterprise never leaves the drawing-board.

Secondly, it is worth reading because it is worth reading: just as anthropologists are brought up on the classics of ethnographic fieldwork, so students of the past can benefit from the richness of European ethnography revealed in Annaliste writing. Because of the dominance of conventional history, the study of European peasant societies has often been marginalized as "folklife," and relegated to museums of dead industries and bygone rural life. It has taken a transatlantic interest, for instance from John Cole and Eric Wolf studying ecology and ethnicity in an Alpine valley (1973), or Jane and Peter Schneider studying culture and political economy in western Sicily (1976), to bring such studies back into the main stream.

This is an area being simultaneously colonized from two sides: history and anthropology converge in practice, even when their theoreticians are still discussing the blueprints. The results are exemplified in publications such as the Studies in Social Discontinuity series of Academic Press or the *Editions de la Maison des Sciences de l'Homme* published in co-edition with Cambridge University Press. Archaeology fits naturally into such an enterprise, examining the microstructures of daily life from settlement excavations, as exemplified for instance by Linda Therkorn's sensitive interpretation (1987) of protohistoric houses from north Holland, with their cattle symbolism, building orientations, house-offerings and foundation deposits. These provide a point of contact both with the anthropology of Bourdieu, the fine-grained historical ethnography of recent Annalistes, and the hitherto despised insights of folklore and rural geography; and archaeology provides a dimension of evidence that could be recovered in no other way.

Thirdly it (and especially the example of Lombard and Braudel) offers an encouragement to work on a large scale, placing these individual bundles of information in a wider spatio-temporal framework. Braudel and V. G. Childe share the same sweep (A. G. Sherratt 1990), comprehending the variety of the world in AD 1500 or 1500 BC without reducing it to the court intrigues of Philip II or Tuthmosis III: though the world would have been different without either of them. As Knapp describes (this volume), the Late Bronze Age archaeology of the Levant is a dialectic between local developments and influences and interventions from Egypt – a microcosm of the kinds of situation which were occurring all across the world by AD 1500 (Wolf 1982). Such interactions form a continuing story in the Old World from the Bronze Age onwards, and have to be appreciated both from the political context of the literate (and necessarily propagandist) centers of power (Larsen 1979) and from the active responses and independent interests of the indigenous peoples on whom they impinged.

Areas affected by these processes, but still essentially prehistoric, suffer from a kind of archaeological schizophrenia: for instance the later prehistoric Levant and the Aegean swing between the paradigms of "traditional history" and "prehistory," affecting not only their interpretative models but their whole methodology (E. S. Sherratt 1990). Can pottery-based chronologies achieve the resolution required to deal with "events" in "real time," or only a statistical conflation of typical occurrences within the span of several lifetimes? The idea of "process" which is needed to describe the latter differs, on the one hand, from the universal processes of the neo-evolutionists, and on the other from the event-based narratives of conventional historiography (which still tend to dominate ancient history). The Braudelian scale of analysis offers an appropriate approach to these problems: although "The Mediterranean in the Age of Tuthmosis III" remains to be written, Nancy Sandars' book *The Sea Peoples* (1978) offers a good example of the necessary mixing of ancient history and prehistoric archaeology, while the *Annales*-based work of Italian scholars such as Mario Liverani (e.g., 1987) provides a complementary discussion of the social dynamic behind the kinds of events recorded in the texts. While Braudel may be unsophisticated from the point of view of the fact-saturated modern historian or the philosophical subtleties of metahistory, his example may still inspire those with bigger and cruder problems – which are typical of much larger areas of the past. The chapters by Smith and Duke (this volume) show how this is as true of the New World as of the Old.

Fourthly, Annaliste historians have explored large themes as well as large situations; and these cut across the divisions between archaeological and textual or iconic evidence. The study of wheeled vehicles is a case in point. Richard Bulliet's *Annales* paper of 1969 (Bulliet, this volume) grew to a monograph – which he was too modest to mention – called *The Camel and the Wheel* (1975). This, too, I count among the stimulating works of recent historiography which have informed my own work (e.g., Sherratt 1981: 275). Its thesis, in brief, was that wheeled vehicles all but disappeared over large areas of the Near East after the Arab conquests, as wheel-going cities became dominated by camel-riding elites from what had previously been the interstices of the settled landscape – a world turned inside out. Not only is this description of the historical situation highly suggestive for the interpretation of earlier episodes (the eruption of the Aramaeans in the Levant at the end of the Bronze Age as described by Liverani [1987: 69–70], for instance), but it situates technological change within social conceptions of ethnicity and ideology: "appropriate behavior" within a particular socio-political context.

It is interesting that precisely the same change occurred in relation to wine-drinking, which, like the use of the wheel, had been part of Near Eastern urban civilization from the beginning. The proscription of alcohol by Muhammad (and its replacement by cannabis) parallels the replacement of the wheel by the camel in the new ideology of Islam. This symbolic dimension to the use of wheeled vehicles (as of drinking) is well brought out by Stuart Piggott's study (1983) of carts and chariots from prehistoric Europe, from purely archaeological evidence; and it parallels recent studies of other areas of material culture such as cloth and clothing (Weiner and Schneider 1989; Barber 1991) or metallurgy (Herbert 1984; Lechtman 1984).

Finally, the rich metaphorical content of Braudel's writing evidently evokes imaginative responses and applications, as can be judged by several chapters in this volume (notably those of Fletcher and Smith, as well as the editor). This may be more a matter of reception theory than textual criticism, for the meanings which they find in Braudel's phrases and ideas (or in those of Annalistes generally) are generated as much by the archaeological contexts in which they are applied as by the original intentions of their author. But what greater tribute could be offered to a writer than to propagate and diversify his chains of meaning, while adapting them to new ends which he could never have envisaged? Archaeology will have come of age when historians arrange symposia and assemble essays on what historians can learn from archaeologists; when we, in turn, may be surprised at what they find of value in the things we do and write.

Notes

1 The phrase "New Archaeology" causes problems in characterizing the 'sixties generation in Britain. I include here the Cambridge palaeoeconomy school centered on Eric Higgs as a more typical British representative of what I describe than David Clarke.

2 It is interesting to note that the series in which Febvre's (1932) *Geographical Introduction to History* was published, "The History of Civilisation" edited by C. K. Ogden, contained two books by Gordon Childe (as well as works which he had translated), as well as by J. L. Myres. The French series on which it was based was called "L'Evolution de l'humanité."

3 Though not entirely unconsciously – witness the discussion of structure and agency in Le Roy Ladurie (1981), and also Duby and Le Goff in Le Goff and Nora (1985).

4 There is a strong evolutionist streak in Braudel, which emerges when he looks for signs of material progress and constantly assesses the standard of living as a calorie count, when the material he discusses could equally be seen as a socially constructed world; the assumptions and interests behind his approach are very much the world of New Archaeology.

5 There is also a path-breaking series of articles in *Annales* itself, dealing with subjects such as timber supply and ship construction in the seventh to the eleventh centuries (reprinted in Lombard 1972).

6 Bloch, of course, is pre-1500, as is Duby; but their focus is primarily agrarian.

7 Including archaeologists such as Salomon Reinach. This accounts for the difficulty which English speakers have in pronouncing what were originally German names with a French accent!

8 The description is by Le Goff, lecture in Oxford, April 1990.

References

Appadurai, A. 1986 Introduction: commodities and the politics of value, in A. Appadurai, ed., *The Social Life of Things*, pp. 3–63. Cambridge: Cambridge University Press.

Barber, E. 1990 *Prehistoric Textiles*. Princeton: Princeton University Press.

Bernal, M. 1987 *Black Athena: The Afroasiatic Roots of Classical Civilisation*. Volume 1, *The Fabrication of Ancient Greece 1785–1985*. London: Free Association Books.

Bloch, M. 1966 *French Rural History: An Essay on its Original Characteristics*. London: Routledge.

Braudel, F. 1972 *The Mediterranean in the age of Philip II*. London: Collins.

1980 *On History*. Chicago: University of Chicago Press.

1981 *The Structures of Everyday Life: The Limits of the Possible* (= *Civilization and Capitalism 15th–18th Century*, volume 1). London: Collins.

1982 *The Wheels of Commerce* (= *Civilization and Capitalism 15th–18th Century*, volume 2). London: Collins.

1984 *The Perspective of the World* (= *Civilization and Capitalism 15th–18th Century*, volume 3). London: Collins.

1988 *The Identity of France*. Volume 1, *History and Environment*. London: Collins.

Bulliet, R. W. 1975 *The Camel and the Wheel*. Cambridge, MA: Harvard University Press.

Cole, J. W. and E. Wolf 1973 *The Hidden Frontier: Ecology and Ethnicity in an Alpine Valley*. New York: Academic Press.

Courbin, P. 1988 *What is Archaeology? An Essay on the Nature of Archaeological Research*. Chicago: University of Chicago Press.

Febvre, L. 1932 *A Geographical Introduction to History*. London: Kegan Paul.

Fink, C. 1989 *Marc Bloch: A Life in History*. Cambridge: Cambridge University Press.

Flon, C. (ed.) 1985 *The World Atlas of Archaeology*. London: Mitchell Beazley.

Herbert, E. 1984 *Red Gold of Africa*. Madison: University of Wisconsin Press.

Himmelfarb, G. 1987 The "Group": British Marxist historians, in G. Himmelfarb, ed., *The New History and the Old: Critical Appraisals and Essays*, pp. 70–93. Cambridge, MA: Belknap Press.

Hodges, R. 1982 *Dark Age Economics*. London: Duckworth.

Hodges, R. and D. Whitehouse 1983 *Mohammed, Charlemagne and the Origins of Europe*. London: Duckworth.

Hufton, O. 1986 Fernand Braudel. *Past and Present* 112: 208–13.

Larsen, M. T. 1979 *Power and Propaganda*. Copenhagen: Akademisk Verlag.

Le Goff, J. 1988 *Medieval Civilisation 400–1500*. Oxford: Blackwell.

Le Goff, J. and P. Nora 1985 *Constructing the Past*. Cambridge: Cambridge University Press.

Le Roy Ladurie, E. 1974 *The Peasants of Languedoc*. Urbana: University of Illinois Press.

1980 *Montaillou: Cathars and Catholics in a French Village 1294–1324*. Harmondsworth: Penguin.

1981 *The Mind and Method of the Historian*. Hassocks: Harvester Press.

Lechtman, H. 1984 Andean value systems and the development of prehistoric metallurgy. *Technology and Culture* 25: 1–36.

Leroi-Gourhan, A. 1964–5 *Le Geste et la Parole* (2 vols.). Paris: Albin Michel.

Lewthwaite, J. 1988 Trial by durée: the application of historical-geographical concepts to the archaeology of settlement on Corsica and Sardinia, in J. L. Bintliff, D. Davidson, and A. Grant, eds., *Conceptual Issues in Environmental Archaeology*, pp. 161–86. Edinburgh: Edinburgh University Press.

Liverani, M. 1987 The collapse of the Near Eastern regional system at the end of the Bronze Age: the case of Syria, in M. Rowlands, M. Larsen, and K. Kristiansen, eds., *Centre and Periphery in the Ancient World*, pp. 66–73. Cambridge: Cambridge University Press.

Lombard, M. 1971 *Monnaie et histoire d'Alexandre à Mahomet* (= *Etudes d'economie médiévale*, volume 1). Civilisations et sociétés 26. Paris: Mouton.

1972 *Espaces et réseaux du haut moyen-âge*. Paris: Mouton.

1974 *Les Métaux dans l'ancien monde du Vè au XIè siècle* (= *Etudes d'economie médiévale*, volume 2). Civilisations et sociétés 38. Paris: Mouton.

1978 *Les Textiles dans le monde musulman du VIIè au XIIè siècle* (= *Etudes d'economie médiévale*, volume 3). Civilisations et sociétés 61. Paris: Mouton.

Myres, J. L. 1923 Primitive Man in geological time; Neolithic and Bronze Age cultures, in J. B. Bury, S. A. Cook, and F. E. Adcock, eds., *The Cambridge Ancient History*. Volume 1, *Egypt and Babylonia to 1580 BC* (first edition), pp. 1–54, 57–110. Cambridge: Cambridge University Press.

Piggott, S. 1983 *The First Wheeled Transport. From the Atlantic Coast to the Caspian Sea*. London: Thames and Hudson.

Ricoeur, P. 1980 *The Contribution of French Historiography to the Theory of History* (Zaharoff Lecture for 1987/8). Oxford: Oxford University Press.

Sandars, N. 1978 *The Sea Peoples*. London: Thames and Hudson.

Schneider, J. 1977 Was there a pre-capitalist world system? *Peasant Studies* 6: 20–9.

Schneider, J. and P. Schneider 1976 *Culture and Political Economy in Western Sicily*. New York: Academic Press.

Sherratt, A. G. 1981 Plough and pastoralism: aspects of the secondary products revolution, in I. Hodder, G. Isaac, and N. Hammond, eds., *Pattern of the Past: Studies in Honour of David Clarke*, pp. 261–305. Cambridge: Cambridge University Press.

1990 Gordon Childe: patterns and paradigms in prehistory. *Australian Archaeology* 30: 3–13.

Sherratt, E. S. 1990 From *Khronos* to *Khronologia*: Warren and Hankey's Aegean bronze age timetable. *Antiquity* 64: 414–15.

Stone, L. 1985 A life of learning. *American Council of Learned Societies Newsletter* 36: 3–22.

Therkorn, L. 1987 The inter-relationship of materials and meanings: some suggestions on housing concerns within Iron Age Noord-Holland, in I. Hodder, ed., *The Archaeology of Contextual Meanings*, pp. 102–10. Cambridge: Cambridge University Press.

Wallerstein, I. 1974 *The Modern World-System: Capitalist Agriculture and the Origins of the European World-Economy in the Sixteenth Century*. New York: Academic Press.

Weiner, A. B. and J. Schneider (eds.) 1989 *Cloth and Human Experience*. Washington: Smithsonian Institution.

Wolf, E. R. 1982 *Europe and the People without History*. Berkeley and Los Angeles: University of California Press.

1987 An interview with Eric Wolf (by Jonathan Friedman). *Current Anthropology* 28: 107–18.

Index

For EU product safety concerns, contact us at Calle de José Abascal, 56–1°,
28003 Madrid, Spain or eugpsr@cambridge.org.

www.ingramcontent.com/pod-product-compliance
Ingram Content Group UK Ltd.
Pitfield, Milton Keynes, MK11 3LW, UK
UKHW030856150625
459647UK00021B/2785

* 9 7 8 0 5 2 1 1 0 2 6 0 5 *